War and Ideas

This book collects the key essays, together with updating notes and commentary, of Professor John Mueller on war and the role of ideas and opinions.

Mueller has maintained that war (and peace) are, in essence, merely ideas, and that war has waned as the notion that 'peace' is a decidedly better idea has gained currency. The first part of the book extends this argument, noting that as ideas have spread, war is losing out not only in the developed world, but now in the developing one, and that even civil war is in marked decline. It also assesses and critiques theories arguing that this phenomenon is caused by the rising acceptance of democracy and/or capitalism.

The second part argues that the Cold War was at base a clash of ideas that were seen to be threatening, not of arms balances, domestic systems, geography, or international structure. It also maintains that there has been a considerable tendency to exaggerate security threats—currently, in particular, the one presented by international terrorism—and to see them in excessively military terms.

The third section deals with the role public opinion plays in foreign policy, and argues that many earlier conclusions about opinion during the Korean and Vietnam Wars, including especially ones concerning the importance of casualties in determining popular support for war, apply to more recent military ventures in the Persian Gulf, Bosnia, Iraq, and Afghanistan. It also assesses the difficulties leaders and idea entrepreneurs often encounter when they try to manage or manipulate public opinion.

This book will be of much interest to students of international relations, security studies, foreign policy and international history.

John Mueller is Professor of Political Science and holds the Woody Hayes Chair of National Security Studies, Mershon Center, Ohio State University. He is author/editor of 13 books on politics and international security.

War and Ideas

Selected essays

John Mueller

 Routledge
Taylor & Francis Group

LONDON AND NEW YORK

First published 2011
by Routledge
2 Park Square, Milton Park, Abingdon, Oxon OX14 4RN

Simultaneously published in the USA and Canada
by Routledge
711 Third Avenue, New York, NY 10017

Routledge is an imprint of the Taylor & Francis Group, an informa business

British Library Cataloguing in Publication Data
A catalogue record for this book is available from the British Library

Library of Congress Cataloging in Publication Data
Mueller, John E.
  War and ideas : selected essays / John Mueller.
    p. cm.
  1. Politics and war.   2. War—Public opinion.   I. Title.
  JZ6385.M84 2011
  355.02—dc22

                                        2010049139
ISBN: 978-0-415-78176-3 (hbk)
ISBN: 978-0-415-78177-0 (pbk)

Typeset in Times New Roman
by RefineCatch Limited, Bungay, Suffolk

Printed and bound in Great Britain by
CPI Antony Rowe, Chippenham, Wiltshire

Contents

Acknowledgements and synopses

To Judy
To Karl, Michelle, Karen, Erik, Susan, Kraig
To Timothy, Sam, Clara, Kara, Malcolm, Atticus, Lida
To Lois and Phyllis
And to the memory of Alexander Stephan

The author and publishers wish to acknowledge the following publications from which the relevant articles were taken.

Chapter 1: "The obsolescence of major war," from 21 *Bulletin of Peace Proposals* 321–28 (September 1990).
A summary of the argument in Retreat from Doomsday.

Chapter 2: "Policing the remnants of war," from 40 *Journal of Peace Research* 507–18 (September 2003).
A summary of the argument in The Remnants of War.

Chapter 3: "War has almost ceased to exist: An assessment," from 124 *Political Science Quarterly* 297–321 (Summer 2009).
Evaluates trends in warfare and discusses what this suggests about the theories and explanations about the causes of war (most have been wrong).

Chapter 4: "Why isn't there more violence?," from 13 *Security Studies* 191–203 (Spring 2004).
Looks broadly at the incidence of domestic and international violence, concluding that it has been far less common than usually assumed with implications about the "state of nature" and about the condition of "international anarchy."

Chapter 5: "What was the Cold War about? Evidence from its ending," from 119 *Political Science Quarterly* 609–31 (Winter 2004–05).
Argues that the Cold War was entirely about a clash of ideas or ideologies, not about weapons, power, the Soviet domination of Eastern Europe, or Communism per se.

Chapter 6: "Simplicity and spook: Terrorism and the dynamics of threat exaggeration," from 6 *International Studies Perspectives* 155–73 (May 2005).
Considers a variety of perceived national security threats since World War II and concludes that they have been consistently and often destructively inflated.

Chapter 7: "Faulty correlation, foolish consistency, and fatal consequence: Democracy, peace, and theory in the Middle East," in Steven W. Hook (ed.), *Democratic Peace in Theory and Practice* (Kent, OH: Kent State University Press, 2010). Some corrections to the original have been made.
Assesses democratic peace theory and its questionable validity and its even more questionable application to policy in the Mideast and Iraq War.

Chapter 8: "American foreign policy and public opinion in a new era: Eleven propositions," in Barbara Norrander and Clyde Wilcox (eds), *Understanding Public Opinion*, 2nd edn (Washington, DC: CQ Press, 2002), pp. 149–72.
Investigates the relevance of, and the ups and downs of, foreign policy ideas and concerns that have captured the American public's attention since 1945.

Chapter 9: "The Iraq War and the management of American public opinion," in James Pfiffner and Mark Phythian (eds), *Intelligence and National Security Policy Making in Iraq: British and American perspectives* (Manchester, UK: Manchester University Press, 2008), pp. 126–48.
Evaluates the American public's opinion on the Iraq War and compares the patterns to earlier ones, particularly for the Korean and Vietnam wars.

Preface
Marketing mousetraps

"Build a better mousetrap," Ralph Waldo Emerson supposedly once said, "and the world will beat a path to your door." Since the modern mousetrap wasn't really invented until several years after his death, the statement has understandably been presumed to be apocryphal. However, Emerson did say something similar about building better chairs or crucibles or church organs, so whoever manipulated his wording got his essential meaning right.

The implication of the homely homily, however, is savagely mistaken: that all you have to do is create a better product and people will eagerly snap it up without further effort on your part. In fact, according to John Lienhard, there have been well over 4,400 patents issued for mousetraps in the United States and, although at least *some* of them must represent decided improvements, only a few have made any money. Far less naïve is the gloss on Emerson's fabricated aphorism that was penned by the brilliant lyricist Johnny Mercer, an important character in a book I wrote a quarter century ago. As Mercer points out, just because you do everything right—kiss better, squeeze better, tease better, lie bigger—doesn't guarantee that you'll make the sell, that you'll make an impression on her, that something will "happen" to you.

Throughout history a great many people—idea entrepreneurs I call them—have come up with a lot of ideas and have tried to market them like mousetraps hoping that something will "happen." Some of the ideas have gained acceptance, and those that have been embraced have often had considerable consequences for better or worse. Among the better ones, in my view, are those holding democracy to be a superior form of government, capitalism to be a good way to organize the economy, science to be a productive method of inquiry, and war to be a really terrible idea. Among the worse ones, again in my view, have been Communism, fascism, and the notions that there are Communists under my bed (1945–1989) and that Osama bin Laden and his little band of squirrely fanatics present an existential threat to the United States, to the modern state system, to civilization (2001–).

In various ways, the essays collected in this volume explore the marketing of ideas. Part I focuses on the selling of the idea of war aversion. Part II deals with the clash of ideas that was at the core of the Cold War, with the selling of national security threats, and with faulty extrapolations about the nature of democracy that helped impel the war in Iraq. And Part III assesses the customers, the people who, in a process often mysterious, decide whether and what they are going to buy and embrace. Each essay (a few of which borrow from each other now and then) is followed by some related, and sometimes updated, reflections including the occasional shameless plug for some of my other publications.

Preoccupied as it is with describing and assessing the process by which ideas are marketed, this book is, I guess, something of an exercise in "constructivism," a word (and a field) that didn't, however, exist when I began my explorations.

A key problem is that, like those seeking to peddle the better mousetrap or squeeze the better squeeze, idea entrepreneurs (including fear-mongers) are at the mercy of the whims and caprices of those they are seeking to "manipulate," and they fail far more often than they succeed. As the legendary impresario Sol Hurok once allegedly philosophized after one of his expertly promoted acts bombed at the box office, "If people don't want to come, nothing will stop them." Indeed, if extensive purposeful promotion could guarantee acceptance, we'd all be driving Edsels and drinking New Coke. Or, put another way, at any time there are myriad ideas swirling around, and anyone who can accurately and consistently anticipate which of these are actually going to turn people on would not be writing about it (like me, right now), but would move to Wall Street to become in very short order the richest person on the planet.

But the process by which ideas are marketed can be at least partially explicated and explained. For example, it seems to me that it was highly significant that idea entrepreneurs managed to get the (essentially new) idea of war aversion into the intellectual atmosphere in the few decades before the First World War, so that they could profit (or become the mainstream) when the war experience abruptly rendered their customers much more receptive. These efforts, it seems to me, have been substantially responsible for the historically unprecedented absence of war among developed states for most of a century now. Similarly, over the course of the last couple of centuries other idea entrepreneurs sought to market the ideas that democracy is the most desirable form of government and that free-market capitalism is the best way to organize the economy, in each case with what looks today to have been a fair amount of success.

A focus on idea entrepreneurs and on what Robert Dahl calls "the historical movement of ideas" recommends itself because it is often difficult to come up with material reasons to explain important historical developments. For example, slavery declined over the nineteenth century even though the Atlantic slave trade was then entering what was probably the most dynamic and profitable period in its existence. And democracy began to take root in substantial countries by the end of the eighteenth century even though it had been known as a form of government for millennia and even though there seem to have been no technological or economic advances at the time that impelled its acceptance.

At any rate, given the crucial role ideas have often played in history, it is important to assess the process by which the people seeking to market them fail or succeed. Beliefs, ideas, ideologies, and attitudes are often, as Dahl has noted, "a major independent variable," and they must remain in the consideration. Yet, "because of their concern with rigor and their dissatisfaction with the 'softness' of historical description, generalization, and explanation, most social scientists have turned away from the historical movement of ideas. As a result, their own theories, however, 'rigorous' they may be, leave out an important explanatory variable and often lead to naive reductionism."

Ideas are very often forces themselves then, not flotsam on the tide of broader social or economic patterns. Francis Fukuyama has pointed to what he calls "the autonomous power of ideas," or as Ernest Gellner has put out, "a great deal can happen without being necessary," without being "inscribed into any historic plan." In various ways, the essays in this collection seek to explore and develop that notion.

References

Robert A. Dahl, *Polyarchy*. New Haven, CT: Yale University Press, 1971.

Francis Fukuyama, The End of History? *National Interest*, Summer 1989.

Ernest Gellner, Introduction. In *Europe and the Rise of Capitalism*, ed. Jean Baechler, John A. Hall and Michael Mann. London: Basil Blackwell, 1988.

John H. Lienhard, *Inventing Modern: Growing up with X-rays, Skyscrapers, and Tailfins*. Oxford and New York: Oxford University Press, 2003.

Part I

War, ideas, and peace

Introduction

One rather good thing about publishing a book contending that major war—war among developed states—may be obsolescent is that even those who disagree with you hope you're right. That certainly happened to me in 1989 when my book *Retreat from Doomsday* came out—reviews were peppered with words like "hopeful" and "encouraging."

In an important respect, that very phenomenon underscored a central message of the book. Had it been published a century earlier, it would have been met by a rash of derisive reviews reacting with horror that anyone would have the temerity to suggest that war could in any sense be on the way out—that a beautiful, honorable, holy, sublime, heroic, ennobling, natural, virtuous, glorious, cleansing, manly, necessary, and progressive institution might be in the process of being replaced by something as debasing, trivial, and rotten as perpetual peace characterized by crass materialism, artistic decline, repellant effeminacy, rampant selfishness, base immorality, petrifying stagnation, sordid frivolity, degrading cowardice, corrupting boredom, and utter emptiness.

The central message of the book is that war is merely an idea, and that the decline of major war has been chiefly due to the way attitudes toward the value and efficacy of war have changed, roughly following the pattern by which the ancient and once-formidable institution of formal slavery became discredited and then obsolete. Key to the process has been the machinations of idea entrepreneurs, not changes in wider-ranging social, economic, or technological developments or in institutions, trade, or patterns of interdependence—which often seem to be more nearly a consequence of peace and of rising war aversion than their cause. The first article reprinted below, "The obsolescence of major war," summarizes the argument of that book.

Beyond the hope, there was quite a bit of strong agreement in 1989, most notably and gratifyingly in a front-page review in the Sunday *Washington Post Book World* by McGeorge Bundy. However, the book certainly attracted some distinguished detractors as well. Harvard's Samuel Huntington assessed it along with then-current discussions about the apparent end of the Cold War and with Francis Fukuyama's famous essay "The End of History?" Labeling the collective phenomenon "endism," he pronounced it the "intellectual fad of 1989." Although willing to concede that "the probability of hot war between the two superpowers is as low as it has ever been" and that war between any of the advanced industrialized democracies was "even more unlikely," Huntington warned that endism tended to ignore the "weakness and irrationality of human nature" and stressed that human beings were "often stupid, selfish, cruel, and sinful." Endism, he concluded, provided "an illusion of well-being," invited "relaxed complacency," and was accordingly "dangerous and subversive." Meanwhile, in the *New York Times* the prominent military and diplomatic historian Michael Howard reviewed the book with considerable skepticism (although with less alarm) about its central thesis. "One would like to believe Mr. Mueller," he wrote, but the "prudent reader will check that his air raid shelter is in good repair."

In the ensuing years, the ranks of the "dangerous and subversive" have expanded to include, among others, Robert Jervis in a book in this series, and the developed world seems to have continued, even accelerated, its retreat from doomsday—a word that has picked up a slight aura of quaintness over the ensuing two decades. And, however imprudently, air raid shelters do seem to have been allowed to lapse into disrepair.

However, *Retreat from Doomsday* has little to say about civil war, the kind of war that was by far the most common then and has continued to be so since. So in 2004 I published *The Remnants of War*, which sought to assess not only major war, but warfare of all sorts including especially those of the civil variety. It develops a distinction between criminal and disciplined warfare, contending that most (though not all) civil wars, far from stemming from "clashes of civilizations" (Huntington again), more nearly resemble criminal predation or the clashes of thugs. Although developed countries have tried to use military intervention in the wake of the Cold War to deal with civil conflicts and with regimes that are dangers to their own populations, the book identifies bad governance as the chief effective cause of most civil conflict and good governance as the key antidote. The second article reprinted in this section, "Policing the remnants of war," summarizes much of the argument.

When that book was published, a notable dwindling in the frequency of all forms of war, especially civil war, was evident, and "War has almost ceased to exist: An Assessment" summarizes my overall argument about war in its various forms while updating the data to 2009. It finds that, despite headline-grabbing wars in Iraq and Afghanistan, the decline of war, as conventionally defined, continues. Although it is far too early to be certain about this trend, particularly with regard to civil war, it is likely, again, that those who disagree with me will hope I am right.

That article also engages in a bit of speculation. If war is in such pronounced decline, many of the explanations spewed out over the centuries for the institution's existence and persistence may be found wanting. War seems to be waning, but there seem to have been few changes in many of the variables that have often been seen to be causally consequential, whether they stem from biology, psychology, economics, or structural or institutional analysis. Nor are explanations stressing weaponry, resentment, trade, communication, or technology doing very well. In my view, in a phrase I'm afraid I've used more than once, war is not a trick of fate, a thunderbolt from hell, a natural calamity, or a desperate plot contrivance dreamed up by some sadistic puppeteer on high. It is merely an idea, an institution that has been grafted onto human existence. Like dueling and formal slavery, it may be natural in some sense, but it is not necessary.

The final article in Part I, "Why isn't there more violence?" extrapolates on that last consideration. While violence may make use of natural proclivities, it seems to be remarkably infrequent, especially considering the ease with which it can be committed, and non-violence is more nearly the natural, or normal, condition. Violence, in other words, is an aberration (which is why, in part, it garners so much attention), and people seem to be able to live quite well without it. The article also suggests that, while Hobbesian states of nature may exist, they are not conditions in which everyone is the enemy of everyone else, but situations where people unwillingly come under the control of bands, often very small ones, of criminal predators. This perspective can also lead to a re-evaluation of meaning of international "anarchy."

References

McGeorge Bundy, World Without War, Amen. *Washington Post Book World*, March 12, 1989.

Francis Fukuyama, The End of History? *National Interest*, Summer 1989.

Michael Howard, A Death Knell for War? *New York Times Book Review*, April 30, 1989.

Samuel P. Huntington, No Exit: The Errors of Endism. *National Interest*, Fall 1989.

Samuel P. Huntington, *The Clash of Civilizations and the Remaking of the World Order*. New York: Touchstone, 1996.

Robert Jervis, *American Foreign Policy in a New Era*. New York: Routledge, 2005.

1 The obsolescence of major war

1 Introductory remarks

In discussing the causes of international war, commentators have often found it useful to group theories into what they term levels of analysis. In his classic work *Man, the State and War*, Kenneth N. Waltz organizes the theories according to whether the cause of war is found in the nature of man, in the nature of the state, or in the nature of the international state system. More recently Jack Levy, partly setting the issue of human nature to one side, organizes the theories according to whether they stress the systemic level, the nature of state and society, or the decision-making process.[1]

In various ways, these level-of-analysis approaches direct attention away from war itself and toward concerns which may influence the incidence of war. However, war should not be visualized as a sort of recurring outcome that is determined by other conditions, but rather as a phenomenon that has its own qualities and appeals. And over time these appeals can change. War, in this view, is merely an idea, an institution, like dueling or slavery, that has been grafted onto human existence. Unlike breathing, eating, or sex, war is not something that is somehow required by the human condition, by the structure of international affairs, or by the forces of history.

Accordingly war can shrivel up and disappear, and this can come about without requiring that there be any notable change or improvement on any of the level-of-analysis categories. Specifically, war can die out without changing human nature, without modifying the nature of the state or the nation-state, without changing the international system, without creating an effective world government or system of international law, and without improving the competence or moral capacity of political leaders. It can also go away without expanding international trade, interdependence, or communication; without fabricating an effective moral or practical equivalent; without enveloping the earth in democracy or prosperity; without devising ingenious agreements to restrict arms or the arms industry; without reducing the world's considerable store of hate, selfishness, nationalism, and racism; without increasing the amount of love, justice, harmony, cooperation, good will, or inner peace in the world; without establishing security communities; and without doing anything whatever about nuclear weapons.

Not only *can* such a development take place, but it has been taking place for a century or more, at least within the developed world, an area which was once a cauldron of international and civil war. Conflicts of interest are inevitable and continue to persist within the developed world. But the notion that war should be used to resolve them has increasingly been discredited and abandoned there. War, it seems, is becoming obsolete, at least in the developed world: in an area where war was once often casually seen as beneficial, noble, and glorious, or at least as necessary or inevitable, the conviction has now become widespread that war would be intolerably costly, unwise, futile, and debased.[2]

Some of this may be suggested by the remarkable developments in the Cold War that took place at the end of the 1980s. The dangers of a major war in the developed world clearly declined remarkably, yet this can hardly be attributed to an improvement in human nature, to the demise of the nation-state, to the rise of a world government, or to a notable improvement in the competence of political leaders.

2 Two analogies: dueling and slavery

It may not be obvious that an accepted, time-honored institution which serves an urgent social purpose can become obsolescent and then die out because a lot of people come to find it obnoxious. But the argument here is that something like that has been happening to war in the developed world. To illustrate the dynamic, it will be helpful briefly to assess two analogies: the processes by which the once-perennial institutions of dueling and slavery have all but vanished from the face of the earth.

2.1 Dueling

In some important respects war in the developed world may be following the example of another violent method for settling disputes, dueling, which up until a century ago was common practice in Europe and America among a certain class of young and youngish men who liked to classify themselves as gentlemen.[3] Men of the social set that once dueled still exist, they still get insulted, and they still are concerned about their self-respect and their standing among their peers. But they don't duel. However, they do not avoid dueling today because they evaluate the option and reject it on cost-benefit grounds. Rather, the option never perco-lates into their consciousness as something that is available. That is, a form of violence famed and fabled for centuries has sunk from thought as a viable, conscious possibility.

The Prussian strategist, Carl von Clausewitz, opens his famous 1832 book, *On War*, by observing that "War is nothing but a duel on a larger scale."[4] If war, like dueling, comes to be viewed as a thoroughly undesirable, even ridiculous, policy, and if it can no longer promise gains or if potential combatants no longer come to value the things it can gain for them, then war can fade away as a coherent possi-bility even if a truly viable substitute or "moral equivalent" for it were never formulated. Like dueling, it could become unfashionable and then obsolete.

2.2 Slavery

From the dawn of prehistory until about 1788 slavery, like war, could be found just about everywhere in one form or another, and it flourished in every age.[5] At that point, however, the anti-slavery forces began to argue that the institution was repulsive, immoral, and uncivilized, and this sentiment gradually picked up adherents. Remarkably, at exactly the time that the anti-slavery movement was taking flight, the Atlantic slave economy, as Seymour Drescher notes, "was entering what was probably the most dynamic and profitable period in its existence."[6]

Thus the abolitionists were up against an institution that was viable, profitable, and expanding, and one that had been uncritically accepted for thousands—perhaps millions—of years as a natural and inevitable part of human existence. To counter this powerful, time-honored institution, the abolitionists' principal weapon was a novel argument: it had recently occurred to them, they said, that slavery was no longer the way people ought to do things.

As it happened, it was an idea whose time had come. The abolition of slavery required legislative battles, international pressures, economic travail, and, in the United States, a cataclysmic war (but it did *not* require the fabrication of a functional equivalent or the formation of an effective supranational authority). Within a century slavery, and most similar institutions like serfdom, had been all but eradicated from the face of the globe. Slavery became controversial and then obsolete.

2.3 War

Dueling and slavery no longer exist as effective institutions and have largely faded from human experience except as something one reads about in books. While their re-establishment is not impossible, they show after a century of neglect no signs of revival. Other once-popular, even once-admirable, institutions in the developed world have been, or are being, eliminated because at some point they began to seem repulsive, immoral, and uncivilized: bear-baiting, bare-knuckle fighting, freak shows, casual torture, wanton cruelty to animals, burning heretics, flogging, vendetta, deforming corseting, laughing at the insane, the death penalty for minor crimes, eunuchism, public cigarette smoking.

War may well be in the process of joining this list of recently discovered sins and vices. War is not, of course, the same as dueling or slavery. Like war, dueling is an institution for settling disputes, but it was something of a social affectation and it usually involved only matters of "honor," not ones of physical gain. Like war, slavery was nearly universal and an apparently inevitable part of human existence, but it could be eliminated area by area: a country that abolished slavery did not have to worry about what other countries were doing, while a country that would like to abolish war must continue to be concerned about those that have kept it in their repertory.

On the other hand, war has against it not only substantial psychic costs, but also very obvious and widespread physical ones. Dueling brought death and destruction but, at least in the first instance, only to a few people who had specifically volunteered to participate. And while slavery may have brought moral destruction, it was generally a considerable economic success.

In some respects then, the fact that war has outlived dueling and slavery is curious. But there are signs that, at least in the developed world, it has begun, like them, to succumb to obsolescence.

3   Trends against war before 1914

There were a number of trends away from war in the developed world before World War I. Two of these deserve special emphasis.

3.1   The Hollandization phenonomon

As early as 1800 a few once-warlike countries in Europe, like Holland, Switzerland, and Sweden, quietly began to drop out of the war system. While war was still generally accepted as a natural and inevitable phenomenon, these countries found solace (and prosperity) in policies that stressed peace. People who argue that war is inherent in nature and those who see war as a recurring, cyclic phenomenon need to supply an explanation for these countries. Switzerland, for example, has avoided all international war for nearly 200 years. If war is inherent in human nature or if war is some sort of cyclic inevitability, the Swiss ought to be roaring for a fight by now.

3.2   The rise of an organized peace movement

While there have been individual war opponents throughout history, the existence of organized groups devoted to abolishing war from the human condition is quite new. The institution of war came under truly organized and concentrated attack only after 1815, and this peace movement developed real momentum only by the end of the century.[7]

War opponents stressed various arguments against war. Some, like the Quakers, were opposed to war primarily because they found it immoral. Others stressed arguments that were essentially aesthetic: war, they concluded, was repulsive, barbaric, and uncivilized. Still others, such as the British liberals, stressed the futility of war: particularly from an economic standpoint, they argued, even the winners of war were worse off than if they had pursued a policy of peace. These protesters were joined by socialists and others who had concluded that war was a capitalistic device in which the working class was used as cannon fodder. Among their activities, the various elements of the antiwar movement were devoted to exploring alternatives to war such as arbitration and international law and organization, and to developing mechanisms, like disarmament, that might reduce its frequency or consequences.

Peace advocates were a noisy gadfly minority by 1900, and they had established a sense of momentum. Their arguments were inescapable, but for the most part they were rejected and derided by the majority which still held to the traditional view that war was noble, natural, thrilling, progressive, manly, redemptive, and beneficial.[8] Up until 1914, as Michael Howard has observed, war "was almost universally considered an acceptable, perhaps an inevitable and for many people a desirable way of settling international differences."[9]

4 The impact of World War I

The holocaust of World War I turned peace advocates into a pronounced majority in the developed world and destroyed war romanticism. The war marked, as Arnold Toynbee points out, the end of a "span of five thousand years during which war had been one of mankind's master institutions." Or as Evan Luard observes, "the First World War transformed traditional attitudes toward war. For the first time there was an almost universal sense that the deliberate launching of a war could now no longer be justified."[10]

World War I was, of course, horrible. But horror was not invented in 1914. History had already had its Carthages, its Jerichos, its wars of thirty and a hundred years. Seen in historic context, in fact, World War I does not seem to have been all that unusual in its duration, destructiveness, grimness, political pointlessness, economic consequences, breadth, or intensity. It does seem to be unique in that it was the first major war to be preceded by substantial, organized antiwar agitation, and in that, for Europeans, it followed an unprecedentedly peaceful century during which Europeans had begun, perhaps unknowingly, to appreciate the virtues of peace.[11]

Obviously, this change of attitude was not enough to prevent the wars that have taken place since 1918. But the notion that the institution of war, particularly war in the developed world, was repulsive, uncivilized, immoral, and futile—voiced only by minorities before 1914—was an idea whose time had come, and it is one that has permeated most of the developed world ever since.

5 World War II

It is possible that enough war spirit still lingered, particularly in Germany, that another war in Europe was necessary to extinguish it there. But analysis of opinion in the interwar period suggests that war was viewed with about as much horror in Germany as any place else on the continent.[12] To a remarkable degree major war returned to Europe only because of the astoundingly successful machinations of Adolf Hitler, virtually the last European who was willing to risk major war. As Gerhard Weinberg has put it, "Whether any other German leader would indeed have taken the plunge is surely doubtful, and the very warnings Hitler received from some of his generals can only have reinforced his belief in his personal role as the one man able, willing, and even eager to lead Germany and drag the world into war."[13] That is, after World War I, a war in Europe could only be brought about through the maniacally dedicated manipulations of an exceptionally lucky and spectacularly skilled entrepreneur; before World War I, any dimwit—e.g. Kaiser Wilhelm—could get into one.

The war in Asia was, of course, developed out of the expansionary policies of distant Japan, a country which neither participated substantially in World War I nor learned its lessons. In World War II Japan got the message most Europeans had received from World War I.

6 The Cold War, the long peace, and nuclear weapons

Since 1945 major war has been most likely to develop from the Cold War that has dominated postwar international history. The hostility of the era mostly derives from the Soviet Union's ideological—even romantic—affection for revolution and for revolutionary war. While this ideology is expansionistic in some respects, it has never visualized major war in the Hitler mode as a remotely sensible tactic.[14]

East and West have never been close to major war, and it seems unlikey that nuclear weapons have been important determinants of this—insofar as a military deterrent has been necessary, the fear of escalation to a war like World War I or II supplies it. Even allowing considerably for stupidity, ineptness, miscalculation, and self-deception, a large war, nuclear or otherwise, has never been remotely in the interest of the essentially contented, risk-averse, escalation-anticipating countries that have dominated world affairs since 1945. This is not to deny that nuclear war is appalling to contemplate and mind-concentratingly dramatic, particularly in the speed with which it could bring about massive destruction. Nor it is to deny that decision makers, both at times of crisis and at times of non-crisis, are well aware of how cataclysmic a nuclear war could be. It is simply to stress that the horror of repeating World War II is not all that much less impressive or dramatic, and that leaders essentially content with the status quo will strive to avoid anything that they feel could lead to either calamity. A jump from a fiftieth-floor window is probably quite a bit more horrible to think about than a jump from a fifth-floor one, but anyone who finds life even minimally satisfying is extremely unlikely to do either.[15]

In general the wars that have involved developed countries since World War II have been of two kinds, both declining in frequency and relevance. One of these concerns lingering colonial responsibilities and readjustments. Thus the Dutch got involved in (but did not start) a war in Indonesia, the French in Indochina and Algeria, the British in Malaya and the Falklands.

The other kind relates to the Cold War contest between East and West. The Communists have generally sought to avoid major war, not so much because they necessarily find such wars to be immoral, repulsive, or uncivilized, but because they find them futile—dangerous, potentially counterproductive, wildly and absurdly adventurous. However, for decades after 1945 they retained a dutiful affection for what they came to call wars of national liberation—smaller wars around the world designed to further the progressive cause of world revolution. The West has seen this threat as visceral and as one that must be countered even at the cost of war if necessary. Wars fought in this context, such as those in Korea and Vietnam, have essentially been seen to be preventive—if Communism is countered there, it won't have to be countered later on more vital, closer turf.

The lesson learned (perhaps overlearned) from the Hitler experience is that aggressive threats must be dealt with by those who abhor war when the threats are still comparatively small and distant; to allow the aggressive force to succeed only brings nearer the day when a larger war must be fought. Thus countries which abhor war have felt it necessary to wage wars in order to prevent wider wars.

7 The consequences of the demise of the Cold War

Because of economic crisis and persistent ideological failure, it now appears that the Cold War has ended as the Soviet Union, following the lead of its former ideological soulmate, China, abandons its quest for ideological expansion and quests after prosperity and a quiet, normal international situation. Unless some new form of conflict emerges, war participation by developed countries is likely to continue its decline.

As tensions lapse between the two sides in what used to be known as the Cold War, there is a natural tendency for the arms that backed, and in a sense measured, that tension to atrophy. Both sides have begun what might be called a negative arms race. Formal arms negotiations will probably only slow and pedantify this natural process, and might best be abandoned at this point. It may also be time to confederate the East–West alliances (rather than allowing them to fragment) with the combined organization serving to regulate the remarkable changes going on in Europe.[16]

The demise of the Cold War should also facilitate further expansion of international trade and interdependence. Trade and interdependence may not lead inexorably to peace, but peace does seem to lead to, or at any rate facilitates, trade, interdependence, and economic growth. That is, peace ought to be seen not as a dependent, but rather as an independent variable in such considerations. The 1992 economic unity of Europe and the building of a long-envisioned channel tunnel are the consequences of peace, not its cause.

Left alone, enterprising business people will naturally explore the possibilities of investing in other countries or selling their products there. Averse to disastrous surprises, they are more likely to invest if they are confident that peace will prevail. But for trade to flourish, governments must stay out of the way not only by eschewing war, but also by eschewing measures which unnaturally inhibit trade.

Furthermore, if nations no longer find it sensible to use force or the threat of force in their dealings with one another, it may be neither necessary nor particularly desirable to create an entrenched international government or police force (as opposed to ad hoc arrangements and devices designed to meet specific problems). This is because an effective international government could be detrimental to economic growth since, like domestic governments, it could be manipulated to reward the inefficient, coddle the incompetent, and plague the innovative.

8 War in the Third World

War has not, of course, become fully obsolete. While major war—war among developed countries—seems to be going out of style, war obviously continues to flourish elsewhere. The demise of the Cold War suggests that the United States and the Soviet Union, in particular, are likely to involve themselves less in these wars. Moreover, it is possible that the catastrophic Iran–Iraq war will sober people in the Third World about that kind of war. And it does seem that much of the romance has gone out of the concept of violent revolution as Third World countries increasingly turn to the drab, difficult, and unromantic task of economic development.

Thus it is possible that the developed world's aversion to war may eventually infect the rest of the world as well (international war, in fact, has been quite rare in Latin America for a century). But this development is not certain, nor is its pace predictable. As slavery continued to persist in Brazil even after it had been abolished elsewhere, the existence of war in some parts of the world does not refute the observation that it is vanishing, or has vanished, in other parts.

9 Imperfect peace

War, even war within the developed world, has not become, nor could it ever become, impossible. When it seems necessary, even countries like the United States and Britain, which were among the first to become thoroughly disillusioned with war, have been able to fight wars and to use military force—often with high morale and substantial public support, at least at first. The ability to make war and the knowledge about how to do so can never be fully expunged—nor, for that matter, can the ability or knowledge to institute slavery, eunuchism, crucifixion, or human sacrifice. War is declining as an institution not because it has ceased to be possible or fascinating, but because peoples and leaders in the developed world—where war was once endemic—have increasingly found war to be disgusting, ridiculous, and unwise.

The view presented in this article is based upon the premise that, in some important respects, war is often taken too seriously. War, it seems, is merely an idea. It is not a trick of fate, a thunderbolt from hell, a natural calamity, or a desperate plot contrivance dreamed up by some sadistic puppeteer on high. And if war begins in the minds of men, as the UNESCO charter insists, it can end there as well. Over the centuries war opponents have been trying to bring this about by discrediting war as an idea, and the argument here is that they have been substantially successful at doing so. The long peace since World War II is less a product of recent weaponry than the culmination of a substantial historical process. For the last two or three centuries, major war—war among developed countries—has gradually moved toward terminal disrepute because of its perceived repulsiveness and futility.

It could also be argued that, to a considerable degree, people have tended to take *peace* too seriously as well. Peace is merely what emerges when the institution of war is neglected. It does not mean that the world suddenly becomes immersed in those qualities with which the word, "peace," is constantly being associated: love, justice, harmony, cooperation, brotherhood, good will. People still remain contentious and there still remain substantial conflicts of interest. The difference is only that they no longer resort to force to resolve their conflicts, any more than young men today resort to formal dueling to resolve their quarrels. A world at peace would not be perfect, but it would be notably better than the alternative.

Notes

1 Kenneth N. Waltz, *Man, the State and War* (New York: Columbia University Press, 1959); Jack S. Levy, "The Causes of War: A Review of Theories and Evidence," in Philip E. Tetlock, Jo L. Husbands, Robert Jervis, Paul C. Stern, and Charles Tilly (eds.), *Behavior, Society, and Nuclear War*, Vol. 1 (New York: Oxford University Press, 1989), pp. 209–333. See also J. David Singer, "The Levels of Analysis Problem in International Relations," in Klaus Knorr and Sydney Verba (eds.), *The International System* (Princeton, NJ: Princeton University Press, 1961), pp. 77–92; and James N. Rosenau, "Pre-theories and Theories of Foreign Policy," in R. B. Farrell (ed.), *Approaches to Comparative and International Politics* (Evanston, IL: Northwestern University Press, 1966), pp. 27–92.
2 For a further development of these arguments, see John Mueller, *Retreat from Doomsday: The Obsolescence of Major War* (New York: Basic Books, 1989).
3 For other observations of the analogy between war and dueling, see Bernard Brodie, *War and Politics* (New York: Macmillan, 1973), p. 275; Norman Angell, *The Great Illusion* (London: Heinemann, 1914), pp. 202–3; G. P. Gooch, *History of Our Time, 1885–1911* (London: Williams and Norgate, 1911), p. 249; J. E. Cairnes, "International Law," *Fortnightly Review*, Vol. 2 (November 1, 1865), p. 650n.
4 Carl Von Clausewitz, *On War* (Princeton, NJ: Princeton University Press, 1976), p. 75.
5 See Orlando Patterson, *Slavery and Social Death: A Comparative Study* (Cambridge, MA: Harvard University Press, 1982); Stanley Engerman, "Slavery and Emancipation in Comparative Perspective: A Look at Some Recent Debates," *Journal of Economic History*, Vol. 46, No. 2 (June 1986), pp. 318–19. For another comparison of the institutions of war and slavery, see James Lee Ray, "The Abolitition of Slavery and the End of International War," *International Organization*, Vol. 43, No. 3 (Summer 1989), pp. 405–39.
6 Seymour Drescher, *Capitalism and Antislavery: British Mobilization in Comparative Perspective* (New York: Oxford University Press. 1987), p. 4. See also David Eltis, *Economic Growth and the Ending of the Transatlantic Slave Trade* (New York: Oxford University Press, 1987); Engerman, "Slavery and Emancipation," pp. 322–33, 339.
7 For a useful history, see A. C. F. Beales, *The History of Peace: A Short Account of the Organised Movements for International Peace* (New York: Dial, 1931).
8 For an excellent discussion, see Roland N. Stromberg, *Redemption by War: The Intellectuals and 1914* (Lawrence, KS: Regents Press of Kansas, 1982).
9 Michael Howard, *The Causes of Wars and Other Essays* (Cambridge, MA: Harvard University Press, 1984), p. 9.
10 Arnold J. Toynbee, *Experiences* (New York: Oxford University Press, 1969), p. 214; Evan Luard, *War in International Society* (New Haven, CT: Yale University Press), p. 365.
11 For a further development of this argument, see John Mueller, "Changing Attitudes Toward War: The Impact of World War I," *British Journal of Political Science*, forthcoming.
12 For a discussion of the antipathy felt by the German people toward war in the 1930s, see Ian Kershaw, *The "Hitler Myth"* (Oxford: Oxford University Press, 1987), pp. 122–47, 229, 241; Marlis G. Steinert, *Hitler's War and the Germans: Public Mood and Attitude During the Second World War* (Athens, OH: Ohio University Press, 1977), pp. 40–41, 315, 341.

13 *The Foreign Policy of Hitler's Germany* (Chicago, IL: University of Chicago Press, 1980), p. 664.
14 For a valuable discussion, see Frederic S. Burin, "The Communist Doctrine of the Inevitability of War," *American Political Science Review*, Vol. 57, No. 2 (June 1963), pp. 334–54.
15 For a further development of this argument, see John Mueller, "The Essential Irrelevance of Nuclear Weapons: Stability in the Postwar World," *International Security*, Vol. 13, no. 2 (Fall 1988), pp. 55–79.
16 On these two policy proposals, see John Mueller, "A New Concert of Europe," *Foreign Policy* (Winter 1989–90), pp. 3–16.

REFLECTIONS

Hitler as a necessary cause of World War II

I have further developed the notion that Adolf Hitler was a necessary cause of the war in Europe in *The Remnants of War*. There was, it seems to me, no momentum toward another world war in Europe, historical conditions in no important way required that contest, and the major nations of Europe were not on a collision course that was likely to lead to war. In order to bring about another continental war it was necessary for Germany to desire to expand into areas that would inspire military resistance from other major countries and to be willing and able to pursue war when these desires were so opposed.

Although the somewhat mystical notion that Germany needed *Lebensraum*, living space, in the non-German lands to its east had been around for quite a while, there was nothing remotely natural or inevitable about the process by which they came to dominate German foreign policy in the 1930s. Moreover, to get his policies adopted Hitler had not only to mislead his own public but to override the objections of some of his most important cronies and collaborators. As he put it late in 1938, "Circumstances have forced me to talk almost exclusively of peace for decades." Moreover, whatever interest there may have been in the abstract for Hitler's policy of expansion, the notion that war should be used to carry out that policy attracted very little support. In Germany, as in the West, there was a great fear of war: some people had come to reject war entirely and in principle, while others opposed it because they anticipated huge costs like those suffered in World War I and/or because they believed Germany would lose. Nor was there notable enthusiasm for continental war within the German military.

It also seems clear that Hitler possessed extraordinary qualities as a leader. He had enormous energy and stamina, an exceptional capacity to persuade, an excellent memory, strong powers of concentration, an overwhelming craving for power, a fanatical belief in his mission, a monumental self-confidence, a unique daring, a spectacular facility for lying, a mesmerizing oratorical style, and an ability to be utterly ruthless to anyone who got in his way or attempted to divert him from his intended course of action. Hitler also appears to have been utterly unique in his belief that he could intimidate his opponents into standing idly by as he carried off some dramatic conquests.

Clearly, if history's greatest cataclysm came about only because one spectacularly skilled, lucky, and determined man willed it into existence, this circumstance has substantial implications. The experience obviously demonstrates how vital key individuals can be in shaping history. It suggests as well that World War II in Europe was not a continuation of World War I, nor was the interwar international "system" intrinsically unstable or its institutions catastrophically ill designed. Moreover, Germany's democracy was probably not particularly less admirable or less viable than others at the time: if a consolidating leader had instead come along to put things back into order, the era would have been seen merely as a colorful growing period. Nor did World War II grow out of the depression of the 1930s: economic troubles may have helped Hitler gain office in Germany, but war came only after he had apparently pulled the country out of the depression. And the war in Europe does not appear to have emerged out of the militarism of German society or character: for all their oratory and ritual, for all their fulminations and parades, for all their flag-waving and solemn ceremony, Hitler and his Nazis were never able to get the German people to view war with anything other than horror and foreboding.

In addition, appeasement may have gained an undeservedly bad reputation. The appeasers' strategy of accommodation might well have worked with any other German leader and they might today be celebrated as great visionaries. Moreover, the Great War of 1914–1918 might have lived up to its billing as the war to end all war (at least war of that type) and we might now be celebrating—or taking for granted—nearly a century of peace in Europe.

The experience further suggests that, contrary to the post-World War II visions of George Orwell and containment theorists, totalitarianism neither requires war to function nor does it necessarily lead to war. But for Hitler's maniacal expansionary zeal and extreme willingness to accept risk, even a totalitarian Nazi Germany would not have gone to war.

Moreover, although the Soviet Union was a totalitarian state with visions of changing the world, its ideology focused on revolutionary processes over major war, and its tactics stressed subversion, revolution, diplomatic and economic pressure, seduction, guerrilla warfare, local uprising, and civil war. The Communists never subscribed to a Hitler-style theory of direct, Armageddon-risking conquest. In addition, their revolutionary methodology contained a strong sense of cautious pragmatism: a good revolutionary moves carefully in a hostile world, striking when the prospects for success are bright and avoiding risky undertakings. Given their global game plan stressing revolutionary upheaval and given their experience with two disastrous world wars, a major war in Europe or against the United States, whether conventional or nuclear, scarcely made any sense whatever.

The essential irrelevance of nuclear weapons

This proposition, first presented as an op-ed and then as an article in *International Security*, has been much developed and expanded in my *Atomic Obsession* of 2010. The book argues not only that nuclear weapons were not necessary to prevent World War III but that, whatever their impact on activist rhetoric, strategic theorizing, defense budgets, and political posturing, nuclear weapons have had at best a quite limited effect on history, have been a substantial waste of money and effort, do not seem to have been terribly appealing to most states that do not have them, are out of reach for terrorists, and are unlikely materially to shape much of our future, even as nuclear proliferation, while not necessarily desirable, is unlikely to prove to be a major danger or to accelerate.

In addition, a set of essays, one of them by me, examining the essential irrelevance thesis from a number of angles has been published under the editorship of John Lewis Gaddis, Philip Gordon, Ernest May, and Jonathan Rosenberg.

The waning of major war

The notion that major war may be obsolescent has also been subject to a series of essays, assessing the merits of the proposition and evaluating its implications. Among these are an article by Christopher Fettweis and a book edited by Raimo Väyrynen that includes ruminations by Marie Henehan, Kalevi Holsti, Patrick Morgan, T. V. Paul, Paul Schroeder, Hendrik Spruyt, William Thompson, Martin van Creveld, John Vasquez, Peter Wallensteen, Väyrynen, and me.

Reflections references

Chrisopher J. Fettweis, A Revolution in International Relations Theory? *International Studies Review* 8(4), December 2006.

John Lewis Gaddis, Philip H. Gordon, Ernest R. May, and Jonathan Rosenberg, eds., *Cold War Statesmen Confront the Bomb: Nuclear Diplomacy Since 1945*. Oxford, UK: Oxford University Press, 1999.

George Orwell, *Nineteen Eighty-Four*. London: Secker and Warburg, 1949.

Raimo Väyrynen, ed., *The Waning of Major War: Theories and Debates*. New York: Routledge, 2006.

2   Policing the remnants of war

Introduction

In some very important respects, the institution of war is clearly in decline. Certain standard, indeed classic, varieties of war – particularly major war or wars among developed countries – have become so rare and unlikely that they could well be considered to be obsolescent, if not obsolete. Also in notable decline, it appears, are conventional war more generally, conventional civil war, colonial war, and ideological civil war.[1]

Moreover, much, but not all, of what remains of war, sometimes labeled 'new war', 'ethnic conflict', or, most grandly, 'clashes of civilizations', is more nearly opportunistic predation waged by packs – often remarkably small ones – of criminals, bandits, and thugs. To a substantial and perhaps increasing degree, then, warfare has been reduced to its remnants – or dregs – and thugs are the residual combatants. And history and recent experience suggest that much of this could be, and perhaps is being, reduced or substantially eliminated by disciplined police and military forces. The key to dealing with these wars lies more with the development of competent domestic governments than with the application of international policing. This article explores these themes.

The remnants of war

Most contemporary war is civil war and almost all of it occurs in poor countries.[2] A survey of the three dozen or so wars that have been waged since the end of the Cold War suggests that many, often most, of the combatants in these wars are criminals and thugs who engage in warfare in much the same way as they often did in medieval and early modern Europe: as mercenaries recruited or dragooned by weak (or even desperate) state governments or as warlord gangs developed within failed or weak states. A few contemporary civil wars, however, do variously betray elements of disciplined, if mainly unconventional, conflict, as does much terrorism.[3]

Criminal warfare: The mercenary approach

The wars in former Yugoslavia illustrate the mercenary process best (Mueller, 2000a, b). It is important to note that the Serbian (or Yugoslav) army rather substantially disintegrated early in the hostilities and this, as Burg and Shoup (1999: 137) observe, 'led all sides to rely on irregulars and special units'.[4] Specifically, like many of the lords and kings of medieval Europe, the politicians recruited criminals and hooligans to get into the action. As part of this process, it appears that thousands of prison inmates, promised shortened sentences and enticed by the prospect that they could 'take whatever booty you can', were released in Serbia for the war effort (Borger, 1997; Cohen, 1998: 192, 410–411). Similarly, the initial fighting forces of Bosnia and of Croatia were also substantially made up of small bands of criminals and violent opportunists recruited or self-recruited from street gangs.

Thus, the key dynamic of the conflicts was not in the risings of neighbor against neighbor, still less in the clashings of civilizations. Rather, it was in the focused predations of comparatively small groups of violent, and very often drunken, thugs and criminals recruited and semi-coordinated by politicians. Identity, ethnicity, nationalism, civilization, culture, and religion proved to be more nearly an excuse, pretext, or general organizing principle for their predations rather than an independent cause of them.

Other instances in which governments and armies have recruited criminals and thugs essentially as mercenary forces include some of the 'death squads' in Latin America and elsewhere (Campbell & Brenner, 2000). Particularly in the last years of its occupation of East Timor, the Indonesian army found it useful to band together and coordinate the activities of East Timorese 'toughs' and 'musclemen', as Moore (2001) calls them, into paramilitary units. In Somalia, warlord Mohammed Aidid ran his fiefdom with a few dozen hired guns paid in part with drugs (Bowden, 1999: 109, 368), and a large number of criminals were recruited into the national guard of Chechnya (Lieven, 1998: 61–62, 75, 81).

Criminal warfare: The brigand approach

When governments become weak, it is likely (almost by definition) that criminal activity will increase, and sometimes the resulting criminality will be organized enough to look like war. Often the government itself – or even one from a neighboring country – can essentially become one of the criminal or warlord bands (Keen, 1998: ch. 2; Reno, 1998; Gamba & Cornwell, 2000; Berkeley, 2001). Several wars in Africa illustrate the brigand process best. As Berkeley (2001: 15) puts it, 'Ethnic conflict in Africa is a form of organized crime', and the 'warring factions are best understood not as "tribes" but as racketeering enterprises'.

A weakened regime in Liberia was toppled by an armed group initially of 100 or so led by an accused embezzler ($922,382) and jailbreak artist, Charles Taylor, and by a somewhat larger group that had spun off from Taylor's forces, led by a psychopathic, hymn-singing drunk named Prince Yormi Johnson (Ellis, 1999: 2–4, 10, 15, 67–68, 74–75, 319; Reno, 1998: 92). Life as a combatant was routinely facilitated by alcohol and drugs, and it is estimated that 25–30% emerged from the war with a serious drug problem (Ellis, 1999: 134).

To put down a rebellion in neighboring Sierra Leone, the government rapidly expanded its not-very-good army of 3,000 to a really terrible one of 14,000. This rag-tag force, consisting mostly of 'drop-outs and robbers' according to a prominent Sierra Leonean human-rights campaigner, was sent, underpaid, undertrained, and underfed, into combat under commanders who had a distinct preference for leading from the rear (Keen, 1998: 26–28; Reno, 1998: 125). Rather than taking the rebels on, the troops quickly fragmented into bandit gangs and sought to profit from the chaos. Similar patterns of conflict and mayhem have taken place in Nigeria (Reno, 1998), Sudan (Berkeley, 2001), Angola (Gamba & Cornwell, 2000), and Congo (Reno, 1998; Berkeley, 2001), and various countries in the Caucasus and central Asia (Lieven, 1998: ch. 1).[5]

In some respects, the long war in Colombia also fits this pattern. The FARC guerrillas act much like a brigand force (Rabasa & Chalk, 2001: 47–51; Keen, 1998: 35). In opposition are paramilitaries, some of whom work as mercenaries for landowners or business people, while others go off on their own, applying guerrilla tactics against the guerrillas, claiming turf and setting up private fiefdoms. Many of these forces, like the guerrillas, engage in criminal activities such as drug trafficking, kidnapping for ransom, or setting up protection rackets (Sánchez, 2001: 20–25; Rabasa & Chalk, 2001: xvi, 53–55, 58–59).

Disciplined warfare

Although few, if any, of the armed civil conflicts in the post-Cold War era seem clearly and unambiguously to be disciplined wars, differentiating criminal from disciplined warfare is not always easy. Almost all wars – particularly civil wars – contain elements of both. Moreover, at various times disciplined combatants can degenerate into opportunistic criminal predators, while criminal armies can sometimes get their act together and perform like disciplined ones – standing, fighting, and risking their lives for a cause or agenda.

A good case in point is Afghanistan. Reacting to the Soviet invasion of 1979, Afghan warriors fought a guerrilla war with tenacity and discipline against the well-armed but often ill-led and incompetent invaders, causing them to withdraw in 1989. In the aftermath of that victory, however, the former disciplined combatants disintegrated into dozens of squabbling and corrupt warlord and bandit gangs, plundering the population they had once defended (Rashid, 2000: chs. 1–2). A similar pattern seems to have held in the 1994–96 war in Chechnya.

Today, substantial elements of disciplined warfare can be seen in the lengthy, persistent conflict in Sri Lanka in which a tenacious guerrilla group, the Tamil Tigers, is battling for secession. Some Kurdish rebels in Turkey may fit the same pattern. In the second war in Chechnya, begun in 1999, many of the defending combatants seem once again to have reverted from banditry to disciplined, dedicated warfare against the massively destructive Russian army. Moreover, the attacks against Israel by various Arab groups may now have become so continuous and organized that what is going on there can be called disciplined warfare rather than terrorism.

Policing the remnants of war

'The Clausewitzian analysis is breaking down,' writes Keegan (2001: 39). 'War is escaping from state control, into the hands of bandits and anarchists.' Therefore, 'the great work of disarming tribes, sects, warlords and criminals – a principal achievement of monarchs in the 17th century and empires in the 19th – threatens to need doing all over again'. War, of course, is not escaping anyone's control in the once war-prone developed world – quite the reverse. But there are substantial areas in the developing world where it clearly has.

The intimidating, opportunistic, and very often drugged or drunken thugs have been successful mainly because they are the biggest bullies on the block. However, like most bullies (and sadists and torturers), they tend not to be particularly interested in engaging a formidable opponent. Moreover, they substantially lack organization, discipline, coherent tactics or strategy, deep motivation, broad popular support, or ideological commitment.

Therefore, a sufficiently large, impressively armed, and well-disciplined policing force can be effective in pacifying those conflicts which are thug-dominated. The thugs would still exist of course, but insofar as they remained unpacified, they would be reduced to sporadic and improvised crime and violence, not town mastery. For example, during the post-Cold War period, disciplined forces were up against criminal ones in Panama, Somalia, Haiti, East Timor, Sierra Leone, Croatia, and Bosnia.[6] In all cases, the disciplined forces triumphed easily and at remarkably low cost in casualties – though in Somalia the peace-keepers found that cost to be insufficiently low given the value of the stakes.

Policing by developed countries

In their new era of essential consensus in the wake of the Cold War, the developed countries have been free to explore various devices for managing the world. Some of these devices are diplomatic, social, or economic, but the judicious application of military force is also potentially available. Freed of disagreements among themselves – at least of disagreements that could lead to violent conflict between them – they are free to carry out the 'great work' that Keegan calls for, in a series of what might be called 'policing wars'.

It seems unlikely, however, that the developed states will be able to respond to this opportunity by creating mechanisms for systematically dealing with civil warfare. They are likely to intervene with any sort of reliability either by themselves or through international bodies only where their interests are or seem to be importantly engaged or where they manage to become self-entrapped. And even then, they are likely to intervene with enormous concern about suffering too many casualties of their own.

From time to time, their attention may be arrested by concerns about international terrorism, about the dispersion of 'weapons of mass destruction' to what are sometimes called 'rogue states', about the flow of illegal drugs to their own populations, and about refugee flows that cause them trouble and cost them money. Thus, armed ventures may be launched to push back international aggression, as in the Persian Gulf in 1991, or to relieve the peoples of Afghanistan and Iraq of vicious and unpopular regimes a decade later. But these ventures are primarily impelled and justified by fears about terrorist or international threats that seem to emanate from those countries, not by humanitarian concerns about the conditions of their peoples. For the most part, then, developed countries are likely to see most civil conflicts as essentially irrelevant to their interests and thus to remain aloof.[7]

International bodies and consortiums of developed countries can often be useful to broker ceasefires and peace settlements, and they can sometimes assist with humanitarian aid and economic and political development once peace has been achieved. However, a truly effective solution to the problem of residual warfare lies elsewhere. And there may be one.

Policing by effective governments

It seems likely that the key to controlling the remnants of war is the establishment of competent domestic military and policing forces, tracing a process Europe went through in the middle of the last millennium. After all, it was not efforts by the international community that brought warfare, particularly civil warfare, under control in Europe, but rather the development of capable governments.[8] And, to a very substantial degree, much of the civil warfare that persists in the world today is a function of the extent to which inadequate governments exist.

As one study finds (Hegre et al., 2001), civil wars are least likely to occur in stable democracies and in stable autocracies – that is, in countries with effective governments and policing forces (see also Oberschall, 2001: 135–136; Russett & Oneal, 2001: 70; Marshall & Gurr, 2003: 19–20, 25; Fearon & Laitin, 2003: 85, 88; Tilly, 2003: ch. 2). Stable democracies, almost by definition, have effective policing forces, and they deal with grievance by bringing the aggrieved into the process (as long as it is expressed peacefully) and listening to the grievance. Stable autocracies also have capable policing forces – in fact, they are often called 'police states'. They rule through the selective, but persistent, application of terror – through vigilant domestic spying and through effective, if often brutal, suppression. North Korea and Cuba provide contemporary examples.

In fact, in an important sense, many civil wars have effectively been *caused* by inept governments. Because of closed political systems and policing methods in which excessive and indiscriminate force is employed to try to deal with relatively small bands of troublemakers, inept governments can turn friendly or indifferent people into hostile ones and vastly increase the size of the problems they are trying to deal with. As Keen (1998: 21) has observed, 'the aggression of counter-insurgency forces has repeatedly alienated their potential civilian supporters, and this has often continued even when evidently counter-productive from a military point of view'.

The spectacularly counterproductive effort of the Serbs to police small bands of Albanian terrorists in their Kosovo province supplies a pertinent case in point. Although the terrorists of the Kosovo Liberation Army (KLA) did not enjoy great support among the Albanians, particularly in the cities, the Serb depredations, carried out mainly by special paramilitary units under the direction of the ministry of the interior in Belgrade, greatly increased the support for the terrorists by essentially forcing Albanians to choose between rule by brutish racist thugs from their own ethnic group or rule by brutish racist thugs from the other ethnic group (Hedges, 1998; O'Connor, 1998; Judah, 1999). The KLA, which numbered no more than 150 before the massacres, quickly increased to an estimated 12,000 (Steele, 1998; Hedges, 1999: 34–36).

Similarly counterproductive was the Indonesian military invasion and occupation of East Timor in 1975. Coming on the heels of a brief civil conflict, the Indonesians could probably have obtained a degree of support from one side as well as acquiescence from the majority of the population. But the invaders instead engaged in an orgy of indiscriminate brutality, torture, murder, rape, massacre, looting, and pillage. This forced much of the population into rebel territory, hardened resistance, and led to an on-and-off guerrilla conflict that lasted 24 years and ended in an internationally supervised loss of the conquest. It is notable that when the Portuguese controlled East Timor, they did so with a military force of no more than 1,500, while the Indonesians needed forces in the tens of thousands (Dunn, 1995: 65–72).

Similar processes have taken place in Algeria (Kalyvas, 1999: 261), Sierra Leone (Keen, 1998: 26–28), Liberia (Ellis, 1999: 76–79, 113; Howe, 1996/97: 149), Chechnya (Lieven, 1998: 126–134), Lebanon (Mackey, 1989: 175, 204), Guatemala (Stoll, 1993; Valentino, 2003), and elsewhere.

Something comparable can happen when the police and government, either through incompetence or lack of will, are unable to protect minorities from rioters who purport to represent the majority. In Sri Lanka, for example, Tamils have variously identified themselves by their origin of emigration or by the region of the country in which they lived. But gangs of Sinhalese, reacting to incidents of Tamil terrorism, rioted against Tamils in Colombo and elsewhere in 1983, looting, killing, and setting fires while the police mainly stood by in effective, and sometimes actual, complicity. Tamils of all varieties then fled to safety in one potentially secessionist corner of the country, one that came to be controlled by Tamil terrorists acting as warlords (Tambiah, 1986: 21; Kloos, 2001). Something similar happened in Azerbaijan in 1988 (Kaufman, 2001: 64).

Prosperity may be beneficial if it helps to develop, or comes associated with, competent governments and police forces, but wealth itself is not the key operative factor. Thus, it is entirely possible to imagine Bosnian-like chaos in prosperous Quebec or Northern Ireland if the Canadian or British authorities had attempted to deal with conflicts there through murderous rampage rather than through patient policing and political accommodation.

Indeed, when poor countries adopt sound and accommodating political policies, they often do quite well. Thus, ethnic violence has been avoided in Bulgaria and Romania even though those countries are hardly more developed than Serbia or Bosnia and even though they have experienced considerably greater ethnic tension.[9] And the most impressive case is Macedonia, former Yugoslavia's poorest province. In 1991, Kaplan (1991: 104) ominously declared that 'Macedonia is once again poised to erupt. . . . Rarely has the very process of history been so transparent and cyclical.' Over the course of a tense decade, despite those 'transparent and cyclical' threats, Macedonian political leaders deftly and successfully sought calm accommodation and substantially achieved it (Ackermann, 2000; Lund, 2000). Things became more difficult later with the rise of an armed insurgency based outside the country – in Kosovo – after the war there of 1999. There were some very rough moments, particularly when the government seemed on the verge of sending Slav gangs into the action (Wood, 2001). However, in part because of active work by the European Community, the Macedonian leadership again was able to keep things under control (Pearson, 2002). Its experience strongly suggests that the disasters in the more prosperous areas of former Yugoslavia, far from being inevitable, could very likely have been avoided if politicians and police had behaved more sensibly.

Thus, the establishment of effective government or, more specifically, of coherent and responsive political systems and disciplined military and policing forces, is the key to engendering and maintaining civil peace – to policing the thugs, brigands, bandits, highwaymen, goons, bullies, criminals, pirates, mercenaries, robbers, adventurers, hooligans, and children who seem to be the chief remaining perpetrators of a type of violence that can be said to resemble war.

Effective government and trends in residual warfare

People who carefully track the incidence of various forms of violent conflict generally agree on the overall pattern of warfare and armed conflict since World War II. There was something of a tapering-off after that conflict, a rise (mainly in civil warfare) beginning in the 1960s or so that peaked in the early 1990s, and a decline since then (see Eriksson, Wallensteen & Sollenberg, 2003; Gleditsch et al., 2002; Marshall & Gurr, 2003: 12–14; Fearon & Laitin, 2003; 77–78; Tilly, 2003: ch. 3).

Obviously, these broad patterns mask all kinds of subtlety and variety, but their overall shape does conform fairly well to the discussion above. The key to the amount of residual (mainly criminal) warfare in the world, it has been argued, is not the degree to which there is hatred, grievance, or ethnic or civilizational cleavage, but rather the degree to which governments function adequately.

And it appears that the trends in warfare track rather well the existence of weak governments. With the decolonization of the late 1950s and 1960s, a group of poorly governed societies came into being, and, in part because of the processes outlined above, many found themselves having to deal with civil warfare. Moreover, as civil wars became criminal enterprises, they tended to become longer and to accumulate in number (Keen, 1998: ch. 2; Fearon & Laitin, 2003: 77–78). This pattern may have been embellished by another phenomenon: democratization, which is often accompanied by a period in which governments become weak (see also Collier, 2000: 98, 108; Hegre et al., 2001; Snyder, 2000). Most of the datasets document a notable rise – or acceleration in the upward trend – in civil war after 1975, a pattern that coincides rather closely with the rise in democracy that began at that time.

Then, in the aftermath of the Cold War in the early 1990s, there was a further increase in the number of incompetent governments as weak, confused, ill-directed, and sometimes criminal governments emerged in many of the post-Communist countries, replacing comparatively competent police states. In addition, with the end of the Cold War, the developed countries no longer had nearly as much interest in financially propping up some Third World governments and helping them police themselves – an effect particularly noticeable in Africa (Reno, 1998: ch. 2; Keen, 1998: 23; Bates, 2001: ch. 5).

By the mid-1990s, however, a large number of countries had managed to get through the rough period and had achieved a considerable degree of democratic stability – especially in Latin America, post-communist Europe, and East and Southeast Asia – and relatively effective governments had emerged in most of them. Moreover, lingering ideological civil wars inspired or exacerbated by the Cold War contest died out (or became transmogrified into criminal ones) with its demise.

POGG

Experience suggests, then, that the essential, and long-term, solution to the problems of civil warfare lies not in ministrations by the international community – so often half-hearted, half-vast, and half-coherent – but rather in the establishment of competent domestic governments in the many places that do not now have them.

The Canadians, as it happens, have the appropriate slogan. Many countries and institutions have mottoes designed to get the blood flowing, ones that cry for, and are often delivered through, a thicket of exclamation points. There is, for example, 'Liberty! Equality! Fraternity!', or 'Duty! Honor! Country!', or 'One Reich! One People! One Führer!' Canada's national slogan, by contrast, is one of studied modesty: 'Peace, Order and Good Government'.

But whatever the slogan's failings, POGG, as embarrassed Canadians sometimes flippantly put it, is what people throughout the world seem to need and to be yearning for. There is plenty of 'ethnic conflict' in Canada – between Francophones and Anglophones – but that conflict over the course of a third of a century resulted in exactly one death (Horowitz, 2001: 561). And there is a reason for that: Good Government.

As it happens, the world is not a teeming mass of frustrated, angry, hate-filled fanatics seeking to express their ethnic, religious, cultural, or civilizational angst in cataclysmic violence against each other in a Hobbesian state of nature. There are small numbers of people, it is true, who are drawn to violence and yearn to experience its exhilarations and its potential profits. Some of these are, indeed, fanatics and true believers, but most are criminals and thugs, and small, unpoliced, or badly policed bands of these people can cause vastly more devastation than their numbers would seem to imply.[10] What is needed to keep them in check – to establish peace and order – is good government, following the path the developed world fell upon in the middle of the last millennium.

But for the most part, the establishment of peace and order through good government – which is perhaps the way the Canadian motto should be read – needs to be accomplished by people within the countries themselves. Sometimes, international authorities, working out of or under the direction of the developed countries, have been able to aid or speed the process. And they can certainly be of assistance when a country sincerely desires to develop the kinds of competent military and police forces that have helped bring peace and prosperity to the developed world. Moreover, the example of the developed societies – civil, prosperous, flexible, productive, and free from organized violent conflict – can be most attractive, as indicated by the masses of people from the developing world who are trying to immigrate there, abandoning in fear and disgust the turmoil and violence of their home countries. However, unless the developed world wants once again to engage in a form of colonialism, it is likely that exercises in nation-building that are productive of peace and order will have to be accomplished – and, ultimately, with results that are most likely to be lasting – by forces that are domestic.

Over the course of the last few decades, there seems to have been an increase in the developing world in the number of countries that are led by effective people who, instead of looting and dissipating their country's resources like Zaire's Mobutu, seem to be dedicated to adopting policies that will further its orderly development – something Rotberg (2002) labels 'positive leadership'. This has happened in almost all of Latin America as well as in many places in Asia – areas that, not coincidentally, have also experienced a considerable decline in warfare.

Whether Africa – the area that continues to be most plagued by civil warfare – will follow that pattern is yet to be determined, but there are at least some hopeful signs. Quite remarkable changes have taken place in South Africa, which managed to move to coherent, responsive democracy from a condition that was part democracy and part police state – although huge problems remain. Central to that remarkable accomplishment was the judicious leadership of the country's first elected post-apartheid president, Nelson Mandela.

The Mandela approach may be gradually replacing the Mobutu one in Africa and elsewhere (Reno, 2000: 59; Berkeley, 2001: 226–242; Rotberg, 2002). Among the potential candidates variously suggested as 'new leaders' are Musaveni in Uganda, the younger Kabila in Congo, Kagame in Rwanda, Obasanjo in Nigeria, Deby in Chad, Konare and perhaps Touré in Mali, Wade in Senegal, and Karzai in Afghanistan. Whether such people will proliferate in other countries, whether these people will truly follow the Mandela route rather than the Mobutu one, and whether they will really be able to improve the situation in their countries remains to be seen, of course. But since competent government seems to be vital to controlling civil warfare, this development could be of profound importance.[11]

There are signs, then, that in an increasing number of places fanatics, criminals, and thugs, the chief authors and organizers of what remains of war in the world, are being brought under control or sometimes aptly coopted by effective governments. Criminality and criminal predation will still exist (there is some of that even in Canada) and so will terrorism which, like crime, can be carried out by individuals or very small groups. And there will certainly be plenty of other problems to worry about – famine, disease, malnutrition, pollution, corruption, poverty, politics, and economic travail.

However, while far from certain, a further (or continuing) decline in a most common remaining kind of war does seem to be an entirely reasonable prospect.

Notes

1   For an assessment of this process, see Mueller (1989, 1995: chs. 8–9). See also Mueller (forthcoming).
2   For recent tabulations of the relative frequency of armed conflicts, see Gleditsch et al. (2002), Eriksson, Wallensteen & Sollenberg (2003), and Marshall & Gurr (2003). By one calculation, a poor country is 85 times more likely to experience violent conflict than a rich one (Ellingsen, 2000: 243). See also Collier (2000: 97, 109–110), Hegre et al. (2001: 37, 40), Mack (2002: 521), Fearon & Laitin (2003: 83).
3   For the argument that these remaining wars are anything but 'new' in form or substance, see Kalyvas (2001).
4   This process is almost too vividly illustrated by the experience of General Slavko Lisica, who tried to shame Serb conscripts in Croatia into fighting by declaring that all those who were not prepared to 'defend the glory of the Serbian nation' should lay down their arms and take off their uniforms. To his astonishment, 'they all did, including their commanding officer'. Furious, he shouted at them 'to remove everything including their underpants, and with the exception of one man they all removed their military issue underpants and marched off completely naked'. Later, he says, the recruits managed to commandeer a cannon and used it to shell his headquarters (Doder & Branson, 1999: 97–98).
5   Assessing the warlord predation that is taking place in several countries in Africa, Keen (2000: 26) describes a process in which 'one avoids battles, picks on unarmed civilians, and makes money'. He calls this 'war', but his characterization seems much more nearly to be a description of crime. In fact, many of these 'low-intensity wars' seem more nearly to be high-intensity crime.
6   While Serb forces in Croatia and Bosnia remained criminal-dominated, their enemies developed disciplined, non-criminal forces (Mueller, 2000a: 64–65).
7   Under the administration of George W. Bush, the United States, unchallenged militarily in the world after the Cold War, explored the possibility of taking out perceived threats to itself by unilateral or near-unilateral military measures in Afghanistan in 2001 and in Iraq in 2003. Whether this constitutes a new application of war for what the United States, at least, would take to be policing purposes remains to be seen. The messy aftermaths of these two wars suggest its appeals are likely to be limited.
8   Of course, the attainment of civil order did not keep European governments from engaging in international wars. However, the present aversion to international war should continue to limit such wars even in a world filled with competent states – as it has in once-warlike Europe.
9   On Bulgaria, see Ganev (1997) and Barany (2002). On Romania and Slovakia, see Linden (2000). On Kazakhstan, see Kaufman (2001: 78–80).

10 In a review of several studies of 'ethnic' war, Fearon and Laitin (2000: 869) observe that 'what is described as ethnic violence looks very much like gang violence with no necessary ethnic dimension' in which what is required is simply the 'availability of mobilizable thugs'. They then muse: 'One might ask if there has been a great upsurge in ethnic war since the end of the Cold War, or whether more insurgencies are not labeled "ethnic" due to opportunistic redescriptions and salesmanship by rebel leaders seeking support from great power patrons newly disposed to see ethnic rather than Left–Right conflict.' Indeed, one might very well ask that.

11 That such a change is possible and can happen quite quickly is suggested by the experience in Latin America, where military leaders became increasingly convinced that military dictatorship was a thing of the past, and country after country became democratic.

References

Ackermann, Alice, 2000. *Making Peace Prevail: Preventing Violent Conflict in Macedonia*. Syracuse, NY: Syracuse University Press.

Barany, Zoltan, 2002. 'Bulgaria's Royal Elections', *Journal of Democracy* 13(2): 141–155.

Bates, Robert H., 2001. *Prosperity and Violence: The Political Economy of Development*. New York: Norton.

Berdal, Mats & David M. Malone, eds, 2000. *Greed and Grievance: Economic Agendas in Civil Wars*. Boulder, CO: Lynne Rienner.

Berkeley, Bill, 2001. *The Graves Are Not Yet Full: Race, Tribe and Power in the Heart of Africa*. New York: Basic Books.

Borger, Julian, 1997. 'The President's Secret Henchmen', *Guardian Weekly*, 16 February: 8.

Bowden, Mark, 1999. *Black Hawk Down: A Story of Modern War*. New York: Atlantic Monthly Press.

Burg, Steven L. & Paul S. Shoup, 1999. *The War in Bosnia-Herzegovina: Ethnic Conflict and International Intervention*. Armonk, NY: Sharpe.

Campbell, Bruce B. & Arthur D. Brenner, eds, 2000. *Death Squads in Global Perspective: Murder with Deniability*. New York: St. Martin's Press.

Cohen, Roger, 1998. *Hearts Grown Brutal: Sagas of Sarajevo*. New York: Random House.

Collier, Paul, 2000. 'Doing Well out of War: An Economic Perspective', in Berdal & Malone (91–111).

Doder, Dusko & Louise Branson, 1999. *Milosevic: Portrait of a Tyrant*. New York: Free Press.

Dunn, James, 1995. 'The Timor Affair in International Perspective', in Peter Carey & G. Carter Bentley, eds, *East Timor at the Crossroads: The Forging of a Nation*. Honolulu, HI: University of Hawai'i Press (59–72).

Ellingsen, Tanja, 2000. 'Colorful Community or Ethnic Witches' Brew?', *Journal of Conflict Resolution* 44(2): 228–249.

Ellis, Stephen, 1999. *The Mask of Anarchy: The Destruction of Liberia and the Religious Dimension of an African Civil War*. New York: New York University Press.

Eriksson, Mikael, Peter Wallensteen & Margareta Sollenberg, 2003. 'Armed Conflict, 1989–2002', *Journal of Peace Research* 40(5): 593–608.

Fearon, James D. & David D. Laitin, 2000. 'Violence and the Social Construction of Ethnic Identity', *International Organization* 54(4): 845–877.

Fearon, James D. & David D. Laitin, 2003. 'Ethnicity, Insurgency, and Civil War', *American Political Science Review* 97(1): 75–90.

Gamba, Virginia & Richard Cornwell, 2000. 'Arms, Elites, and Resources in the Angolan Civil War', in Berdal & Malone (157–172).

Ganev, Venelin I., 1997. 'Bulgaria's Symphony of Hope', *Journal of Democracy* 8(4): 125–139.

Gleditsch, Nils Petter, Peter Wallensteen, Mikael Eriksson, Margareta Sollenberg & Håvard Strand, 2002. 'Armed Conflict 1946–2001: A New Dataset', *Journal of Peace Research* 39(5): 615–637.

Hedges, Chris, 1998. 'Kosovo Rebels' New Tactic: Attack Serb Civilians', *New York Times*, 24 June: A1.

Hedges, Chris, 1999. 'Kosovo's Next Masters?', *Foreign Affairs* 78(3): 24–42.

Hegre, Håvard, Tanja Ellingsen, Scott Gates & Nils Petter Gleditsch, 2001. 'Toward a Democratic Civil Peace? Democracy, Political Change, and Civil War, 1816–1992', *American Political Science Review* 95(1): 33–48.

Horowitz, Donald L., 2001. *The Deadly Ethnic Riot*. Berkeley, CA: University of California Press.

Howe, Herbert, 1996/97. 'Lessons of Liberia: ECOMOG and Regional Peacekeeping', *International Security* 21(1): 145–176.

Judah, Tim, 1999. 'KLA Is Still a Force To Be Reckoned With', *Wall Street Journal*, 7 April: A22.

Kalyvas, Stathis N., 1999. 'Wanton and Senseless? The Logic of Massacres in Algeria', *Rationality and Society* 11(3): 243–285.

Kalyvas, Stathis N., 2001. ' "New" and "Old" Civil Wars: A Valid Distinction?', *World Politics* 54(1): 99–118.

Kaplan, Robert D., 1991. 'History's Cauldron', *Atlantic Monthly* 267 (June): 93–104.

Kaufman, Stuart J., 2001. *Modern Hatreds: The Symbolic Politics of Ethnic War*. Ithaca, NY: Cornell University Press.

Keegan, John, 2001. 'The Threat from Europe', *Spectator*, 24 March: 38–39.

Keen, David, 1998. *The Economic Functions of Violence in Civil Wars*. London: International Institute for Strategic Studies, Adelphi Paper No. 320.

Keen, David, 2000. 'Incentives and Disincentives for Violence', in Berdal & Malone (19–41).

Kloos, Peter, 2001. 'A Turning Point? From Civil Struggle to Civil War in Sri Lanka', in Bettina E. Schmidt & Ingo W. Schröder, eds, *Anthropology of Violence and Conflict*. London: Routledge (176–196).

Lieven, Anatol, 1998. *Chechnya: Tombstone of Russian Power*. New Haven, CT: Yale University Press.

Linden, Robert H., 2000. 'Putting on Their Sunday Best: Romania, Hungary, and the Puzzle of Peace', *International Studies Quarterly* 44(1): 121–145.

Lund, Michael S., 2000. 'Preventive Diplomacy for Macedonia, 1992–1999: From Containment to Nation Building', in Bruce W. Jentleson, ed., *Opportunities Missed, Opportunities Seized: Preventive Diplomacy in the Post-Cold War World*. Lanham, MD: Rowman & Littlefield (173–208).

Mack, Andrew, 2002. 'Civil War: Academic Research and the Policy Community', *Journal of Peace Research* 39(5): 515–525.

Mackey, Sandra, 1989. *Lebanon: Death of a Nation*. New York: Congdon & Weed.

Marshall, Monty G. & Ted Robert Gurr, 2003. *Peace and Conflict, 2003: A Global Survey of Armed Conflicts, Self-determination Movements, and Democracy*. College Park, MD: Center for International Development and Conflict Management, University of Maryland.

Moore, Samuel, 2001. 'The Indonesian Military's Last Years in East Timor: An Analysis of its Secret Documents', *Indonesia* 72 (October): 9–44.

Mueller, John, 1989. *Retreat from Doomsday: The Obsolescence of Major War*. New York: Basic Books (http://psweb.sbs.ohio-state.edu/faculty/jmueller/links).

Mueller, John, 1995. *Quiet Cataclysm: Reflections on the Recent Transformation of World Politics*. New York: HarperCollins (http://psweb.sbs.ohio-state.edu/faculty/jmueller/links).

Mueller, John, 2000a. 'The Banality of "Ethnic War" ', *International Security* 25(1): 42–70.

Mueller, John, 2000b. 'The Banality of "Ethnic War": Yugoslavia and Rwanda', paper presented at the Annual Meeting of the American Political Science Association, Washington, DC, 2 September (http://psweb.sbs.ohio-state. edu/faculty/jmueller/links).

Mueller, John, forthcoming. *The Remnants of War*. Ithaca, NY: Cornell University Press.

Oberschall, Anthony, 2001. 'From Ethnic Cooperation to Violence and War in Yugoslavia', in Daniel Chirot & Martin E. P. Seligman, eds, *Ethnopolitical Warfare: Causes, Consequences, and Possible Solutions*. Washington, DC: American Psychological Association (119–150).

O'Connor, Mike, 1998. '12,000 Flee Serb Attack on a Town in Kosovo'. *New York Times*, 22 July: A6.

Pearson, Brenda, 2002. *Putting Peace into Practice: Can Macedonia's New Government Meet the Challenge?* Special Report. Washington, DC: United States Institute of Peace.

Rabasa, Angel & Peter Chalk, 2001. *Colombian Labyrinth: The Synergy of Drugs and Insurgency and its Implications for Regional Stability*. Santa Monica, CA: RAND.

Rashid, Ahmed, 2000. *Taliban: Militant Islam, Oil and Fundamentalism in Central Asia*. New Haven, CT: Yale University Press.

Reno, William, 1998. *Warlord Politics and African States*. Boulder, CO: Lynne Rienner.

Reno, William, 2000. 'Shadow States and the Political Economy of Civil Wars', in Berdal & Malone (43–68).

Rotberg, Robert, 2002. 'New Breed of African Leader', *Christian Science Monitor*, 9 January: 9.

Russett, Bruce M. & John R. Oneal, 2001. *Triangulating Peace: Democracy, Interdependence, and International Organizations*. New York: Norton.

Sánchez, G. Gonzalo, 2001. 'Problems of Violence, Prospects for Peace', in Charles Bergquist, Ricardo Peñarand & Gonzalo G. Sánchez, eds, *Violence in Colombia: Waging War and Negotiating Peace*. Wilmington, DE: Scholarly Resources (1–38).

Snyder, Jack, 2000. *From Voting to Violence: Democratization and Nationalist Conflict*. New York: Norton.

Steele, Jonathan, 1998. 'Kosovo Fighters Set No-go Areas', *Guardian Weekly*, 17 May: 4.

Stoll, David, 1993. *Between Two Armies in the Ixil Towns of Guatemala*. New York: Columbia University Press.

Tambiah, Stanley J., 1986. *Sri Lanka: Ethnic Fratricide and the Dismantling of Democracy*. Chicago, IL: University of Chicago Press.

Tilly, Charles, 2003. *The Politics of Collective Violence*. New York: Cambridge University Press.

Valentino, Benjamin, 2003. *Final Solutions*. Ithaca, NY: Cornell University Press.

Wood, Nicholas, 2001. 'Killer Gangs Plot Revenge in Macedonia', *Observer* (London), 6 May. Observer website special report (http://www.observer.co.uk/Print/0,3858,418 1792,00.html).

REFLECTIONS

War, love, and the combat high

At base, war is a hopeless problem, but it does not seem to be a serious one. The problem is hopeless because it is clearly impossible to make war impossible. It may be true that on some perfectly reasonable level war is a ludicrous, even childish, enterprise. The experience of millennia, however, has shown that people, if effectively organized and inspired, will dutifully embrace the absurdity and march off to slaughter each other in large numbers, that they will accept the experience as appropriate and sensible, and that they will often find it fascinating. The knowledge about how to make war and the capacity to do so, in other words, will always be with us—they can never be fully expunged.

The problem would be a serious one if war were also somehow necessary—if it were a natural requirement of the human condition. However, although war exploits natural qualities and proclivities it is neither necessary nor inevitable, a proposition I have explored more fully in *The Remnants of War* and in an essay in *Quiet Cataclysm*.

One emotional or natural element that makes war possible is the appeal of the combat high. At least for some soldiers, battle turns out to be extremely exhilarating—war, as William James once observed, is "supremely thrilling excitement" and "the supreme theater of human strenuousness." Vietnam veteran William Broyles has come to a similar conclusion: "War is ugly, horrible, evil, and it is reasonable for men to hate all that. But I believe that most men who have been to war would have to admit, if they are honest, that somewhere inside themselves they loved it too, loved it as much as anything that has happened to them before or since." It is "an experience of great intensity"; it "replaces the difficult gray areas of daily life with an eerie, serene clarity"; "if you come back whole [a notable qualification] you bring with you the knowledge that you have explored regions of your soul that in most men will always remain uncharted"; "war may be the only way in which most men touch the mythic domain of our soul. It is . . . the initiation into the power of life and death." "Most men who have been to war . . . remember that never in their lives did they have so heightened a sexuality. War is, in short, a turn-on."

There is another key emotion that makes war possible. In order to make men actually engage in combat, a number of devices have been applied over the centuries such as bribery, liquor, drugs, religion, appeals to patriotism, and sheer, murderous compulsion. Studies of combat motivation generally conclude, however, that the most reliable quality inspiring people to risk deadly, dangerous combat is love, or more specifically a quality variously known as small group loyalty, unit cohesion, primary group solidarity, male bonding, or the buddy system. For Broyles, the most "enduring emotion of war" is "comradeship" and "brotherly love," a "utopian experience" in which "individual possessions and advantage count for nothing, the group is everything."

But while these two qualities may help in an important way to make war *possible*, they do not make it inevitable or necessary. This is because there seems to be no natural requirement that people must necessarily experience either the combat high or the intense love of comradeship under fire. Moreover, after battle, soldiers seem to be able to live out the rest of their lives without ever again engaging in these emotional experiences, no matter how exhilarating and "utopian" they once found them to be. Broyles makes this clear: "I never want to fight again," and "I would do everything in my power to keep my son from fighting." Indeed, the argument can be made even stronger. After experiencing the intense love and the heady high of the combat experience, soldiers must be able, like Broyles, to slump back into drab peacetime endeavors without seeking to recreate the combat experience on their own (those few unable to make the transition are locked up in prisons or mental institutions). Were this not the case, no one would go to war in the first place because in the longer run they would trigger qualities that would destroy their own societies.

The appeals of love and of the combat high that permit war to happen should be seen as tools or capacities of human nature that can be exploited rather than as dynamic natural forces that must be unleashed, diverted, or bottled up. And tools that no longer seem useful or have become out of date can—like a rusty old rake—simply be neglected with neither anxiety nor remorse.

Developing armies: recruiting criminals and ordinary men

None of this should lead to the conclusion that recruiting, retaining, and motivating a combatant force is easy. The appeals of love and of the combat high may be real, but recruiting has often failed miserably, and desertion and defection have been exceedingly common in warfare even when, as is very often the case, the penalty is death. That is, the central problem in warfare through the ages has been to keep men from flagrantly disobeying orders by deserting at the earliest opportunity.

Moreover, the problem in constituting armies is not simply to create forces that will conduct themselves well during the violence of combat, but ones that can also endure the long periods of boring and uncomfortable languor between engagements. The combat experience consists of long periods of tedium punctuated by episodes of sheer terror, and the prosecution of war requires the recruitment, retention, and motivation of men who can withstand both challenges. They must be able to live with and to commit intense violence, but they must also be able to endure long intervals—months at least, often years—of various kinds of deprivation. Among the problems: lice, maggots, leeches, and other vermin; debilitating and very often fatal battles with dysentery and other diseases; the absence of women; terrible, even inedible, food; germ-ridden water; stale cigarettes; bone-deep fatigue; syphilitic prostitutes; watered or even poisonous liquor; sleep deprivation; family separation and homesickness; absence of privacy; constant and often brutal and pointless harassment or physical abuse by superiors and by the incoherent system; exposure to extremes of weather; masturbatory fantasies that become decreasingly stimulating; and boredom that can become cosmic, overwhelming, stupefying—an emotion, only rarely remarked upon that is far more common in war than the rush that comes with combat.

Broadly speaking, there seem to be two methods for developing armies— for successfully cajoling or coercing collections of men into engaging in the violent, profane, sacrificial, uncertain, masochistic, and essentially absurd enterprise known as war.

Intuitively, it might seem that the easiest (and cheapest) method for recruiting combatants would be to enlist people who revel in violence and regularly employ it to enrich themselves—people who, it might appear, are most likely to relish the combat high. We have in civilian life a name for such people—criminals—but the category would also encompass people popularly known as bullies, hooligans, toughs, goons, and thugs.

It happens, however, that criminals and thugs tend to be undesirable warriors, however much they may be drawn to combat by their inclination to relish violence or to find profit in it. To begin with, they are often difficult to control. They tend to be troublemakers: unruly, disobedient, and mutinous, committing unauthorized crimes while on (or off) duty that can be detrimental or even destructive of the military enterprise. This natural unruliness can be enhanced by the deprivation and boredom that commonly envelop the long periods between military action. Most importantly, criminals are often disinclined to stand and fight when things become truly dangerous, and they often simply desert when whim and opportunity coincide. The motto for the criminal, after all, is not a variation of "semper fi," "all for one and one for all," "duty, honor, country," "Banzai," or "remember Pearl Harbor," but "take the money and run." In general, then, although thugs do seem to be more willing to accept risk than ordinary people, and although they can be induced to engage in battle by the appeal of pay or booty and by the prospect of inflicting violence, they will tend reliably to fight only when the probability of being killed is low enough or when they are massively coerced.

The discovery of these problems with the employment of criminals as combatants has historically led to efforts to recruit ordinary men as combatants—people who, unlike criminals and thugs, commit violence at no other time in their lives (though they may watch a lot of it on television). Combat studies, in fact, generally find performance positively correlated with social class, education, intelligence, and personal stability.

The result has been the development of disciplined warfare in which men primarily inflict violence not for fun and profit, but because their training and indoctrination has instilled in them a need to follow orders, to observe a carefully contrived and tendentious code of honor, to seek glory and reputation in combat, to love, honor, or fear their officers, to believe in a cause, to fear the shame, humiliation, or costs of surrender, or, in particular, to be loyal to, and to deserve the loyalty of, their fellow combatants.

Distinguishing between crime, terrorism, and war

A distinction between criminal and disciplined warfare can be used to differentiate between war, crime, and terrorism.

Most definitions of terrorism hold it to be violent activity with some sort of political or policy purpose that targets civilians. This focus on the terrorist's victims can be problematic because terrorists often target the military or police. More helpful may be to concentrate on the intensity and frequency of the violence.

Terrorism and criminal activity are similar in that they are carried out sporadically by small groups and individuals. They differ in their goals and in the willingness of the perpetrators to risk death. Terrorists operate in pursuit of a political goal and are frequently willing to die in the effort, while criminals are in the game for fun and profit and are distinctly unwilling to die in the process.

When criminal bands become significant enough in size or when governments enlist significant numbers of criminals into their military forces, the activity becomes criminal warfare. When violence focused on a political aim is applied in a disciplined manner by substantial groups and becomes continuous or sustained, it ceases to be terrorism and becomes disciplined warfare.

The distinction applied here between terrorism and disciplined war is essentially quantitative then. Terrorism, like crime, is a relatively petty event—an incidental, isolated act of mayhem perpetrated by individuals or by small groups, violence that generally does a comparatively limited amount of damage. If such activity becomes common and sustained, we no longer call the process terrorism, but insurgency, guerrilla or unconventional warfare, or, simply, war.

Thus, it seems reasonable to consider the Irish Republican Army—whose activities, together with those of its opponents, resulted in the deaths of less than 100 people per year—to be a terrorist force. But by the same token the sustained and far more murderous activities of anti-government and anti-Soviet forces in Afghanistan in the 1980s continue to be best classified as warfare. The situation in Iraq also illustrates the point. For sound political reasons, President George W. Bush frequently referred to the opposition violence there as "terrorism," but most observers prefer "insurgency."

In fact, if the sustained warfare committed by the insurgents in Iraq is considered to be terrorism, a huge number of what have been called civil wars in the past would have to be reclassified as exercises in terrorism such as the decade-long conflict in Algeria in the 1990s in which perhaps 100,000 people perished. And so would most "primitive warfare," which, like irregular warfare more generally, relies mostly on raids rather than on set-piece battles. Indeed, the concept of civil war might have to be retired almost entirely. Most of the mayhem in the American Civil War did take place in set-piece battles between uniformed combatants, but that conflict was extremely unusual among civil wars in this respect—the rebels in most civil wars substantially rely on tactics that are indistinguishable from those employed by the terrorist.

If criminal or terrorist activity becomes widespread and continuous enough to be labeled war, the goal for those engaged in opposing them is to reverse the process by reducing the violence to more bearable levels. When these efforts are successful, "war"—whether disciplined or criminal—will cease to exist, although crime and terrorism may still persist.

At that point, the rules of policing, rather than those of warfare, apply. In neither case, however, does it make much sense to seek to eliminate the violence entirely: because criminal and terrorist violence can be accomplished at any time by individuals or by very small groups, there is no way it can be completely eradicated. This is fully appreciated in the case of crime, where police chiefs seek to achieve a low and essentially bearable crime rate and do not even pretend to be able to reduce it to zero. In the case of terrorism, however, the impossible goal of complete eradication is very often sought, or, at any rate, proclaimed. Since terrorism, unlike crime, is often an exceedingly rare activity in many areas, this goal may seem achievable. However, it is essentially illusory because there is no way to guarantee that an individual or small group might not from time to time launch another attack.

Reflections references

William Broyles, Jr., Why Men Love War. *Esquire*, November 1984.
William James, *Memories and Studies*. New York: Longmans, Green, 1911.

3 War has almost ceased to exist

An assessment

In 1911, the eminent British historian, G.P. Gooch, concluded a book by ele-giacally declaring that "we can now look forward with something like confidence to the time when war between civilized nations will be considered as antiquated as the duel, and when peacemakers shall be called the children of God." And in that year's edition of the *Encyclopedia Britannica*, Sir Thomas Barclay predicted, in the article on "Peace," that "in no distant future, life among nations" would be characterized by "law, order and peace among men."[1]

During the intervening century, the world has, of course, experienced a very large amount of often hugely destructive warfare, and God, far from blessing peacemakers, appears mostly to have decided to fight "on both sides in that encouraging way He has," as A.A. Milne put it bitterly in the interval separating the two largest of those armed conflicts. During that same period, philosopher George Santayana proclaimed, even more bitterly, "Only the dead have seen the end of war."[2] Indeed, some writers have dubbed the decades after 1911 "the century of warfare," and a very large portion of the international relations and political science literature has been focused on the causes and consequences of war, seen, most notably perhaps, in the monumental *A Study of War*, published at the depths of the most devastating war in history by Quincy Wright.[3]

It may be time to revisit the visions and optimism of a century ago and to assess the massive intervening literature on war because we may be reaching a point where war—in both its international and civil varieties—ceases, or nearly ceases, to exist, a remarkable development that has attracted little notice.

This article assesses and seeks to explain this phenomenon, and it speculates about what the development, should it definitely and definitively materialize, might suggest about the various remedies and nostrums that scholars and analysts—both pessimists and optimists—have prescribed over the last century to deal with the problem of war. Most of these, it appears, have been irrelevant to the process.

Definitions

War is very commonly defined as an armed conflict between governments (in the case of international wars) or between a government and an at least somewhat organized domestic armed group (for civil wars) in which at least 1,000 people are killed each year as a direct consequence, or a fairly direct one (caught in the crossfire), of the fighting.[4]

Most of the literature on war, of course, deals with very substantial conflicts like the World Wars, the American Civil War, or the Korean or Franco-Prussian Wars, in which organized combatants have at each other, and it is surely wars like these that were of primary, even exclusive, concern to Gooch, Barclay, Milne, and Wright. In such a context, a 1,000 battle death threshold could be considered to be very low, even minimalist. Indeed, the Falklands/Malvinas War of 1982 between Britain and Argentina, in which about 1,000 battle deaths were inflicted, has gone down in history almost as something of a comic opera exercise, in considerable part because of its comparatively low casualties.[5]

If an armed conflict inflicts fewer than 1,000 battle and battle-related deaths in a year, there has been a tendency to call it exactly that: an armed conflict, not war.[6] Other terms that might sometimes apply would be terrorism, coordinated riots, a high crime rate, brutal policing, or criminal predation.

There are also armed conflicts, particularly civil ones, in which combatants rarely actually fight each other, but instead primarily prey on the civilian population. Although comparatively few battle or battle-related deaths may be inflicted, considerably more—often vastly more—than 1,000 civilian deaths may result each year, consequences that often persist even after any fighting among combatants stops.[7] Very often war, or a war-like condition, greatly facilitates such deadly activity, and sometimes civilians are massacred as part of a military strategy to defeat an insurgency by eliminating its support network.[8] However, keeping classical definitions of war in mind, unless combatants actually fight against each other in sufficient degree, it seems sensible to use words other than "war" to characterize what is going on in these circumstances. Among these might be ethnic cleansing, genocide, mass killing, terrorism, massacre, extensive criminal predation, or simply, applying a term suggested by Peter Wallensteen, one-sided violence. For present purposes, in order to consider deadly activities as warfare, they must be characterized by extensive two-sided violence. This approach generally captures what I think has traditionally been meant by "war" in the vast majority of the vast literature on the subject.

However, it should be noted that other definitions are certainly possible.[9] For example, some analysts have focused on, and tallied, armed conflicts that inflict as few as 25 battle deaths yearly.[10] Others, rather than simply focusing on the frequency of wars, have applied a measure of destructiveness, weighing costly wars more heavily than those less costly.[11] And still others have tallied warfare without including casualty estimates in their definitions at all.[12] Other data sets, particularly those developed over the last 20 years, have focused entirely on civil wars, applying various definitions about casualties and about the wars' beginning and ending dates.[13] However, no matter how defined, the basic trend lines for warfare as portrayed in Figure 3.1—and in particular for the remarkable decline in recent years that is a central area of concern in this article—are found in all these data sets.[14]

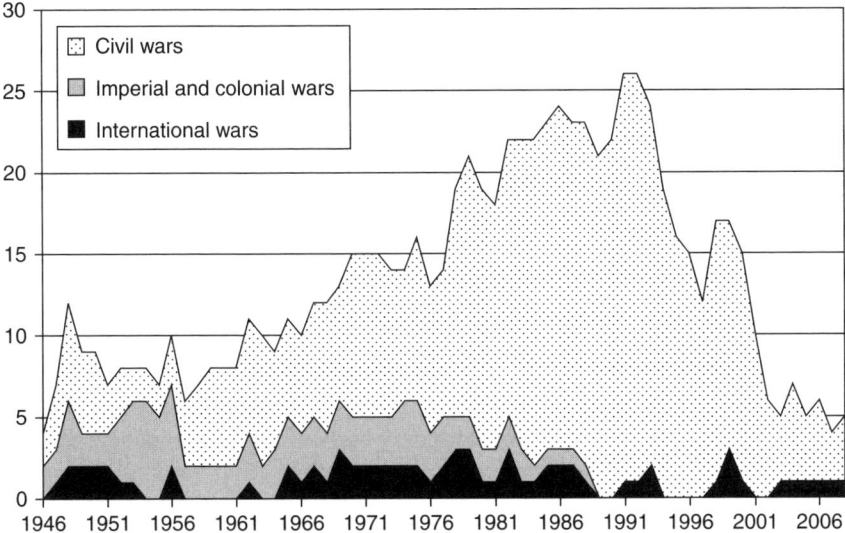

Figure 3.1 Number of ongoing wars by year, 1946–2008.

The data are for "wars," violent armed conflicts that resulted in at least 1,000 military and civilian battle-related deaths in the year indicated.

Sources: www.pcr.uu.se/gpdatabase/search.php; Kristian Gleditsch, "A Revised List of Wars Between and Within Independent States, 1816–2002," *International Interactions* 30 (2004): 231–262; plus additional correspondence with Gleditsch.

Trends

Applying my preferred definition of war—one that is effectively used in perhaps 95 percent of the literature on the subject—Figure 3.1 supplies a frequency distribution for the number of civil, imperial and colonial, and international wars going on in each year in the post-World War II period. To repeat: an armed conflict is considered to be a war if at least 1,000 battle or battle-related deaths are inflicted in the indicated year.

To assess the trends, it is useful to consider four types of war: wars among developed countries, other international wars, colonial and imperial wars, and civil wars.

International war among developed countries: the rise of war aversion

As can be seen in Figure 3.1, international wars during the period have been quite infrequent.

However, the data so arrayed actually mask what is likely to constitute the most significant number in the history of warfare: zero (or near-zero). This is the number of wars that have taken place since 1945 between developed states (or "civilized nations" as Gooch would have it). These are conventionally taken to include the countries of Europe (both Eastern and Western), that continent's offshoots, such as the United States, Canada, Australia, and New Zealand, and a few other countries, such as Japan.

Shattering centuries of bloody practice, these counties have substantially abandoned war as a method for dealing with their disagreements. Until about a hundred years ago, war was widely accepted as a positive thing in that area: as military historian Michael Howard has observed, "Before 1914 war was almost universally considered to be an acceptable, perhaps an inevitable and for many people a desirable way of settling international differences."[15]

Thus, five years before writing his treatise, *Perpetual Peace*, Immanuel Kant held that "a prolonged peace favors the predominance of a mere commercial spirit, and with it a debasing self-interest, cowardice, and effeminacy, and tends to degrade the character of the nation." Somewhat later Alexis de Tocqueville concluded that "war almost always enlarges the mind of a people and raises their character," and Frederick the Great observed, "War opens the most fruitful field to all virtues, for at every moment constancy, pity, magnanimity, heroism, and mercy shine forth in it." In 1895, the distinguished American jurist Oliver Wendell Holmes, Jr., told the Harvard graduating class that a world without the "divine folly of honor" would not be endurable, and the one thing he found to be "true and adorable" was "the faith . . . which leads a soldier to throw away his life in obedience to a blindly accepted duty, in a cause which he little understands, in a plan of campaign of which he has no notion, under tactics of which he does not see the use."

For some, it followed that periodic wars were necessary to cleanse the nation from the decadence of peace. According to Friedrich Nietzsche, "It is mere illusion and pretty sentiment to expect much (even anything at all) from mankind if it forgets how to make war," and J.A. Cramb, a British professor of history, proclaimed that universal peace would be "a world sunk in bovine content." In 1871, a French intellectual, Ernest Renan, called war "one of the conditions of progress, the cut of the whip which prevents a country from going to sleep, forcing satisfied mediocrity itself to leave its apathy." In 1891, novelist Émile Zola found war to be "life itself. . . . We must eat and be eaten so that the world might live. It is only warlike nations which have prospered: a nation dies as soon as it disarms." Or, as Russian composer Igor Stravinsky put it simply, war is "necessary for human progress."[16]

European attitudes toward war changed profoundly at the time of World War I. There is no way to quantify this change except perhaps through a rough sort of content analysis. Before that war, it was very easy, as suggested above, to find serious writers, analysts, and politicians in Europe and the United States exalting war as desirable, inevitable, natural, progressive, and necessary. After the war, however, such people became extremely rare, though the excitement of the combat experience continued (and continues) to have its fascination for some.

This abrupt and remarkable change has often been noted by historians and political scientists. In his impressive study of wars since 1400, Evan Luard observes that "the First World War transformed traditional attitudes toward war. For the first time there was an almost universal sense that the deliberate launching of a war could now no longer be justified." Bernard Brodie points out that "a basic historical change had taken place in the attitudes of the European (and American) peoples toward war." Arnold Toynbee called it the end of a "span of five thousand years during which war had been one of mankind's master institutions."[17]

Obviously, this change of attitude was not enough to keep developed countries out of all wars altogether. Most disastrously, it did not prevent the war of 1939–1945—although the European half of that conflagration might not have been in the cards in any sense, and was mostly the product of the machinations of a single man—or atavism—Adolf Hitler.[18] In addition, developed countries, while avoiding war with each other since that cataclysm, have engaged in three other types of war: colonial wars, wars generated in peripheral areas by the Cold War of 1945–1989, and what I call "policing wars" in the post-Cold War era. These three kinds of wars are discussed separately below.

However, the existence of these wars should not be allowed to cloud an appreciation for the shift of opinion that occurred at the time of the First World War, one that was dramatically reinforced by the Second. In the process, a standard, indeed classic, variety of war—war among developed countries—has become so rare and unlikely that it could well be considered to be obsolescent, if not obsolete. Reflecting on this phenomenon, Howard mused in 1991 that it had become "quite possible that war in the sense of major, organized armed conflict between highly developed societies may not recur, and that a stable framework for international order will become firmly established." Two years later, the military historian and analyst John Keegan concluded, in his *A History of Warfare*, that the kind of war he was principally considering could well be in terminal demise: "War, it seems to me, after a lifetime of reading about the subject, mingling with men of war, visiting the sites of war and observing its effects, may well be ceasing to commend itself to human beings as a desirable or productive, let alone rational, means of reconciling their discontents." By the end of the century, Mary Kaldor was suggesting that "the barbarity of war between states may have become a thing of the past," and by the beginning of the new one, Robert Jervis had concluded that war among the leading states "will not occur in the future" or, in the words of Jeffrey Record, may have "disappeared altogether."[19]

Other international wars: war aversion spreads?

Figure 3.1 also suggests that international war of any kind—not simply wars among developed countries—has become rather rare.

The Cold War of 1945–1989 generated several international wars waged between developed states and states or entities in the developing world. Of these, three were particularly notable and costly—the Korean War (1950–1953), the American war in Vietnam (1965–1975), and the Soviet Union's war in Afghanistan (1979–1989). This kind of war died out, of course, with the Cold War.

There were also international wars outside the Cold War. Between 1948 and 1973, several were waged between Israel and its neighbors, but none since (though Israel has had armed conflicts with Arab substate groups). Nor, except perhaps for a brief, localized flare-up over Kashmir in 1999, has there been a direct war between India and Pakistan over the same span of time. Indeed, of the international wars waged since the end of the Cold War in 1989, there was only one that fits cleanly into the classic model in which two countries have it out over some issue of mutual dispute, in this case territory: the almost unnoticed, but quite costly, conflict between Ethiopia and Eritrea that transpired between 1998 and 2000.

It should also be noted that there was a considerable expansion during the period in the number of independent states. When these states were colonies, they could not, by definition, engage in international war with each other. It is particularly impressive that there have been so few international wars during a period in which the number of entities capable of conducting them increased so greatly.

In addition to the conflict between Ethiopia and Eritria, the international wars tallied in Figure 3.1 for the post-Cold War period include aspects of the post-Communist conflicts in the Balkans and in the Caucasus region, that confrontation between India and Pakistan in 1999, and a few "policing wars," militarized efforts by developed countries designed to bring order to civil conflicts or to deal with thuggish regimes.

Policing wars substantially emerged when the Cold War ended (though the Suez War of 1956 and the Congo intervention in the early 1960s could be seen, perhaps, to be precursors). Because developed countries came basically to see the world in much the same way and because there was little or no fear of war between them, they were left free to explore devices for managing the world. Some of these devices are diplomatic, social, or economic, but the judicious application of military force—or something that looks a great deal like war—is also potentially available.

The problem with war is not so much in the institution in the abstract—it does often settle differences—but rather in its consequences: the death and destruction that inevitably ensue. International war may be under some degree of control, but two very notable sources of artificial or human-made death and destruction continue to persist. One of these is civil war, the chief remaining form of war, as Figure 3.1 makes clear, and many of these have been highly destructive. For example, in the late 1990s, a semi-internationalized civil war—or set of civil wars—in the Congo resulted in the deaths, by some estimates, of three million people, mostly from the disruption and disease it caused. The second is government. In fact, over the course of the bloody twentieth century, far more people were killed by their own governments than were killed by all wars put together.[20] During the 1990s, for example, the government of Rwanda systematically tried to kill off a minority group, a venture that resulted in upwards of half a million deaths; in North Korea at the same time, the regime so mismanaged and exacerbated famine conditions that hundreds of thousands of people died, with some careful estimates putting the number at over two million.

In principle, the international community is ill-prepared to deal with civil conflict and with vicious or destructively incompetent domestic governments because it is chiefly set up to confront problems that transcend international borders, not those that lurk within them. However, having substantially abandoned war and armed conflict among themselves, the developed countries can, if they so desire, expand their efforts and collaborate on international police work to deal with civil war and with vicious domestic regimes. And, indeed, the Security Council of the United Nations does appear in recent years to have developed or evolved the legal ability legitimately to authorize military intervention to police civil wars or to oust a state government deemed too incompetent or too venal to be allowed to continue to exist.[21]

In fact, since the Cold War, there have been a number of instances in which developed countries, with or without a Security Council mandate, have applied, or credibly threatened to apply, military force against other countries to seek to correct conditions they considered sufficiently unsuitable. These have included interventions in Panama in 1989, in Kuwait and Iraq in 1991, in Somalia in 1992–1993, in Haiti in 1994, in Bosnia in 1995, in Kosovo and East Timor in 1999, in Sierra Leone in 2000, in Afghanistan in 2001, and in Iraq in 2003. Some of these ventures have been sufficiently costly in lives to tally as international wars in Figure 3.1. Except for the last two, however, the developed countries were able to engage in these ventures at remarkably little cost to themselves, particularly in casualties, and, since they were most focused on thuggish regimes or on thug-dominated civil wars, they were generally successful.[22]

However, despite a degree of success, the post-Cold War phenomenon of policing wars, rather tentative at best, seems more likely to wane than to grow. There are several reasons for this, among them a lack of interest, an extremely low tolerance for casualties in military missions that are essentially humanitarian, and an aversion to long-term policing. The experience of the wars in Iraq and, increasingly, Afghanistan is likely to further magnify a reluctance to intervene unless the outside countries perceive a clear threat to their own interests. Thus, when depredations by government-inspired armed bands caused ethnic cleansing and tens of thousands of deaths in western Sudan, the international community, after 10 years of mea culpa breast-beating over its failure to intervene in Rwanda, responded with little more than huffing and puffing, pressure on the Sudan government, and the setting up of inadequate and underfunded refugee camps.[23] And for years, they largely stood by as Robert Mugabe's agile and destructive dictatorship progressively impoverished and brutalized the once-promising country of Zimbabwe.

Imperial and colonial war and the demise of conquest: a consequence of war aversion

Throughout the last two centuries, there have been a large number of wars resulting from the efforts of imperial countries to gain and then to maintain their hold on distant, or sometimes attached, colonial territories. Indeed, fully 199 of the 244 wars Luard identifies as having taken place between 1789 and 1917 were wars of colonization or decolonization.[24] Another analysis enumerates 149 colonial and imperial wars waged between 1816 and 1992.[25] One of the great, if often undernoted, changes during the Cold War was the final demise of the whole idea of empire—previously one of the great epoch-defining constants in human history.[26] Colonialism's demise has meant, of course, an end to its attendant wars, and Figure 3.1 documents that phenomenon.

To a considerable degree, this remarkable development is a consequence of rising war aversion that led, essentially, to a demise in the acceptance of the idea of conquest.

Throughout history, international wars have been variously motivated, but those motivations have generally been expressed in a quest to conquer and to possess territory. Thus, suggests John Vasquez, territory is "a general underlying cause of war," and he stresses that "of all the possible issues states can fight over, the evidence overwhelmingly indicates that issues involving territory ... are the main ones prone to collective violence." And "few interstate wars are fought without any territorial issues being involved in one way or another."[27]

To the degree to which that is true, it would appear that a potential cure for international war would be to disallow territorial expansion by states. Accordingly, building on efforts conducted after World War I, the peacemakers of 1945 declared international boundaries to be essentially sacrosanct—that is, unalterable by the use or threat of military force—no matter how illogical or unjust some of them might seem to interested parties. And the peoples residing in the chunks of territory contained within them would be expected to establish governments that, no matter how disgusting or reprehensible, would then be dutifully admitted to the all-inclusive club of "sovereign" states known as the United Nations. Efforts to change international frontiers by force or the threat of force were pejoratively labeled "aggression" and sternly declared to be unacceptable.

Remarkably, this process has, for various reasons and for the most part, worked. Although many international borders were in dispute, although there remained vast colonial empires in which certain countries possessed certain other countries or proto-countries, and although some of the largest states quickly became increasingly enmeshed in a profound ideological and military rivalry known as the Cold War, the prohibition against territorial aggression has been astoundingly successful. In the decades since 1945, there have been many cases in which countries split through internal armed rebellion (including anti-colonial wars). Reversing the experience and patterns of all recorded history, however, there have been scarcely any extensive alterations of international boundaries through force—though, as noted above, there have been legitimized violations of sovereignty in most of the policing wars of the post-Cold War era. Indeed, the only time one United Nations member tried to conquer another to incorporate it into its own territory was when Iraq "anachronistically" (to apply Howard's characterization) attempted to seize Kuwait in 1990, a venture that was soon reversed by military force.[28]

The norm against conquest and its associated institutional structure stress peace, but they are not so much the cause of the desire for peace as its result. That is, the norm was specifically fabricated and developed because war-averse countries, noting that disputes over territory had been a major cause of international war in the past, were seeking to enforce and enshrine the norm. Its existence did not cause them to be war averse, but rather the reverse.

Civil war

As Figure 3.1 vividly demonstrates and as noted above, civil war has been by far the most common type of war since World War II. Most civil wars have taken place in the poorest countries of the world, and many have been labeled "new war," "ethnic conflict," or, most grandly, "clashes of civilizations." But, in fact, most, though certainly not all, have been more nearly opportunistic predation waged by packs—often remarkably small ones—of criminals, bandits, and thugs engaging in armed conflict either as mercenaries under hire to desperate governments or as independent or semi-independent warlord or brigand bands.[29]

The existence and increasing frequency of civil war up until the early 1990s can be attributed to several factors. With the decolonization of the late 1950s and 1960s, a group of poorly governed societies came into being, and many found themselves having to deal with civil warfare. Moreover, as many of these civil conflicts became criminal enterprises, they tended to become longer and to accumulate in number. This pattern may have been embellished by another phenomenon, democratization, which often is accompanied by a period in which governments become weak.[30] Then, in the aftermath of the Cold War in the early 1990s, there was a further increase in the number of incompetent governments, as weak, confused, ill-directed, and sometimes criminal governments emerged in many of the post-Communist countries, replacing comparatively competent police states. In addition, with the end of the Cold War, the developed countries, including former colonialist France, no longer had nearly as much interest in financially propping up some third-world governments and in helping them police themselves—an effect particularly noticeable in Africa.[31]

To a very substantial degree, then, much civil warfare is essentially the result of inadequate government.[32] Civil wars are least likely to occur in stable democracies and in stable autocracies—that is, in countries with effective governments and policing forces.[33] They are most common—almost by definition—in what has come to be called "failed states." In fact, in an important sense, many civil wars have effectively been *caused* by inept governments, which tend to apply excessive and indiscriminate force to try to deal with relatively small bands of troublemakers, often turning friendly or indifferent subjects into hostile ones.

Many of these civil wars have endured for years, and the growth pattern through the early 1990s is mostly the result of a process of cumulation.[34] In recent years, however, this process seems to have reversed itself: many of these wars—or competitive criminal enterprises—have exhausted themselves, and new ones have failed to arise in sufficient numbers to maintain the same frequency.

A fully satisfactory explanation for this remarkable decline has yet to be developed. Exhaustion may explain why some of the wars finally ended, but that hardly explains why new wars haven't sprung up in places previously free of them. Conceivably, the miserable experience through the mid-1990s with these disastrous wars has finally been successfully transmitted more widely, with the result that civil war, following the pattern found with international war in the developed world, is going out of style. But it is clearly far too early to be certain about anything like that, and, even if this conclusion is valid, the precise process by which this has come about would be difficult to divine.

Although the end of the Cold War tended to increase the problem of civil war, as noted above, lingering ideological civil wars inspired or enhanced by the Cold War contest died out (or became transmogrified into criminal ones) with its demise. But this can explain only a small portion of the decline in civil war.

One key may have been in the rise of competent governments that have increasingly been able to police domestic conflicts, rather than exacerbating them, as frequently happened in the past. A considerable number of countries did manage to get through the rough period and have achieved a degree of stability—especially in Latin America, post-Communist Europe, and East and Southeast Asia—and relatively effective governments have emerged in most of them. Moreover, there is some suggestive but by no means conclusive evidence that governments are becoming generally more effective, even in the poorest areas of the world, and thus that criminal warfare (and criminal regimes) may, like international warfare, be in terminal decline.[35] Certainly the number of first-class tyrannies has diminished greatly in the last decades.

Some argue that peacekeeping efforts by international organizations have often proved effective at keeping the wars from reigniting.[36] International bodies and consortiums of developed countries can often be useful to broker cease-fires and peace settlements, and they can sometimes assist with humanitarian aid and economic and political development once peace has been achieved. That is, they may not be able to stop a war when the combatants are determined to continue fighting, but they can usefully seize the opportunity to stabilize a shaky peace when the combatants have become exhausted. However, it seems clear that a truly effective, long-term solution to the problems presented by civil warfare and vicious regimes does not lie in the ministrations of the international community, but rather in the establishment of competent domestic military and policing forces.

The present condition

No matter how defined, then, there has been a most notable decline in the frequency of wars over the last years. As Table 3.1 suggests, between 2002 and 2008, few wars really shattered the 1,000 battle or battle-related death threshold.[37] Beyond the wars in Iraq and Afghanistan, violent flare-ups have exceeded the yearly battle death threshold during the period in Kashmir, Nepal, Colombia, Burundi, Liberia, Chechnya, Sri Lanka, Afghanistan, Chad, Somalia, Pakistan and Uganda. Almost all of these have just barely done so. Indeed, if the yearly threshold were raised to a not-unreasonable 3,000, almost the only war of any kind that has taken place anywhere in the world since 2001 would be the one in Iraq.

Table 3.1 Battle death estimates for wars, 2002–2008

2002	
Burundi	1,000
Uganda	1,032
Colombia	1,156
Sudan	2,021
India (Kashmir)	1,500–3,000
Nepal	2,500
2003	
Nepal	1,064
India (Kashmir)	1,246–1,894
Liberia	1,661
Sudan	1,999
Iraq	8,313–15,213
2004	
India (Kashmir)	1,075
Chechnya	1,141
Colombia	1,230
Nepal	1,596
Uganda	1,600
Iraq	1,987
Sudan	3,295
2005	
India (Kashmir)	1,058
Afghanistan	1,267
Colombia	1,379
Nepal	1,397
Iraq	2,299
2006	
India (Kashmir)	702–1,116
Sudan	1,002
Chad	1,249
Sri Lanka	1,969
Afghanistan	3,146
Iraq	3,537
2007	
Somalia	1,393
Iraq	1,851
Sri Lanka	2,488
Afghanistan	5,818
2008	
Somalia	1,483
Iraq	2,090
Pakistan	2,996
Afghanistan	4,489
Sri Lanka	8,396

Source: Uppsala Conflict Data Program Database at http://www.pcr.uu.se/gpdatabase/search.php.

Several of these intermittent armed conflicts could potentially rise above the violence threshold in the future, though outside of Afghanistan, most of these seem to be declining in violence. Ethiopia and Eritrea continue to glare at each other, and plenty of problems remain in the Middle East, where in 2006 and again in 2009, Israel took on a substate group based in another country, and where the Iraq conflict could have spillover effects. And, of course, new wars could emerge in other places: concerns about China and the Taiwan issue, for example, are certainly justified, and many in the developed world advocate the application of warfare as a last resort to prevent the acquisition of nuclear weapons by undesirable countries.[38] Moreover, there has been "intercommunal" or "substate" violence in countries like Nigeria (and Iraq) that often certainly resembles warfare, but is removed from consideration here by the definitional requirement that something labeled a "war" must have a government on at least one side.

However, war, as conventionally, even classically, understood, has, at least for the time being, become a remarkably rare phenomenon. Indeed, if civil war becomes (or remains) as uncommon as the international variety, war could be on the verge of ceasing to exist as a substantial phenomenon.

Explanations

If this happens—and it is obviously much too early to be certain—it would constitute one of the most monumental developments in the history of the human race. As yet, however, the prospect has excited remarkably little comment or even notice. In 2004, the United Nations promulgated a press release, "10 stories the world should hear more about," and one of these was called "The Peacekeeping Paradox," in which it was observed that many civil wars had of late ended, providing many hopeful opportunities for international peacekeeping.[39] The story was picked up by the Jim Lehrer *News Hour* program on PBS and by *Business Week*, but that was about all. Newspaper columnist Gwynne Dyer has noted the process in a few columns, and Gregg Easterbrook published a cover story, "The End of War?" in *The New Republic* in 2005 that attracted a very small amount of media attention.[40]

Within the political science community, perhaps the most prominent recent notice of the phenomenon (or potential phenomenon) as it pertains to international war was registered by Robert Jervis in his Presidential Address to the American Political Science Association and in a subsequent book.[41] Among scholars who have been leaders in assessing and measuring war and conflict, Monty Marshall and Ted Gurr have produced an extensive discussion, while Canadian political scientist Andrew Mack has done so in well-received reports that prominently make use of data sets produced by Norwegian and Swedish researchers.[42] In addition, Raimo Väyryen has edited a set of essays that speculate on the potential waning of international war, and Christopher Fettweis has investigated that issue as well.[43]

It would seem, however, that the process should have excited more comment. Should war really prove to be in terminal demise, this would suggest that quite a few revered notions about the causes of—and antidotes to—war ought to be reexamined. And, although the notion is still speculative, it is perhaps not too soon to suggest that if war is really receding, many of the explanations for war so extensively promulgated and discussed over the last century may come to be found wanting. A brief and somewhat cursory survey may help to illustrate the point.

Biology and psychology

As Kenneth Waltz points out, one set of explanations for war has stressed that they arise from the essential nature of the human creature.[44] "I'm not so naïve or simplistic," proclaimed former Secretary of Defense Robert S. McNamara, "[as] to believe we can eliminate war. We're not going to change human nature any time soon."[45] And on confronting the argument in 1989 that at least some kinds of war might be in the process of notable decline, Samuel Huntington deemed that to be quite implausible, due in part to the "weakness and irrationality of human nature," not to mention the human capacity for behavior that is "stupid, selfish, cruel, and sinful."[46]

Yet war may be disappearing without much in the way of perceptible changes— or improvements—in human nature. Nor has the "aggressive drive" been notice-ably attenuated. Testosterone levels seem to be as high as ever, and the thrill and exhilaration that war and combat often incite do not seem to have diminished. Nor has any sort of psychic "moral equivalent" to war—or for that matter a practical one—been fabricated.

Some observers have seen the impetus for war not so much in human nature as in the nature of political leadership. However, it does not seem likely that today's leaders are more rational or competent than the leaders of old, that they are less susceptible to bias and misperception, or that they lust less for power. Evolu-tionary theories about the value and persistence of war do not seem to be doing very well either, and they are likely to have little to say about the important, remarkably abrupt, and quite recent decline in civil warfare.

Resentments

Nationalism, religious extremism, ethnic tension, and social inequalities seem to be about as common as ever, and there do not appear to be notable reductions in the world's considerable store of hate, selfishness, and racism. Extrapolating from the apparently ethnically based conflict in Bosnia in the early 1990s, Huntington promulgated a notion about "clashes of civilizations."[47] However, although there is no reason to think that civilizational angst has decreased since his book appeared in 1996, civil warfare stemming from that (or any other) condition has declined remarkably. And for well over a decade now, Bosnia has managed to remain completely at peace, despite all those supposedly consequential subliminal hatreds we heard so much about in the early 1990s.

Looking at the issue from the opposite perspective, there does not seem to have been a notable surge in the amount of love, justice, harmony, cooperation, brotherhood, good will, or inner peace in the world. Yet war has declined without benefit of such developments.

Weaponry

There has been no great growth in the number of ingenious agreements to restrict arms or the arms industry—indeed, arms seem to be everywhere, and international trade in them continues to flourish. That is, the arms industry, deemed in a vast literature to be peculiarly nefarious and a source, inspiration, instigator, or facilitator of war, continues to do quite nicely, even as war itself slumps in frequency.

Moreover, although there has been some reduction in the number of nuclear weapons in the possession of major countries since the end of the Cold War, they still retain impressive arsenals. In addition, nuclear weapons continue to proliferate, albeit at a pace much slower than has often been feared. If arms races somehow lead to war, they continue in many places.

On the other hand, many analysts have argued that nuclear weapons have actually kept the world from stumbling helplessly into a repeat of World War II.[48] This contention holds that although the people in charge of world affairs since that event have been the same people or the intellectual heirs of the people who tried assiduously, frantically, desperately, and, as it turned out, pathetically, to prevent it, they were so obtuse, depraved, flaky, desperate, or stupid that only visions of mushroom clouds could lead them to conclude that a repeat performance of that catastrophe would be distinctly unpleasant. However, whatever value there may be in this perspective, it hardly explains the infrequency of international war in the periphery, the several instances in which nuclear countries have been directly challenged militarily (Falklands, Yom Kippur, Afghanistan, Vietnam, Iraq, Hungary), or, in particular, the remarkable decline of colonial and civil war.

Those difficulties also hold for the broader idea that war has become rare because of its rising costs.[49] A particular problem in this case is that many earlier wars were hugely destructive, and, as Alan Milward observes, measured as a proportion of the increasing gross national product of the combatants, war "has not shown any discernible long term trend towards greater costliness."[50]

Economics, technology, communication, trade

If the demise of war is dependent on economic development or on the achievement of some sort of economic equality among (or within) nations, as many have postulated, there seems to be a long way to go: the earth has hardly been enveloped in prosperity, while miserable poverty and spectacular economic inequalities remain. There have been notable increases in international trade and in economic interdependence, but there clearly is a long way to go on this as well. International communications have also greatly improved, but the connection between this still rather limited development and the decline of war is difficult to divine.

However, shifting attitudes toward the desirability of war may have been notably enhanced over the last couple of centuries by economic thinking.[51] Specifically, to the degree that economists have been able to get across a pair of key ideas, the result could be an enhanced desire for peace.

One of these holds that the growth of economic well-being should be a dominant goal. Historically, non-economic values have often been deemed more worthy than economic growth, and an important area in which non-economic values have usually dominated is war. For the most part, in fact, economic motivations often seem like a rationale for impulses that are actually more nearly moral, aesthetic, emotional, or psychological.[52] It seems likely, then, that if people with business motivations had actually been running the world, its history would have been quite a bit different (and generally better). By helping to teach the world to value economic well-being above passions that are often economically absurd, economists and their like-minded allies have made an important contribution.[53]

Economists have also been in the lead in advancing a second idea, one holding that wealth is best achieved through exchange, not through conquest. In this regard, Richard Rosecrance cites the striking and important examples of two recent converts: "Today West Germany and Japan use international trade to acquire the very raw materials and oil that they aimed to conquer by military force in the 1930s. They have prospered in peaceful consequence." Among "trading states" like that, Rosecrance observes, "the incentive to wage war is absent."[54] Put another way, free trade furnishes the economic advantages of conquest without the unpleasantness of invasion and the sticky responsibility of imperial control.

Thus, war is unlikely if countries take prosperity as their chief goal *and* if they come to believe that trade is the best way to achieve that goal. Thanks in part to the success of economists, both ideas have now gained wide currency.

Although trade alone may enhance the prospects for peace, a better case could perhaps be made for the opposite causal proposition: peace often leads to, or at any rate facilitates, trade. That is, peace ought to be seen not as a dependent, but rather as an independent, variable in such considerations. The long and historically unprecedented absence of war among the nations of Western Europe, for example, has not been caused by their increasing economic harmony. Rather, economic harmony has been caused, or at least substantially facilitated, by the long and historically unprecedented peace they have enjoyed. Put the other way, international tensions and the prospect of international war have a strong dampening effect on trade, since each threatened nation has an incentive to isolate itself from the rest of the world economically in order to ensure that it can survive if international exchange is cut off by military conflict. In this respect, the Cold War could be seen in part as a huge trade barrier. With the demise of such politically derived and economically foolish constructs, trade was liberated. But it was the rise of peace that facilitated the trade, not the opposite.

Whatever application economic arguments about trade and communication may have to international war, they do not seem to have much relevance to civil conflicts, which are far more common and which are characteristically fought between groups that know each other only too well and trade with each other only too much.[55]

Structure and institutions

Many international relations scholars have rooted the causes of war in the state or in the "structure" of the state system with its permissive condition of "anarchy." As Waltz concludes, "Force is a means of achieving the external ends of states because there exists no consistent, reliable process of reconciling the conflicts of interest that inevitably arise among similar units in a condition of anarchy."[56]

Working from this perspective, it has often been concluded that wars, particularly international wars, would persist unless effective international organizations or a world government were to be fashioned to deal decisively with them. At times, hopes for this have been placed in the United Nations and its provocatively named "Security Council." The United Nations may deserve credit for a number of achievements over its history, but no one is likely to accuse it of having become an effective world government, and therefore "anarchy" persists. Actually, in a condition in which international war does not take place, anarchy might come to be desirable: a condition where states could peacefully go about their business without being hampered by arbitrary government regulation.[57]

Similarly, coherent and effective systems of international law have hardly been developed—indeed, many prominent law schools, such as Harvard University and the University of Chicago, still do not even have people teaching the subject on their regular faculty. Effective moral prohibitions, including the legal renouncing or outlawing of war, also do not seem to have been achieved, nor has anything resembling a cohesive and enforced code of international justice enveloped the world.

In like manner, if war really is ceasing to exist, various system- and power-related explanations for war may need, to varying degrees, to be reassessed. These would include those focusing on polarity, hierarchy, hegemony, hegemonic stability, power status, power cycles, alliance patterns, border insecurities, security dilemmas, power transitions, patterns of contiguity or proximity, capability and offense–defense balances, rivalry patterns, unequal growth, geopolitics, and processes of contagion and diffusion.[58] Moreover, almost all of these relate to international war and have little application to declines in civil and colonial war.

Nor does the essential nature of the state or of the nation-state seem to have been mellowed or modified notably. Some subsets of countries have willingly entered into what Karl Deutsch once labeled "security communities," in which they explicitly or implicitly agree to avoid using force or the threat of force in their dealings with each other.[59] Such developments seem to be more nearly the result of the desire for peace than its cause, but, regardless, the vast majority of states remain outside such unions.

Democracy, many have argued, is conducive to peace, or at least to peace between democratic states. This notion was central to Woodrow Wilson's quest to "make the world safe for democracy." He and many others in Britain, France, and the United States had become convinced that, as Britain's Lloyd George put it later, "Freedom is the only warranty of Peace."[60] This is an important suggestion, and it has of late generated a vast literature that can hardly be fully surveyed here.

However, although there has been a considerable increase in the number of democratic countries in the world, trends in the demise of war seem, as with the case of increased trade and communications, to have considerably outrun it. That is, peace seems to be in the process of breaking out between and within all countries, not just democracies. Moreover, as Miriam Fendius Elman suggests after surveying the literature on the subject, "the important consideration" has to do with ideas, not institutions: it is not "whether a country is democratic or not, but whether its ruling coalition is committed to peaceful methods of conflict resolution." As she further points out, the countries of Latin America and most of Africa have engaged in very few international wars even without the benefit of being democratic (for a century before its 1982 adventure, Argentina, for example, fought none at all).[61] And, of course, the long peace enjoyed by developed countries since World War II includes not only the one that has prevailed between democracies, but also the even more important one between the authoritarian East and the democratic West. Even if there is some connection, whether causal or atmospheric, between democracy and peace, it cannot explain this latter phenomenon

And, as with many of the other arguments assessed above, the democracy explanation has focused almost entirely on international wars. It does not seem to be terribly helpful in explaining the remarkable decline in civil war, by far the most common form of armed conflict.

Responses

Many people still consider war to be normal and an inevitable part of international and domestic life. Effectively, even if they accept the trend I have outlined as genuine, they are inclined to see it simply as a readily reversible blip. As one commentator put it to me, "You may be right, but I still have faith in my fellow man."

And of course, I have no way to be certain that the trend in warfare, particularly civil warfare, will continue on its notable, but only rather recent, downward trajectory. After all, Gooch was writing in a period when international war was quite rare and seemed to be becoming even more so, and there were other periods of comparative quiet in the century before World War I.[62] Perhaps we have today slumped only temporarily into a similar sort of hiatus even as hideous explosions await us around the corner. Indeed, Colin Gray has recently published a book, *Another Bloody Century*, confidently asserting that war "will always be with us," that it "is a permanent feature of the human condition," and that "interstate war, including great power conflict, is very much alive and well."[63]

Nevertheless, the incredible, completely unprecedented, and now remarkably long-term absence, or near-absence, of international war in Europe, that once most warlike of continents, suggests that something new may indeed be afoot.

Moreover, the relatively peaceful periods in Europe before 1914 were far shorter than the present one, and they were accompanied, as noted earlier, by routine and profuse fulminations about the glories and the sublime benefits of war. Also significant is the near-absence for the last few decades of international wars in which states directly go after each other in the classic manner over matters of dispute such as territory. Moreover, the frequency of civil war, by far the most common form of warfare over the last half-century, has now remained at low levels for several years. Although it is obviously far too soon to be completely confident that these levels will continue, there does not seem to be a large number of countries about to descend into internal armed conflict.[64]

At base, it may turn out that war is merely an idea, an institution that has been grafted onto human existence, rather than a trick of fate, a thunderbolt from hell, a natural calamity, a systemic necessity, or a desperate plot contrivance dreamed up by some sadistic puppeteer up high. And the institution may be in pronounced decline, as attitudes toward it have changed, roughly following the pattern according to which the ancient and once-formidable institution of formal, state-sponsored slavery became discredited and then obsolete. All this could conceivably come about without changing human nature; without creating an effective world government or system of international law; without modifying the nature of the state or the nation-state; without expanding international trade, interdependence, or communication; without fabricating an effective moral or practical equivalent to war; without enveloping the earth in democracy or prosperity; without devising ingenious agreements to restrict arms or the arms industry; without reducing the world's considerable store of hate, selfishness, nationalism, religious intolerance, and racism; without increasing the amount of love, justice, or inner peace in the world; without altering the international system; without establishing security communities; without improving the competence of political leaders; and without doing much of anything about nuclear weapons.

Even if war fades, however, all sorts of other calamities will persist: the decline of war hardly means that everything will be perfect. Indeed, the one-sided violence committed by predatory militia bands in places like Sudan and Congo can cause more damage and suffering than many wars. But since these bands rarely fight each other—that is, they mostly manage to avoid two-sided violence—the resulting destruction does not constitute warfare by the definition applied in this article.

In addition, crime will still exist, and so will terrorism, which, like crime, can be carried out by individuals or by very small groups.[65] Indeed, if policing wars are in decline, criminals may take advantage of the situation and expand their predations; whether any such developments cumulate to the point where the situation could be considered warfare would be determined primarily by the response of governments. And, of course, there will certainly be plenty of other problems to worry about—famine, disease, malnutrition, pollution, corruption, poverty, politics, economic travail, and the potential for climate change. Moreover, violent intercommunal warfare remains, as noted, rather extensive, a costly phenomenon that is excluded from my definition of war through its requirement that a government be one of the parties in the armed conflict.

But a continuing decline in war does seem to be a fairly reasonable prospect. And it may be at least time to begin to consider not so much that we "ain't gonna study war no more," but rather that, as with formal dueling, as Gooch rather prematurely suggested a hundred years ago, war, as classically defined, may be in the process of becoming a matter mainly of historical interest.

Notes

1 G.P. Gooch, *History of Our Time, 1885–1911* (London: Williams and Norgate, 1911), 248–249; Thomas Barclay, "Peace" in *Encyclopedia Britannica*, 11th ed., vol. 21 (1911), 16. As Geoffrey Blainey points out, the article on "Peace" in the next edition of that *Encyclopedia* "was a long essay on how the victors punished the vanquished at the Peace Conference of 1919." Geoffrey Blainey, *The Causes of Wars* (New York: Free Press, 1973), 24.

2 Alan Alexander Milne, *Peace with Honour* (New York: Dutton, 1935), 222; George Santayana, *Soliloquies in England and Later Soliloquies* (New York: Scribner, 1922), 102. Santayana's statement has frequently been attributed to Plato, as in Colin S. Gray, *Another Bloody Century: Future Warfare* (London: Weidenfeld & Nicolson, 2005), 19—incorrectly so, according to Bernard Suzanne, accessed at plato-dialogues.org/faq/faq008.htm, 8 April 2009.

3 Quincy Wright, *A Study of War* (Chicago, IL: University of Chicago Press, 1942).

4 The 1,000 battle death threshold was proposed by J. David Singer and Melvin Small in their seminal *The Wages of War 1816–1965: A Statistical Handbook* (New York: Wiley, 1972). According to Singer, the 1,000 figure more or less fell out of the analysis when other aspects of what could be considered warfare were assembled, and the number seemed to them to be on the low side. Conversation with J. David Singer, San Diego, 24 March 2006.

5 The desolate, nearly barren territory was populated by less than 2,000 souls, and an Argentine writer has characterized the conflict as "two bald men fighting over a comb." Quoted in Helmut Norpoth, "Guns and Butter and Government Popularity in Britain," *American Political Science Review* 81 (September 1987): 957. However, the costs of the 10-week war, proportionate to the value of the stakes, could be considered to make the war one of the most brutal in history. In the aftermath of the war, the British felt it necessary to send over a protective force larger than the civilian population, and the combined cost of the war and of the post-war defenses built up through the 1980s alone came to over $3 million for every liberated Falklander. Lawrence Freedman, *Britain and the Falklands War* (Oxford, UK: Basil Blackwell, 1988), 116. "Far from proving that aggression does not pay," observed one American official, "Britain has only proved that resisting it can be ridiculously expensive." Quoted in Max Hastings and Simon Jenkins, *The Battle for the Falklands* (New York: Norton, 1983), 339.

6 As, for example, in Nils Petter Gleditsch, Peter Wallensteen, Mikael Eriksson, Margareta Stollenberg, and Håvard Strand, "Armed Conflict 1946–2001: A New Dataset," *Journal of Peace Research* 35 (September 2002): 615–37; Lotta Harbom and Peter Wallensteen, "Armed Conflict and Its International Dimensions, 1946–2004," *Journal of Peace Research* 42 (2005): 623–635.

7 Hazem Adam Ghobarah, Paul Huth, and Bruce Russett, "Civil Wars Kill and Maim People, Long After the Fighting Stops," *American Political Science Review* 97 (May 2003): 189–202.

8 Benjamin Valentino, *Final Solutions: Mass Killing and Genocide in the 20th Century* (Ithaca, NY: Cornell University Press, 2004), chap. 6.

9 Doyle and Sambanis contrast "negative" or "sovereign" peace with "positive" or "participatory" peace. Michael W. Doyle and Nicholas Sambanis, *Making War and*

Building Peace: United Nations Peace Operations (Princeton, NJ: Princeton University Press, 2006), 18. For the purposes of this article, the absence of war means only that negative peace has been achieved.

10 For example, Gleditsch, Wallensteen, Eriksson, Stollenberg, and Strand, "Armed Conflict 1946–2001"; Harbom and Wallensteen, "Armed Conflict and Its International Dimensions."

11 Monty G. Marshall and Ted Robert Gurr, *Peace and Conflict, 2005: A Global Survey of Armed Conflicts, Self-Determination Movements, and Democracy* (College Park, MD: Center for International Development and Conflict Management, University of Maryland, 2005).

12 Klaus Jürgen Gantzel and Torsten Schwinghammer, *Warfare Since the Second World War* (New Brunswick, NJ and London: Transaction, 2000). See also Evan Luard, *War in International Society* (New Haven, CT: Yale University Press, 1986), 7.

13 On this, see James D. Fearon and David D. Laitin, "Ethnicity, Insurgency, and Civil War," *American Political Science Review* 97 (February 2003): 75–90; Nicholas Sambanis, "What Is A Civil War? Conceptual and Empirical Complexities of an Operational Definition," *Journal of Conflict Resolution* 48 (December 2004): 814–858.

14 For specific commentary on this, see Marshall and Gurr, *Peace and Conflict, 2005*; Andrew Mack, *Human Security Report 2005* (New York: Oxford University Press, 2005).

15 Michael Howard, *The Causes of Wars and Other Essays*, 2nd ed. (Cambridge, MA: Harvard University Press, 1984), 9.

16 For sources and for many other similar quotes, see John Mueller, *Retreat from Doomsday: The Obsolescence of Major War* (New York: Basic Books, 1989), chap. 2. See also Roland N. Stromberg, *Redemption by War: The Intellectuals and 1914* (Lawrence: Regents Press of Kansas, 1982).

17 Luard, *War in International Society*, 365; Bernard Brodie, *War and Politics* (New York: Macmillan, 1973), 30; Arnold J. Toynbee, *Experiences* (New York: Oxford University Press, 1969), 214. Attitudes toward war for people in developed states did not change, it appears, because World War I had been peculiarly destructive—there had been plenty of such wars before. Rather, it was because the war was the first before which there had been an active anti-war movement. In many respects, the war caused their point of view to become widely accepted. For an analysis, see John Mueller, *The Remnants of War* (Ithaca, NY: Cornell University Press, 2004), chap. 3. See also James J. Sheehan, *Where Have All the Soldiers Gone? The Transformation of Modern Europe* (Boston, MA: Houghton Mifflin, 2008), chap. 2.

18 For the argument about Hitler, see Mueller, *Remnants of War*, chap. 4.

19 Michael Howard, *The Lessons of History* (New Haven, CT: Yale University Press, 1991), 176; John Keegan, *A History of Warfare* (New York: Knopf, 1993), 59; Mary Kaldor, *New and Old Wars: Organized Violence in a Global Era* (Cambridge, UK: Polity Press, 1999), 5; Robert Jervis, "Theories of War in an Era of Leading-Power Peace," *American Political Science Review* 96 (March 2002): 1; Jeffrey Record, "Collapsed Countries, Casualty Dread, and the New American Way of War," *Parameters* 32 (Summer 2002): 6. See also Luard, *War in International Society*; Michael Mandelbaum, *The Ideas That Conquered the World: Peace, Democracy, and Free Markets in the Twenty-First Century* (New York: Public Affairs, 2002); Andrew Mack, "Civil War: Academic Research and the Policy Community," *Journal of Peace Research* 39 (September 2002): 515–525; Sheehan, *Where Have All the Soldiers Gone?* For contrary views, see Samuel P. Huntington, "No Exit: The Errors of Endism," *National Interest* 17 (Fall 1989): 3–11; Gray, *Another Bloody Century*.

20 Rudolph Rummel, *Death by Government* (New Brunswick, NJ: Transaction, 1994); Valentino, *Final Solutions*, chap. 1.

21 Christine Gray, *International Law and the Use of Force*, 2nd ed. (Oxford, UK: Oxford University Press, 2004), 250–251; Doyle and Sambanis, *Making War and Building*

Peace, 10. On this issue, see also John Rawls, *The Law of Peoples* (Cambridge, MA: Harvard University Press, 1999), 81, 93n; Kofi Annan, "Two Concepts of Sovereignty," *The Economist*, 16 September 1999; and "A More Secure World: Our Shared Responsibility," Report of the High-level Panel on Threats, Challenges and Change, United Nations, 2004, paragraph 203, accessed at http://www.un.org/secureworld/report3.pdf, 15 April 2009.

22 Mueller, *Remnants of War*, chaps. 6–7.

23 Scott Straus, "Darfur and the Genocide Debate," *Foreign Affairs* 84 (January/February 2005): 123–146.

24 Luard, *War in International Society*, 52, 60.

25 Hilde Ravlo, Nils Petter Gleditsch, and Han Dorussen, *Colonial War and Democratic Peace* (Oslo, Norway: International Peace Research Institute, 2001).

26 See Neta C. Crawford, *Argument and Change in World Politics: Ethics, Decolonization, and Humanitarian Intervention* (Cambridge, UK: Cambridge University Press, 2002); James Lee Ray, "The Abolition of Slavery and the End of International War," *International Organization* 43 (Summer 1989): 431–432; Lawrence H. Keeley, *War Before Civilization* (New York: Oxford University Press, 1996), 166–167.

27 John A. Vasquez, *The War Puzzle* (Cambridge, UK: Cambridge University Press, 1993), 151, 293.

28 Michael Howard, *The Invention of Peace: Reflections on War and International Order* (London: Profile Books, 2000), 92. For a discussion of the process and a detailed enumeration of territorial changes since 1945, see Mark Zacher, "The Territorial Integrity Norm: International Boundaries and the Use of Force," *International Organization* 55 (Spring 2001): 215–250. See also Martin van Creveld, "The Future of War" in Robert G. Patman, ed., *Security in a Post-Cold War World* (New York: St. Martin's, 1999), 28–29; Gray, *International Law and the Use of Force*, 59; Kaldor, *New and Old Wars*, 5.

29 However, sometimes such essentially criminal activity can lead to effective state building, as Charles Tilly has pointed out: "War Making and State Making as Organized Crime" in Peter B. Evans, Dietrich Rueschemeyer and Theda Skocpol, eds., *Bringing the State Back In* (Cambridge, UK: Cambridge University Press, 1985), 169–191. See also Mueller, *Remnants of War*, chaps. 2, 6.

30 On the connection between democratization and weak government, see also Paul Collier, "Doing Well Out of War: An Economic Perspective" in Mats Berdal and David M. Malone, eds., *Greed and Grievance: Economic Agendas in Civil Wars* (Boulder, CO: Lynne Rienner, 2000), 98, 108; Håvard Hegre, Tanja Ellingsen, Scott Gates, and Nils Petter Gleditsch, "Toward a Democratic Civil Peace? Democracy, Political Change, and Civil War, 1816–1992," *American Political Science Review* 95 (March 2001): 33–48; Jack Snyder, *From Voting to Violence: Democratization and Nationalist Conflict* (New York: Norton, 2000); Bruce D. Jones, *Peacemaking in Rwanda: The Dynamics of Failure* (Boulder, CO: Lynne Rienner, 2001), 164–165; Marshall and Gurr, *Peace and Conflict, 2005*, 17–20.

31 Robert H. Bates, *Prosperity and Violence: The Political Economy of Development* (New York: Norton, 2001), chap. 5; David Shearer, *Private Armies and Military Intervention* (London: International Institute for Strategic Studies, 1998, Adelphi Paper No. 316), 27–29; David Keen, *The Economic Functions of Violence in Civil Wars* (London: International Institute for Strategic Studies, 1998, Adelphi Paper No. 320), 23; Gray, *International Law and the Use of Force*, 215–217.

32 For an extended development of this point, see Mueller, *Remnants of War*, chap. 9.

33 Hegre, Ellingsen, Gates, and Gleditsch, "Toward a Democratic Civil Peace?" On this point, see also Bruce M. Russett and John R. Oneal, *Triangulating Peace: Democracy, Interdependence, and International Organizations* (New York: Norton, 2001), 70; Monty G. Marshall and Ted Robert Gurr, *Peace and Conflict, 2003: A Global Survey of Armed Conflicts, Self-Determination Movements, and Democracy* (College Park,

MD: Center for International Development and Conflict Management, University of Maryland, 2003), 19–20, 25; Fearon and Laitin, "Ethnicity, Insurgency, and Civil War," 85, 88; James D. Fearon and David D. Laitin, "Neotrusteeship and the Problem of Weak States," *International Security* 28 (Spring 2004): 21–22; Doyle and Sambanis, *Making War and Building Peace*, 19, 35.

34 Fearon and Laitin, "Ethnicity, Insurgency, and Civil War," 77–78.

35 Robert Rotberg, "New Breed of African Leader," *Christian Science Monitor*, 9 January 2002, 9; Peter Ford, "Twilight of the Tyrants," *Christian Science Monitor*, 19 December 2003, 1.

36 Mack, *Human Security Report 2005*; Virginia Page Fortna, *Where Have All the Victories Gone? War Outcomes in Historical Perspective* (New York: Saltzman Institute for War and Peace Studies, Columbia University, 2005); Fearon and Laitin "Neotrusteeship and the Problem of Weak States"; Doyle and Sambanis, *Making War and Building Peace*.

37 If the numbers for the Iraq War in the table seem low, it should be remembered that only battle deaths are being counted, not civilian deaths incurred outside a battle situation (though civilians caught in the crossfire are included). In addition, for the most part, the count does not include inter-communal violence between Shia and Sunni groups because to be counted as a civil war, a conflict must have the government on one side. For a discussion of the various estimates of civilian deaths in the war, see Hannah Fischer, "Iraqi Civilian Deaths Estimates," CRS Report for Congress, Congressional Research Service, Library of Congress, 27 August 2008, accessed at www.fas.org/sgp/crs/mideast/RS22537.pdf, 31 March 2009.

38 For example, Graham Allison, *Nuclear Terrorism: The Ultimate Preventable Catastrophe* (New York: Times Books, 2004), 165–171. In contrast see John Mueller, *Atomic Obsession: Nuclear Alarmism from Hiroshima to Al Qaeda* (New York: Oxford University Press, 2009), chaps. 10–11.

39 Accessed at www.un.org/events/tenstories/06/story.asp?storyID=500, 10 June 2008.

40 For Dyer's columns, see http://www.gwynnedyer.com. Gregg Easterbrook, "The End of War?" *New Republic*, 30 May 2005, 18–21. Media attention: John Tierney, "Give Peace a Chance," *New York Times*, 28 May 2005.

41 Jervis, "Theories of War in an Era of Leading-Power Peace"; Robert Jervis, *American Foreign Policy in a New Era* (New York: Routledge, 2005). See also Robert Jervis, "Symposium," *Perspectives on Politics* 3 (June 2005): 315–316.

42 Marshall and Gurr, *Peace and Conflict, 2005*. Mack, *Human Security Report 2005*. Andrew Mack, *Human Security Brief 2007* (Vancouver: Human Security Report Project, Simon Fraser University, 2008).

43 Raimo Väyryen, ed., *The Waning of Major War: Theories and Debates* (New York: Routledge, 2006); Christopher J. Fettweis, "A Revolution in International Relations Theory?" *International Studies Review* 8 (December 2006): 677–697. See also Ted Robert Gurr, "Ethnic Warfare on the Wane," *Foreign Affairs* 79 (May/June 2000): 52–64; Martin van Creveld, *The Transformation of War* (New York: Free Press, 1991); Joshua S. Goldstein, "The Worldwide Lull in War," *Christian Science Monitor*, 14 May 2002; Steven Pinker, "A History of Violence," *New Republic*, 19 March 2007.

44 Kenneth N. Waltz, *Man, the State and War* (New York: Columbia University Press, 1959).

45 In the film, *The Fog of War*, Sony Picture Classics, 2003.

46 Huntington, "No Exit," 10.

47 Samuel P. Huntington, *The Clash of Civilizations and the Remaking of the World Order* (New York: Touchstone, 1996).

48 On this issue, see Mueller, *Atomic Obsession*, chap. 3.

49 Carl Kaysen, "Is War Obsolete?" *International Security* 14 (Spring 1990): 42–64.

50 Alan J. Milward, *War, Economy and Society, 1939–1945* (Berkeley: University of California Press, 1997), 3.

51 See John Mueller, *Capitalism, Democracy, and Ralph's Pretty Good Grocery* (Princeton, NJ: Princeton University Press, 1999), chap. 5.

52 As Quincy Wright observed after a lifetime of study on this matter, "Studies of both the direct and the indirect influence of economic factors on the causation of war indicate that they have been much less important than political ambitions, ideological convictions, technological change, legal claims, irrational psychological complexes, ignorance, and unwillingness to maintain conditions of peace in a changing world"; Quincy Wright, "War: The Study of War" in David L. Sills, ed., *International Encyclopedia of the Social Sciences*, vol. 16 (New York: Macmillan-Free Press, 1968), 463. For an extensive discussion of the varying role of economics as a motivation, or excuse, for war, see Luard, *War in International Society*.

53 See also Albert O. Hirschman, *The Passions and the Interests* (Princeton, NJ: Princeton University Press, 1977); Donald McCloskey, "Bourgeois Virtue," *American Scholar* 63 (Spring 1994): 180–182.

54 Richard Rosecrance, *The Rise of the Trading State: Conquest and Commerce in the Modern World* (New York: Basic Books, 1986), 16, 24. See also Erik Gartzke, "The Capitalist Peace," *American Journal of Political Science* 51 (January 2007): 166–191.

55 Kenneth N. Waltz, *Theory of International Politics* (Reading, MA: Addison-Wesley, 1979), 138.

56 Waltz, *Man, the State and War*, 238.

57 See also Fettweis, "Revolution in International Relations Theory?" 687.

58 See also Fettweis, "Revolution in International Relations Theory?" 684–691. For a systematic discussion of many of these constructs, see Daniel S. Geller, "Explaining War: Empirical Patterns and Theoretical Mechanisms" in Manus I. Midlarsky, ed., *Handbook of War Studies II* (Ann Arbor: University of Michigan Press, 2000), 407–449.

59 Karl W. Deutsch, *Political Community and the North Atlantic Area* (Princeton, NJ: Princeton University Press, 1957).

60 William E. Rappard, *The Quest for Peace Since the World War* (Cambridge, MA: Harvard University Press, 1940), 42–44. For the contrasting argument that peace causes, or at least facilitates, democracy, see Mark E. Pietrzyk, *International Order and Individual Liberty: Effects of War and Peace on the Development of Governments* (Lanham, MD: University Press of America, 2002); James L. Payne, "Election Fraud: Democracy is an Effect, not a Cause, of Nonviolence," *American Conservative*, 13 March 2006, 11–12; John Mueller, "Faulty Correlation, Foolish Consistency, and Fatal Consequence: Democracy, Peace, and Theory in the Middle East" in Steven W. Hook, ed., *Democratic Peace and Promotion: Critical Perspectives* (Kent, OH: Kent State University Press, forthcoming).

61 Miriam Fendius Elman, ed., *Paths to Peace: Is Democracy the Answer?* (Cambridge, MA: MIT Press, 1997), 484, 496. See also Sebastian Rosato, "The Flawed Logic of Democratic Peace Theory," *American Political Science Review* 97 (November 2003): 585–602.

62 However, some of that, as Kristian Gleditsch points out, was because the number of states in the nineteenth century was considerably undercounted in some approaches. When that is corrected for, the number of wars during that time, particularly international ones, increases considerably; Kristian Gleditsch, "A Revised List of Wars Between and Within Independent States, 1816–2002," *International Interactions* 30 (2004): 231–262. To a degree, this is an issue as well in Figure 3.1: during the post-World War II era, there was, as noted above, a considerable expansion in the number of independent states and therefore in the number of places in which a civil war could take place. However, the basic pattern for civil warfare shown in that figure holds even when one controls for the number of states: see Gleditsch, Wallensteen, Eriksson, Stollenberg, and Strand, "Armed Conflict 1946–2001." Moreover, wars within countries that were not yet independent are not ignored in the figure: they are tallied, of course, in the "colonial war" category.

63 Gray, *Another Bloody Century*, 24, 378, 382. On this issue, see also Peter Wallensteen, "Trends in Major War: Too Early for Waning?" in Väyryen, *Waning of Major War*, 80–93. In 1991, Gray with similar confidence declared it "inconceivable" that Mikhail Gorbachev "could direct and oversee the transformation of the brutal, continental, multinational empire that is the USSR into something so much kinder and gentler that a truly objective basis for a structural improvement in political–security relations would be the consequence": Colin S. Gray, "Do the Changes within the Soviet Union Provide a Basis for Eased Soviet–American Relations? A Skeptical View" in Robert Jervis and Seweryn Bialer, eds., *Soviet–American Relations After the Cold War* (Durham, NC: Duke University Press, 1991), 61.

64 In overall tone, however, a recent book dealing with the end of civil war in Africa is not terribly optimistic about the future: Oliver Furley and Roy May, eds., *Ending Africa's Wars: Progressing to Peace* (Aldershot, UK: Ashgate, 2006).

65 However, terrorism, or at least international terrorism, actually only kills a few hundred people a year worldwide, outside, of course, of 2001. For an assessment, see John Mueller, *Overblown* (New York: Free Press, 2006). See also Mack, *Human Security Brief 2007*.

REFLECTIONS

Is civil war going out of style?

The remarkable decline in civil wars is particularly impressive because, while the increase in civil wars from the 1960s to the early 1990s can be attributed in part (but only in part) to the increasing number of independent states, there has been, of course, no decline in that number during the turnaround that has taken place over the succeeding two decades.

As discussed both in the "War has almost ceased to exist" and in the "Policing the remnants of war" articles, I consider the general improvement in the quality of government to be a key factor in the decline of civil war. But whatever the reason for the decline, it seems possible (though far from certain) that civil war may be going out of style.

During the course of the twentieth century, Europeans came to embrace the idea, first strenuously promoted late in the nineteenth century, that they ought not to do war—or at least war among themselves—anymore. That perspective has held for international war on the continent now for two-thirds of a century, massively shattering all previous precedents. Civil wars in Europe were also almost unknown during that period as well, and when a set of them broke out in the Balkan corner of the continent in the 1990s, the reaction was one of amazement, something that inspired strenuous, if not always particularly effective, efforts to stamp out, or at least to contain, the conflicts. Central to the concern—or outrage—was a doctrine associated with British Prime Minister Tony Blair: "We either stand aside and let this man conduct a policy effectively of racial genocide in a part of Europe or we say 'I'm afraid we're not going to allow that.' " Genocide and war may happen elsewhere, but not *here*. We simply don't do that anymore.

It doesn't seem too much of a stretch to suggest that civil wars may be going out of style in other areas as well. Unlike Europe, Latin America and East Asia have experienced many civil wars since 1945, but there have been a very few there in the last couple of decades. Perhaps relatedly, the number of coups has also declined enormously in these areas.

In like manner, it may be that something similar is happening in Africa and elsewhere. Peoples there seem to have become fed up with the civil warfare they or their neighbors have suffered in recent decades in which small numbers of thugs, often drunken or drugged, have been able to pulverize effective society through their predatory criminal antics, sometimes sustaining them for decades. In consequence of this disgust, there has been a strong willingness to accept and make effective use of outside aid and to establish effective (if hardly perfect) governments, a process that Page Fortna, among others, has interestingly explored. At any rate, the Mobutu to Mandela phenomenon discussed in the article seems to be holding, at least for now, and the number of civil wars going on in the continent remains at low levels.

There may be another way to look at all this. It may be tempting to characterize (or dismiss) the recent remarkable decline in the number of civil wars, as documented in Figure 3.1, as a "blip." But perhaps the "blip" is in the *rise* in the number of such wars that took place from the 1960s to the early 1990s. As noted in the article, much of this seems to have come from rapid decolonization, which led to the creation of a host of countries that were, to put it mildly, ill-governed and therefore prime candidates, in my view, to become civil war arenas. If that is the case, it is the increase of civil war that is the historical peculiarity, and it is one based substantially on a phenomenon that cannot be repeated.

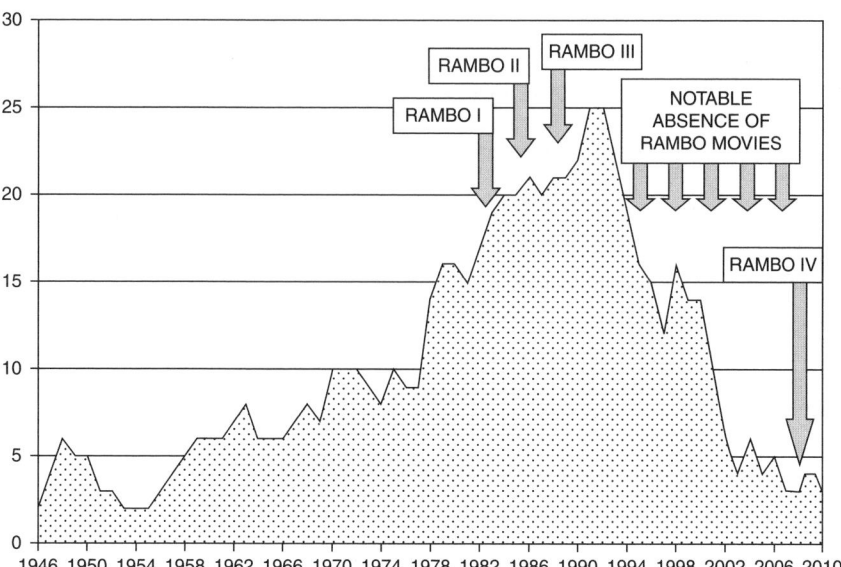

Reflections Figure 3.1 Number of ongoing civil wars by year, 1946–2010.

The *Rambo* phenomenon

There is, however, another explanation for the decline in civil war: the rise in such wars corresponded to the issuance of the *Rambo* movies and the decline to a notable absence of them. The relationship between the movies and the incidence of civil war is documented in Reflections Table 3.1. It is similar to the figure on p. 37 (Figure 3.1), but it only gives the trend for civil wars and it has been updated to 2010.

The *Rambo* connection is not *quite* as absurd as it at first may seem. There are repeated reports of combatants in Africa and the Balkans stoking up not only on booze and drugs in their lairs before beginning a rampage, but mainlining *Rambo* movies as well. For example, a memoir by Ismael Beah, a boy soldier in Sierrra Leone, mentions this repeatedly, and one theater director in Sarajevo not entirely facetiously called for a war crimes trial for Sylvester Stallone: "He's responsible for a lot that has gone on here!" Indeed, one Serbian paramilitary unit actually called itself "The Rambos" and went around in webbed masks and black gloves with black ribbons fetchingly tied around their foreheads.

At any rate, when the latest *Rambo* movie came out in 2008 I checked it out and, for whatever it is worth, updated a chart I had published in *The Remnants of War* on the earlier *Rambo* films. The results are documented in Reflections Table 3.1.

Reflections Table 3.1

	I	II	III	IV
Number of bad guys killed by Rambo with his shirt on	1	12	33	83
Number of bad guys killed by Rambo with his shirt off	0	46	45	0
Total number of bad guys killed by Rambo no matter how attired	1	58	78	83
Number of bad guys killed by accomplices of Rambo	0	10	17	40
Number of good guys killed by bad guys	0	1	37	113
Total number of people killed	1	69	132	236
Number of people killed per minute	0.01	0.72	1.30	2.59
Time at which the first person is killed	29'31"	33'34"	41'9"	3'22"
Number of people killed per minute from that point until the end of the film (not including the ending credits)	0.02	1.18	2.39	3.04
Sequences in which Rambo is shot at without significant result	12	24	38	2
Number of sequences in which good guys are tortured by bad guys	2	5	7	3
Number of sex scenes	0	0	0	0

I: *First Blood* (1982), II: *Rambo: First Blood Part II* (1985), III: *Rambo III* (1988), IV: *Rambo* (2008)

The body count includes only people who visibly fall inert after being bombed; garroted; blasted; stabbed; strangled; blown up by mines, artillery, grenades or other explosives; shot by bullets, artillery or arrows; incinerated by fires or flame-throwers; bludgeoned; stomped or beaten; disemboweled or beheaded; or pushed or tossed off precipices or out of aircraft. It also includes people who had their necks snapped. In a couple of scenes, the action moved very quickly, and bodies became hard to distinguish (such as when a whole bunch of people were mowed down by machine-gun fire), but in most cases the death-toll was clear. In addition, there were many instances in which Rambo blew up occupied tanks, helicopters, cars, trucks, trail passages, guard towers or other buildings. Fatalities from these episodes were not included in the body count unless the people inside were clearly shown to die by, for example, bolting into the open from their erstwhile place of refuge, clutching various body parts and collapsing to the ground.

Whatever its programmed and much escalated mayhem, however, the latest *Rambo* movie has yet to reverse the trend.

Another data set

In a recent book, Meredith Sarkees and Frank Wayman have argued (mainly in the concluding chapter by Sarkees) that war has "a depressing endurance" and does not seem to be in decline. To arrive at this conclusion, they rely solely on yearly data on "war onsets," thereby giving the same weight to a war that dies out in one year as to one that lasts ten.

However, they do provide a list of wars and the years the wars lasted, making it roughly possible to duplicate with their data the number of ongoing wars by year, as applied in my article "War has almost ceased to exist." The results are displayed in Reflections Figure 3.2, and can be compared to those in Figure 3.1 on p. 37. As

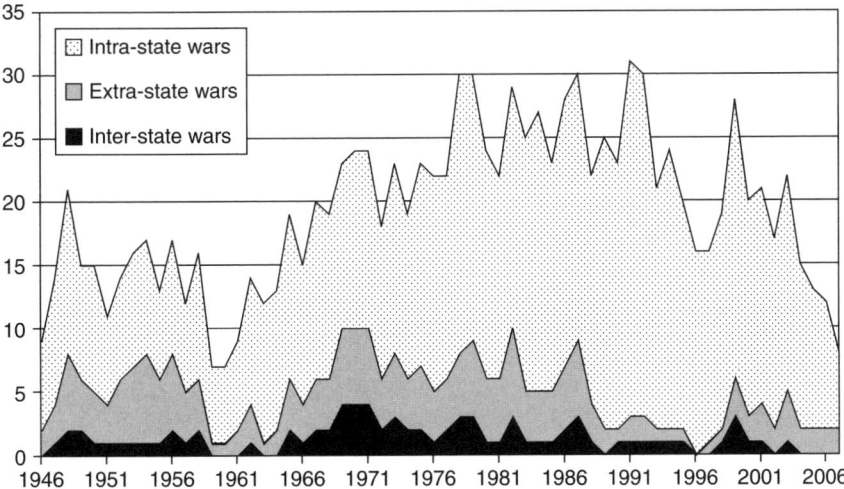

Reflections Figure 3.2 Number of ongoing civil wars, by year, 1946–2007.

can be seen, the patterns are similar to those in the article: an increase of ongoing warfare that peaked in the early 1990s with a distinct, if lumpy, fall-off since. The total number of wars is somewhat larger in the Sarkees/Wayman version because there were years in some of their wars in which 1,000 battle-related deaths were not suffered—for example, Castro's war in Cuba that raged throughout 1958 but that technically ended very early in 1959 is counted in both years even though there were very few casualties in the later year.

Reflections references

Ishmael Beah, *A Long Way Gone: Memoirs of a Boy Soldier*. New York: Farrar, Straus and Giroux, 2007.

Virginia Page Fortna, *Does Peacekeeping Work? Shaping Belligerents' Choices After Civil Wars*. Princeton, NJ: Princeton University Press, 2008.

Meredith Sarkees and Frank Whelon Wayman, *Resort to War: A Data Guide to Inter-State, Extra-State, Intra-State, and Non-State Wars, 1816–2007*. Washington, DC: CQ Press, 2010.

4   Why isn't there more violence?

Benjamin Valentino's masterful book, *Final Solutions*, explores the process by which governments during the twentieth century managed deliberately to kill masses of people. Most of the lessons that emerge from this examination are unsettling. In particular, we learn that mass killing is not all that difficult to carry out.

To begin with, it appears that perpetrating regimes need mainly to set up the killing machinery and organize it with reasonable bureaucratic effectiveness. They do not need to force the executioners to carry out their grim duty nor do they need to propagandize to instill and sustain in the executioners great amounts of hatred or anger toward the victims. For the most part the horrors are carried out in a mechanical process.

Second, the number of people required to perpetrate a mass killing does not need to be large. Over and over again, Valentino finds that the killing machinery was manned by relatively small numbers of people. This means that regimes sometimes need to recruit little more than small bands of sadists or criminals to carry out the task, though there is considerable evidence that, if properly organized and disciplined, ordinary men can also do the killing—or "dirty work," as they may label it.

Third, there is often a great deal of passive acceptance by the general population of systematic destruction of human life being carried out by their government in their name. It is not so much that people approve of the horrors, but that they don't do much of anything to stop them and are inclined instead to look away, sometimes with regret, but effectively with what Valentino calls "negative support."[1]

Fourth, the victims of mass killing rarely put up much in the way of direct resistance. Confused and unorganized, they generally submit to the killing machinery, allowing themselves to be herded and brutalized. The most common kind of "resistance" is to attempt to flee. Sometimes some of those who have been successful in fleeing to safer territory can then organize themselves into an armed resistance force, but this activity little affects the killers in the first instance.

Fifth, though less stressed by Valentino, the perpetrators of mass killing generally suffer little punishment for their acts—sometimes, though certainly not always, this is because the activities have been embedded in wars or in military campaigns. Of course, Adolf Hitler and a number of other top Nazis did not survive the Second World War to meet their fate at the postwar Nuremberg trials, and some sort of punishment may yet be meted out to at least a few of those who perpetrated atrocities in Bosnia or genocide in Rwanda. Yet postwar trials have been mainly a matter of victors' justice, and they take years of effort, are notoriously inconsistent concerning who is arrested and brought to trial, and for the most part are, not unreasonably, biased toward punishing the top leadership, not the vast majority of the perpetrators, who are generally left free to blend back into society. Moreover, most of the leaders of the mass killings examined by Valentino—including Josef Stalin, Mao Zedong, Pol Pot, Turkish leaders in 1915, and counterinsurgents in Afghanistan and Guatemala—died of natural causes.

I would like to extrapolate somewhat from this experience and examine a related question: If violence is so easy to carry out, why isn't there more of it? Despite the horrors detailed by Valentino and those that crowd the headlines daily (not to mention the intuitions of pessimistic visionaries such as Thomas Hobbes), the vast majority of people during the vast majority of their lifetimes never experience much of any violence at all—though they may watch a lot of it on television and at the movies.

Rates of violence

To construct the argument, it would be useful at the outset to estimate how much violence there is in the world and to establish a benchmark for determining whether the amount of violence should be considered to be large or small.

Death by war, government, and automobile

Valentino begins his book by attempting to put his project in broadest context by estimating how many people during the bloody twentieth century died violent deaths in wars and through the systematic use of mass killing by governments. Like others, he concludes that the latter—something Rudolph Rummel has aptly labeled "death by government"—was responsible for a considerably greater amount of death than was the former. Overall, if everything is put together, an estimate—probably somewhat on the high side—of the total number of people who died during the century from wars (both civil and international) and from governmental mass killing would come out to be perhaps 200,000,000.[2] Since around 12,000,000,000 people populated the planet at some time during the century, this would mean that somewhere between 1 and 2 percent of the century's population died from war and mass killing.

It is possible, of course, to regard these violent death rates to be high—1 or 2 percent may sound low, but that adds up to a very large number of deaths overall. A degree of context and something of a benchmark might be established, however, by comparing death rates from automobile accidents. Americans at present drive around in cars designed for safety and very commonly on expensive high-speed highways on which head-to-head crashes and dangerous maneuvers such as left turns are made nearly impossible. Still, an American's chance of dying in an automobile accident over a lifetime is, as it happens, somewhere between 1 and 2 percent.[3] Yet it seems fair to conclude that, judging by their behavior, few Americans consider the chances of dying in an auto crash to be unacceptably high or even worthy of much consideration or consternation, even though the private passenger automobile has been the necessary cause of three million deaths in the United States alone over the course of the twentieth century and, at present rates, will result in four million during the twenty-first.[4]

Of course these rates are only very general ones. War has not been uniformly distributed—one could have mostly avoided it by living in Europe during the last half of the twentieth century or in quite a few other places during the first half. Moreover, certain groups were marked for mass killing and proportionately suffered far more from it: Turkish Armenians, Ukrainian kulaks, European Jews, Rwandan Tutsis, noncommunist Cambodians. Auto accidents, however, are not evenly distributed either. The chances of dying in one are notably lower for those who wear seat belts; who do not drive recklessly or after midnight; who do not drive when drunk, drugged, or very tired; who are not male; and who are not 19 years old.

The key point is that the chances that a randomly selected inhabitant of the twentieth century would die of war or mass killing (something understandably considered tragic and unacceptable) are about the same as the chances that a randomly selected modern American will perish in an automobile accident (a risk considered regrettable, but acceptable). Putting together these two disparate facts, it could be held that, in an important sense, violent death by war or government is remarkably—or perhaps even acceptably—infrequent.

Homicide

Also relevant would be a consideration of homicide rates. Although there are a few cases in which frequencies are even higher, the most murderous societies in all of history have had yearly homicide rates of around 100 in 100,000—that is, ones in which an individual has about one chance in 1,000 per year of being murdered. The vast majority of societies have sustained lower rates: in the United States, it is more like one in 10,000; in Japan and Canada, more like one in a 100,000. Over a lifetime, an individual in the United States has far less than one chance in 100 of being murdered, and even in history's most murderous societies that risk rises only to one in 20. Indeed, crime in total could be considered to be a remarkably uncommon phenomenon. Only a small percentage of the population in most societies becomes a victim of even minor forms of crime in any given year, and violent crime constitutes only a small portion of that.

The chances of becoming a victim of homicide or other crime can, of course, be reduced by living in certain areas, avoiding or getting out of abusive relationships, and remaining distant from the drug trade. Overall, however, it remains rare, even in societies that are considered notably—or at any rate, comparatively—dangerous.

Terrorist violence

Of interest as well is the frequency and effectiveness of another much-discussed form of mayhem: terrorism. Filmmaker Michael Moore happened to remark on the popular CBS news program *60 Minutes* on 16 February 2003 that "the chances of any of us dying in a terrorist incident is very, very, very small." His interviewer, Bob Simon, promptly admonished, "But no one sees the world like that." Both statements, remarkably, are true—the first only a bit more so than the second.

For all the attention it evokes, terrorism, in reasonable context, actually causes rather little damage, and the likelihood that any individual will become a victim in most places is microscopic. The number of people worldwide who die as a result of international terrorism is generally only a few hundred a year—tiny compared to the numbers who die in most civil wars or from automobile accidents. In fact, until 2001, far fewer Americans had been killed in any grouping of years by all forms of international terrorism than were killed by lightning. Furthermore, except in 2001, virtually none of these terrorist deaths occurred within the United States itself.

Even with the September 11 attacks included in the count, however, the number of Americans killed by international terrorism since the late 1960s (which is when the State Department began tracking this data) is about the same as the number killed over the same period by lightning—or by accident-causing deer or by severe allergic reaction to peanuts. In almost all years the total number of people world-wide who die at the hands of international terrorists is not much more than the number who drown in bathtubs in the United States.

Some of this is definitional. When terrorism becomes really extensive, it is generally no longer called "terrorism," but "war." Yet what people are mainly concerned about is random terror, not sustained warfare. Moreover, even using an expansive definition of terrorism and including domestic terrorism in the mix, it is likely that far fewer people were killed by terrorists in the entire world over the last 100 years than died in any of a number of unnoticed civil wars during that period.[5]

Obviously, this could change if international terrorists are able to assemble sufficient weaponry or devise new tactics to kill masses of people and if they come to do so routinely—and this, of course, is the central fear. It should be kept in mind, however, that 9/11 was an extreme event—until that date, no more than 329 people had ever been killed in a single terrorist attack (in a 1985 Air India explosion)—and extreme events often remain exactly that: aberrations, rather than harbingers.[6]

For present purposes, however, the question is this: If terrorism has such a major public impact and evokes such widespread fear, why isn't there more of it? Since 9/11, the United States has been inundated by imaginative speculations about where and how terrorists might strike next. The most spectacular of these stress the exotic: nuclear, chemical, biological, or radiological weapons, all of which take considerable technological sophistication. By contrast, the 9/11 strikes were remarkably low-tech and could have happened long ago: both skyscrapers and airplanes have been around for a century. Given the vastness and apparent vulnerability of the country and the seeming dedication of terrorists and some of their would-be imitators, one would expect there to be a massive number of terrorist attacks following the popular "what's to stop" speculations: what's to stop terrorists from shooting at people in shopping centers, collapsing tunnels, poisoning food, cutting electrical lines, derailing trains, setting forest fires, blowing up oil pipelines, causing massive traffic jams, etc.? Yet, mostly, it does not happen.

Restraints on violence

It is unlikely that the rates of terrorism and of homicide and other crimes are as low as they are because of the remarkable efficiency and effectiveness of the police, criminal justice, and internal security systems. Only a few percent of crimes result in conviction and the perpetrators of the vast majority of terrorist attacks are never found—a consideration that is, of course, irrelevant in the case of suicidal ones. Serial killers characteristically murder a considerable number of people before they are caught, and that usually comes about only because they have established predictable patterns or made key mistakes; if they quit after only a few murders, like Jack the Ripper or the anthrax poisoner of 2001 did, they are unlikely to be apprehended. Other forms of social control may add to the rather limited and inefficient ones presented by the police and security systems. Among these are restraints raised by religious and social proscriptions.

It seems to me, though, that the most reliable restraints on violent behavior—both by individuals and by states—stem from human nature. For the most part, following the Rodney King prescription, we all—or almost all—actually do really want just to get along. There certainly is a quota of jerks out there, but most people most of the time are inclined to avoid conflict—certainly violent conflict. Their key goal is to live in peace and security, and they do this in part by adopting a live-and-let-live philosophy and by sharpening their skills from a very early age for determining whom to trust and befriend.[7] By and large, their instincts predispose them not to belligerence or aggressiveness or even to stand and fight, but rather to flee conflict by removing themselves from threatening situations and moving from neighborhoods that are, or seem, dangerous. What is remarkable about most societies is how small in number, indeed how little in evidence, are the police forces required to maintain acceptable order.

The Hobbesian image

If this is true, it suggests that Hobbes and the Hobbesian perspective on human nature were and are substantially flawed. People in general are not given, or readily driven to, violence or aggression but rather are, for the most part, fairly easy to govern. Indeed, they will tolerate quite a bit of persecution and unpleasantness for a little peace and order. For example, in discussing the dominance that the Canadian government imposed on the often warlike Indians of western Canada,

Lawrence Keeley noted that the restraint they exercised "as they were subjugated and dispossessed is evidence of how much injustice people will tolerate for the sake of peace if they are assured of receiving the means to survive, certain punishment for breaking the peace, and impartial protection of their persons and property if they keep it."[8]

Experience thus suggests that Hobbes—or at least the common Hobbesian image—is wrong, and perhaps profoundly so, in some important respects about the state of nature.[9] Hobbes was obsessed by the chaos and calamity of the English Civil War of 1642–49, which took place during his lifetime, and his important book, *Leviathan*, was, he noted, "occasioned by the disorders of the present time."[10] In particular, he viewed the conflict as a descent into a base state of nature, a "kingdom of darkness" and a "confederacy of deceivers" in which "force and fraud" become "the two cardinal virtues," and where without "a common power to keep them all in awe," people live in a perpetual state of war "where every man is enemy of every man," where there is "continual fear and danger of violent death," and where life, as he famously put it, becomes "solitary, poor, nasty, brutish, and short."[11] Hobbes did acknowledge that people group themselves (so the state of nature may not be quite as "solitary" as his famous description seems to suggest), and thus that the perpetual wars of the state of nature are waged between bands rather than between individuals.[12] The implication of the image, however, at least as it is commonly understood, is one of perpetual and total violence in which all, or virtually all, partake.[13]

Yet the experience of much civil warfare, mass killing, terrorism, and criminal predation calls this image into question. Although the conditions of deep insecurity certainly resemble a Hobbesian state of nature, they come about not because people generally fall into, are manipulated into, or give in to, murderous enmity, but because they are plagued by small numbers of unpoliced criminals or because they unwillingly come under the control of groups, often remarkably small ones, of organized or semi-organized murderers.

As Valentino's discussion suggests, societies can be devastated by the violent maraudings and intimidations of a handful of people. In Bosnia, the much-feared thugs of Arkan's Tigers consisted of a core of some 200 men, and perhaps totaled 500–1,000 overall.[14] Višegrad, a Bosnian city of 50,000, was substantially controlled for years by a returned hometown boy, Milan Lukić, and some 15 well-armed companions.[15] The town of Teslic was controlled, it is estimated, by "five or six men, well placed and willing to use violence."[16] Naser Orić, the Muslim warlord who ruled Srebrenica for several years (and who was mysteriously absent with his gang when Serbian forces overran the town in 1995), led an armed band with a nucleus of only 15 men.[17]

The condition seems quite general, perhaps even universal. For example, during the Dutch Revolt in the middle of the sixteenth century, notes Geoffrey Parker, small numbers of Calvinists were able to topple Catholic authority in many areas, smashing churches and wayside shrines often "in full view of great crowds who watched and lifted not a finger." In the south of the country, the destruction was carried out by a band of between 50 and 100 people—including returned exiles, unemployed manual workers, drunkards, whores, and boys in their early teens—who were hired by the day at the wage of an unskilled laborer.[18] More recently, the forces that ended up shattering Liberia numbered 150 or less at the beginning,[19] and those in Guatemala began with less than 500.[20] According to a priest who lives there, a slum in Kingston, Jamaica, populated by 8,000 people is totally dominated by 30 mobsters.[21] In Somalia, warlord Mohammed Aidid ran his fiefdom with a few dozen hired guns paid in part with drugs.[22] The Rwandan genocide of 1994 is undoubtedly the event that most evokes the Hobbesian neighbor-against-neighbor image in the post-cold war era. Yet the disaster there was perpetrated by perhaps 2 percent of the Hutu male population over the age of 13.[23]

Since Hobbes assumed that every person is, at base, "radically insecure, mistrustful of other men and afraid for his life," he concluded that the only way out of the mess is for everyone permanently to surrender to an authoritarian ruler, one who primarily values glory and stability rather than doctrinal orthodoxy or ideological (or ethnic) purity, and one who will maintain the necessary force to keep people from once again giving in to their natural proclivities for isolation, hostility, and insensitivity to the rights of others.[24]

Experience suggests, however, that this monumental—perhaps even impossible—task is hardly required. As noted, most people most of the time do not have a great deal of difficulty getting along and in fabricating useful rules and patterns of conduct that allow them peacefully to coexist. Police may indeed be needed, even necessary, to maintain order, but they need not normally be numerous nor must their control be Leviathan-like. This is because they mainly need simply to protect the many from the few, rather than everyone from everyone else, as Hobbes—or at least the Hobbesian image—would appear to have it. That is, the policing forces have to deal not with a broad population, but with only a small, violent segment.

At one extreme, the Hobbesian image can lead authorities to reach the essentially racist conclusion that the only effective method for eliminating a threat that emanates from a definable group is to annihilate the group itself. This simple, if horrendous, conclusion has been, as Valentino has demonstrated, a major reason for huge population transfers and for mass killing.[25] At the other extreme, the image can discourage policing by suggesting that the costs would be enormous because one must control directly and completely the entire group, rather than just a small, opportunistic, and often quite cowardly subgroup.

International "anarchy"

Insofar as the realist perspective in international relations takes its cast from a Hobbesian perspective, it may be substantially, even viscerally, in error. Specifically, the notion that countries live in a state of "anarchy" is misleading and could encourage undesirable policy developments.

Technically, of course, the word is accurate: there exists no international government that effectively polices the behavior of the nations of the world. It is, as Kenneth Waltz put it, a condition of "self help."[26] The problem with the word "anarchy" lies in its inescapable connotations: it implies chaos, lawlessness, disorder, confusion, and random violence. It would be equally accurate to characterize the international situation as "unregulated," a word with connotations that are far different, and perhaps far more helpful.[27]

Waltz argued that "interdependent states whose relations remain unregulated must experience conflict and will occasionally fall into violence," or "with many sovereign states, with no system of law enforceable among them, with each state judging its grievances and ambitions according to the dictates of its own reason or desire—conflict, sometimes leading to war, is bound to occur."[28] Realist John Mearsheimer argues further that, in a condition of anarchy, "there is little room for trust among states" and "security will often be scarce."[29]

As suggested above, violence in domestic situations is quite rare, and it seems that this condition primarily derives not from the Leviathan-like capacities of the policing system but rather from human nature, which overwhelmingly tends to eschew violence. People do need protection, but it is not protection from everyone else as Hobbes would have it, but simply from the violent few. Something similar may apply to international society.

Most important in this regard is that in our "anarchic" international system, major wars—wars among developed countries—have become so rare and unlikely that they could well be considered to be obsolescent, if not obsolete. Michael Howard in 1991 found it "quite possible that war in the sense of major, organised armed conflict between highly developed societies may not recur."[30] Two years later, John Keegan concluded in *A History of Warfare* that the kind of war he was principally considering could well be in terminal demise: "War, it seems to me, after a lifetime of reading about the subject, mingling with men of war, visiting the sites of war and observing its effects, may well be ceasing to commend itself to human beings as a desirable or productive, let alone rational, means of reconciling their discontents."[31] By the end of the century, Mary Kaldor was suggesting that "the barbarity of war between states may have become a thing of the past," and by the beginning of the new one, Robert Jervis had concluded that war among the leading states "will not occur in the future" or, in the words of Jeffrey Record, may have "disappeared altogether."[32] In the history of warfare, the most interesting statistic is zero (or near-zero): the number of wars between developed states since 1945.

Not only have developed countries managed to stay out of war with each other, but there has been something of a decline of international wars of any sort since the Second World War. The only truly notable exception between 1975 and the end of the cold war in 1989 (and it is an important one) was the bloody war between Iran and Iraq that lasted from 1980 to 1988. In addition, aside from armed interventions in civil wars in neighboring countries and a few border skirmishes and conflicts, there were regime-changing invasions of Uganda in 1978–79 and of tiny Grenada in 1983, and a brief armed dispute between the United Kingdom and Argentina in 1982 over some remote and nearly barren islands in the South Atlantic. Moreover, it is probably significant that, although armed contests between the Israeli government and Palestinian rebels have remained plentiful, no Arab or Muslim country has been willing since 1973 to escalate the contest to international war by sending its troops to participate directly. After the cold war, there were a number of what might be called "policing wars"—militarized efforts by developed countries to bring order to civil conflicts or to topple thuggish regimes—that reached something of a culminating (and perhaps ending) point with the invasion of Iraq in 2003.[33] Nonetheless, the only really classic sort of international war that has occurred anywhere in the world after 1989 was the conflict between Ethiopia and Eritrea in the late 1990s.

Thus, international war has declined remarkably since 1945 even while international anarchy continues, effectively, to flourish: no one, surely, would confuse the United Nations or other international bodies with a Hobbesian Leviathan.

Experience suggests, then, that alarm about international "anarchy" is much overstressed. Regulation is not normally required, and "anarchy" could become a desirable state.

Notes

1 Benjamin Valentino, *Final Solutions: Mass Killing and Genocide in the Twentieth Century* (Ithaca: Cornell University Press, 2004), 32. Valentino does not deal very much with the notion of sanctions as a form of intentional mass killing (though see p. 88). His point about "negative support," however, is illustrated by the lack of reaction in the United States when America's ambassador to the United Nations, Madeleine Albright, appeared on the nation's most popular television newsmagazine, *60 Minutes*, on 12 May 1996. Asked whether she thought the deaths of perhaps half a million children caused by U.S.-imposed sanctions on Iraq were "worth it," she replied without disputing the number, "I think this is a very hard choice, but the price—we think the price is worth it." This remarkable assertion, ignored in the United States, became famous in the Arab world. See Andrew Cockburn and Patrick Cockburn, *Out of the Ashes: The Resurrection of Saddam Hussein* (New York: HarperCollins, 1999), 263.

2 Valentino, *Final Solutions*, 1–2. See also Rudolph Rummel, *Death by Government* (New Brunswick: Transaction, 1994).

3 David Ropeik and George Gray, *Risk* (Boston: Houghton Mifflin, 2002), 424.

4 The World Health Organization estimates that road crashes currently kill 1.2 million people a year worldwide. See www.who.int/mediacentre/releases/2004/pr24/en (accessed 28 April 2004).

5 The fear of violence, thus, is often much greater than its actuality, and the record with respect to fear about crime suggests that efforts to deal coherently with the risks of terrorism will prove difficult. For example, fear of crime rose notably in the mid-1990s even as statistics were showing that crime was in pronounced decline. When David Dinkins, running for re-election as mayor of New York City, pointed to such numbers, he was accused by A. M. Rosenthal of the *New York Times* of hiding behind "trivializing statistics" that "are supposed to convince us that crime is going down" ("New York to Clinton," *New York Times*, 1 October 1993, A31). New Yorkers did eventually come to feel safer from crime, but this was probably less because crime rates actually declined than because of atmospherics as graffiti, panhandlers, aggressive windshield washers, and the homeless were banished or hidden from view. In the end, it is not clear how one can deal with the public's often irrational fears about remote dangers. Some people say they prefer dangerous forms of transportation such as the private passenger automobile to safe ones such as commercial airliners because they feel they have more

"control." Yet they seem to feel no fear on buses and trains even without having that sense of control and even though derailing a speeding train or crashing a speeding bus are likely to be much easier for a terrorist than downing an airliner—as experience in Israel attests. Furthermore, people tend to be more alarmed by dramatic fatalities—which the 9/11 crashes certainly provided—than by ones that cumulate statistically. Thus the 3,000 deaths of 9/11 inspire far more grief and fear than the 150,000 deaths from auto accidents that have taken place since then. In some respects, fear of terror may be something like playing the lottery except in reverse: the chances of winning the lottery or of dying from terrorism may be microscopic, but for monumental events that are, or seem, random, one can irrelevantly conclude that one's chances are just as good, or as bad, as those of anyone else. The communication of risk, then, is no easy task.

6 On this issue, see John Mueller, "Harbinger or Aberration? A 9/11 Provocation," *National Interest* (fall 2002): 45–50. More generally, see John Mueller, "Simplicity and Spook: Terrorism and the Dynamics of Threat Exaggeration," *International Security Perspectives*, forthcoming.

7 See Robert C. Ellickson, *Order without Law: How Neighbors Settle Disputes* (Cambridge: Harvard University Press, 1991); Lawrence H. Keeley, *War before Civilization: The Myth of the Peaceful Savage* (New York: Oxford University Press, 1996), 178; John Mueller, *Quiet Cataclysm: Reflections on Recent Transformation of World Politics* (New York: HarperCollins, 1994), ch. 8; and John Mueller, *Capitalism, Democracy, and Ralph's Pretty Good Grocery* (Princeton: Princeton University Press, 1999), 38–43.

8 Keeley, *War before Civilization*, 155. People are also strongly inclined to seek governments that seem to be able to provide that sense of safety, even ones that are reprehensible on other grounds. The power of this appeal should never be underestimated. It is fundamental, and people will in desperation often sacrifice almost anything simply to be able to live in peace. Thus, the Taliban succeeded in Afghanistan, despite their theological extremism, in large part because the population was desperate for a force that could bring order to the country. The Nazis came to power in Germany in considerable part because they seemed likely to be able to deal effectively with the political disorder that was endemic in German streets at the time. People in Turkmenistan willingly support a leader who renames months after himself in part because he appears to have kept them from the violent disorder that has infected nearby Tajikistan. Despite the authoritarian cast of his government, Russia's Vladimir Putin remains highly popular in considerable measure because of the perceived stability that has marked his reign—in vivid contrast with the turmoil of the 1990s.

9 This discussion draws upon John Mueller, *The Remnants of War* (Ithaca: Cornell University Press, 2004), 112–16.

10 Thomas Hobbes, *Leviathan* (Indianapolis: Hackett, 1994), 496 (in "Review and Conclusion"). Actually, however, Hobbes had already worked out some of the notions in writings, such as *De Civi*, that were published before the Civil War.

11 Hobbes, *Leviathan*, 76–78 (in ch. 13).

12 Robert P. Kraynak, *History and Modernity in the Thought of Thomas Hobbes* (Ithaca: Cornell University Press, 1990), 148–49.

13 This conclusion may be more Hobbesian than Hobbes, however. Russell Hardin points to a passage in which Hobbes noted that "law was brought into the world for nothing else but to limit the natural liberty of particular men, in such manner, as they might not hurt, but assist one another, and join together against a common enemy." *Leviathan*, 175 (in ch. 26). The suggestion is that the problem is with "particular men," not with the totality of humanity.

14 Miloš Vasić, "The Yugoslav Army and the Post-Yugoslav Armies," in *Yugoslavia and After: A Study in Fragmentation, Despair and Rebirth*, ed. David A. Dyker and Ivan Vejvoda (London: Longman, 1996), 134; and United Nations Commission of Experts, *Final Report of the United Nations Commission of Experts Established Pursuant to*

Security Council Resolution 780 (1992), Annex III. A Special Forces, ed. M. Cherif Bassiouni (New York: United Nations, 28 December 1994), para. 92, 138.

15 Chris Hedges, "From One Serbian Militia Chief, A Trail of Plunder and Slaughter," *New York Times*, 25 March 1996, A1.

16 Mike O'Connor, "Moderate Bosnian Serbs Plot in Secrecy for Unity," *New York Times*, 31 July 1996, A3.

17 David Rohde, *Endgame: The Betrayal and Fall of Srebrenica, Europe's Worst Massacre since World War II* (New York: Farrar, Straus and Giroux, 1997), xiv, 60, 107–9, 354, 355.

18 Geoffrey Parker, *The Dutch Revolt* (London: Allen Lane, 1977), 78–79.

19 William Reno, *Warlord Politics and African States* (Boulder: Lynne Rienner, 1998), 79.

20 Valentino, *Final Solutions*, 206.

21 *60 Minutes* CBS, 14 May 2000.

22 Mark Bowden, *Black Hawk Down: A Story of Modern War* (New York: Atlantic Monthly Press, 1999), 109, 368.

23 Mueller, *Remnants of War*, 100; Valentino, *Final Solutions*, 37; and Bruce D. Jones, *Peace-making in Rwanda: The Dynamics of Failure* (Boulder: Lynne Rienner, 2001), 38–41.

24 Kraynak, *History and Modernity*, 165, 176, 179.

25 Valentino, *Final Solutions*, chs. 4, 5.

26 Kenneth Waltz, *Theory of International Politics* (Reading: Addison-Wesley, 1979), 111.

27 On this issue, see also Mueller, *Quiet Cataclysm*, ch. 2.

28 Waltz, *Theory of International Politics*, 138, 159.

29 John Mearsheimer, "Back to the Future: Instability in Europe after the Cold War," *International Security* 15, no. 1 (summer 1990): 12, 45. See also Robert J. Art and Kenneth N. Waltz, "Technology, Strategy, and the Uses of Force," in *The Use of Force*, ed. Robert J. Art and Kenneth N. Waltz (Lanham: University Press of America, 1983), 3–6.

30 Michael Howard, *The Lessons of History* (New Haven: Yale University Press, 1991), 176.

31 John Keegan, *A History of Warfare* (New York: Knopf, 1993), 59.

32 Mary Kaldor, *New and Old Wars: Organized Violence in a Global Era* (Cambridge: Polity, 1999), 5; Robert Jervis, "Theories of War in an Era of Leading-Power Peace," *American Political Science Review* 96, no. 1 (March 2002), 1; and Jeffrey Record, "Collapsed Countries, Casualty Dread, and the New American Way of War," *Parameters* (summer 2002): 6. See also John Mueller, *Retreat from Doomsday: The Obsolescence of Major War* (New York: Basic Books, 1989).

33 On this phenomenon, see Mueller, *Remnants of War*, chs. 7–8.

REFLECTIONS

The decline in violence

The article seeks to demonstrate that, at least in some important sense, the world is generally not a dangerous place, and, with some spectacular exceptions, never has been. However, it also appears that, whatever its absolute levels of frequency, violence in a wide variety of forms has been in decline over the course of human history. Lawrence Keeley has published an important book demolishing the "peaceful savage" myth and arguing that "primitive warfare" has characteristically been a comparatively vicious and murderous process while, between the frequent wars, homicide rates in those societies have also been very high by the standards of the "civilized world."

Steven Pinker applies a wealth of sources including Keeley's work as well as Benjamin Valentino's *Final Solutions*, the inspiration for my article, and has sought to tackle the issue of the decline of violence more widely. Over the course of human history he charts not only a decline in homicide rates and in the frequency of war, but also in a host of other violent behaviors once widely considered acceptable: infanticide, human sacrifice, blood libel, slavery, superstitious killing of blasphemers and heretics, corporal punishment, torture, feuding, cruelty to animals, capital punishment, and cruel and unusual punishment.

Possible aberrations in the trend

It is tempting to see this, as Pinker does, as part of a sort of "civilizing process," a collective, or collected, attitude change in which violence is increasingly seen to be unacceptable. There appears to be a great deal to this observation.

However, I am more comfortable dealing with attitude streams as independent phenomena in which each is seen to follow its own trajectory. For example, as will be discussed more fully later, the historical processes by which the ideas of democracy, capitalism, and war aversion came to be increasingly accepted are probably best seen to have been ones that are independent, not interdependent or connected. For one thing, although they have paralleled each other, their trajectories have been considerably out of synchronization with each other. For another, there appears to be little in the way of a logical connection between them—although there has been a post hoc tendency to group them under the common rubric of "liberalism" or to credit that rather vaporous historical development, "the enlightenment." By contrast it seems clearly to be quite possible to oppose war but not capital punishment, or the reverse.

Moreover, depending on how one looks at it, there are some distinct countertrends, or at least aberrations, in the general historical decline of violence. Most notably, the increasing acceptance of abortion could be seen—and of course is seen by many—as a strong counter to the trend away from deliberate killing. The eradication of human fetuses was generally condemned as a process of population management as late as the 1960s by such liberal organizations as Planned Parenthood, and that perspective has since been very clearly reversed.

Sorting this out is a bit difficult because abortions became safe (for the mother) only in recent times with the rise of modern medicine. However, suppose there had long been known to be a plant that, if eaten by pregnant women, would cause a fetus to abort. It would seem that a campaign to ban the practice, like the one to ban capital punishment and infanticide and human sacrifice, would be seen to be a progressive, or liberal, one.

Moreover, as David Garland has observed, even though sensibilities have changed so that corporal and capital punishment have been eliminated or greatly reduced and that prisons have become more humane than they used to be, there remains a bland and uncritical tolerance for long-term incarceration which can produce acute mental and psychological suffering, physical deterioration, erosion of social and cognitive skills, social degradation and humiliation, and serious economic and emotional distress for a prisoner's family. But, notes Garland, "because these pains are mental and emotional rather than physical, because they are corrosive over an extended period rather than immediate, because they are removed from public view, and because they are legally disguised as simple 'loss of liberty', they do not greatly offend our sensibilities and they are permitted to form a part of public policy."

Somewhat related may be the indifference, as noted in a footnote in my article, of most of the world to the effects of economic sanctions during the 1990s in Iraq that may have been a necessary cause of more human suffering in an incremental manner than most wars inflict in a direct one. Indeed, if the estimates are even roughly correct, economic sanctions were a necessary cause of the deaths of more people in Iraq than were slain by all the nuclear weapons used in World War II and all the chemical weapons used in World War I combined. There is dispute about the numbers, but at the time they were substantially accepted and they seemed to have moved scarcely anyone. This is all the more impressive because there seems to be remarkably little animosity toward the Iraqi people: responding to a poll question with extreme wording, fully 60 percent of the American public held the Iraqi people to be *innocent* of *any* blame for their leader's policies. The phenomenon could also be seen during the Gulf War of 1991 as discussed in my *Policy and Opinion in the Gulf War*. Extensive pictures and publicity about civilian casualties resulting from an attack on a Baghdad bomb shelter had no impact on attitudes toward US bombing policy in the war. Moreover, the immunity the American public showed to the images of the "highway of death" and to reports at the end of the war that 100,000 Iraqis had died in the war (a figure that is almost certainly much too high) scarcely dampened the enthusiasm of the various "victory" parades and celebrations.

Several explanations for this lack of concern or even much notice during the 1990s are possible. The devastation can be blamed at least in part on Iraqi president Saddam Hussein since he variously refused to comply with many of the sanctioners' demands—though the morality of inflicting pain on one person because another refuses to do one's bidding is, to say the least, a bit shaky. In addition, he sometimes seemed more interested in enhancing the nation's suffering for propaganda purposes (especially with an eye toward getting the sanctions removed) than in relieving it—that is, the people of Iraq essentially became his hostages, and the sanctioners effectively decided to let the hostages suffer rather than to give in to him. There was also hope that the sanctions might hamper Iraq's ability to develop threatening weaponry, and that they might encourage the Iraqis to overthrow Saddam's tyrannical regime. However, in the end, one might be set to wondering, as the United Nations Secretary General put it at the time, "whether suffering inflicted on vulnerable groups in a target country is a legitimate means of exerting pressure on political leaders whose behavior is unlikely to be affected by the plight of their subjects."

Much of the inattention, however, may derive from the fact that economic warfare, like incarceration, generally inflicts pain quietly and incrementally. Deaths are dispersed rather than concentrated, statistical rather than dramatic. In addition, they are of distant, faceless foreigners and are substantially out of sight.

Whatever the trends for the incidence of violence, then, tolerance for this kind of deliberate, if somewhat hidden, suffering seems to have remained remarkably high even in countries at the forefront of the trend away from violence.

Reflections references

David Garland, *Punishment and Modern Society: A Study in Social Theory*. Chicago, IL: University of Chicago Press, 1990.

Lawrence H. Keeley, *War Before Civilization: The Myth of the Peaceful Savage*. New York: Oxford University Press, 1996.

Steven Pinker, *The Better Angels of our Nature: Why Violence has Declined*. New York: Viking, 2011.

Part II

Threat perception, ideas, and foreign policy

Introduction

Retreat from Doomsday deals quite extensively with the Cold War because at the time the book was being written it was generally considered likely that, should a major war take place, it would emerge somehow out of that global contest. The book argues that the Cold War was crucially about ideas and not, in particular, about weapons, especially nuclear weapons which, it seems to me, were "essentially irrelevant" to the process.

In my view, the central motor of the Cold War was Communist ideology which, as developed over the decades, was bent on fomenting worldwide class struggle, but not on anything resembling "aggressive, conquering, Hitlerian war" which "would foolishly risk everything." By 1985, as I was beginning *Retreat from Doomsday*, it appeared to me that, after decades of failure, the new Soviet leadership under Mikhail Gorbachev was in the process of abandoning the class struggle ideology. If ideology (as opposed, for example, to arms balances or Soviet control of East Europe) was its essential driver, the Cold War could be in terminal demise, and it was logical to conclude that we might be coming to the end of the world as we knew it. I presented that argument in a paper at the International Studies Association meetings in March 1986, and then blended the argument into *Retreat from Doomsday* (especially in pp. 211–14) which came out in February 1989 (on this saga, see note 44 in Chapter 5). Throughout this process I was made pleasantly uncomfortable by the fact that Gorbachev was dismantling the Cold War faster than I could write about it.

In later years, I revisited this argument, focusing especially on the rhetoric and actions of the Cold War contestants in the months after the publication of the book. It seems to me that these support my earlier argument, and the first article printed below, "What was the Cold War about? Evidence from its ending," contains the results of those ruminations. About the only thing that was different when the Cold War contestants declared the contest over was the important change in Soviet ideology, suggesting, obviously, that that was what the Cold War was about.

Ideas about threat are key to international politics—indeed, to life—and it is important, therefore, to try to get them right. During the Cold War, there was, it seems to me, a massive, and costly, exaggeration of the Communist threat, in particular the notion that the Communists would be willing to engage in a major, direct military confrontation to carry out their ideological goals.

Threat exaggeration persisted in the post-Cold War era as policymakers have variously obsessed over Japan's economic might, ethnic warfare, the comings and goings of "rogue states," the dangers of "weapons of mass destruction" (even though many of those on the list scarcely warrant such extreme characterizations), and, above all, international terrorism. "Simplicity and spook: Terrorism and the dynamics of threat exaggeration" assesses the process, a concern developed as well in my 2006 book, *Overblown*. Not all threats that could potentially have been seized upon have evoked anxiety and overreaction. But it does appear that every foreign-policy threat in the last several decades that has come to be accepted as significant has then eventually been unwisely exaggerated. In the case of terrorism, this has led to overreactive policies that have been far more costly than any damage committed by terrorists.

The costly war in Iraq has been the most prominent result of the overreaction to terrorism. "Faulty correlation, foolish consistency, fatal consequence: Democracy, peace, and theory in the Middle East" is concerned with this, and it focuses on the interrelationships between ideas and the foreign policies that may stem from these connections. Following the argument in my 1999 book, *Capitalism, Democracy, and Ralph's Pretty Good Grocery*, it contends that democracy is (merely) an idea, a rather good one—or at any rate one that is superior to the alternatives. The institution is at base a messy gimmick for expressing and aggregating policy preferences and, as such, it does not of itself generate specific policy outcomes—it merely sets up the process for determining, for better or worse, what they are to be. However, democracy has come accompanied by a mystique contending that people in democratic countries judiciously avoid war—or at least war with each other. This mystique has generated the conclusion that if a country becomes democratic, it will also become peaceful, an unjustified extrapolation used to rationalize the war in Iraq.

5 What was the Cold War about?

Evidence from its ending

It is important to ascertain when the Cold War ended because such a determination can help to indicate what the Cold War was all about.

Its demise is commonly associated with the collapse of the Soviet empire in Eastern Europe in late 1989 or with the disintegration of the Soviet Union and of Communism in 1991. However, judging from the public rhetoric and actions of important observers and key international actors at the time, the Cold War essentially ended in the spring of 1989, well before these momentous events took place.

If this proposition is true, it suggests that the Cold War was principally (or even entirely) about an ideological conflict in which the West saw the Soviet Union as committed to a threateningly expansionary ideology. Once this menace seemed to vanish with the advent of the policies of Mikhail Gorbachev (similar processes had taken place earlier in Yugoslavia and China), Western leaders and observers began to indicate that the conflict was over. Thus, the Cold War was essentially about ideas. It was not centrally about power or about the military, nuclear, or economic balance—or the distribution of capabilities—between the East and the West. Nor was it about Communism as a form of government, the need to move the world toward democracy and/or capitalism, or, to a degree, Soviet domination of Eastern Europe. The Cold War was not about these concerns because it came to an end before any of them was really resolved.

Two issues should be clarified before beginning the discussion. I wish to argue that the Cold War essentially ended in early 1989, but I do not wish to suggest that the Cold War was necessarily permanently closed down or that it could not have been reinstituted after that date. It was certainly possible for Gorbachev later to change course if he had wanted to. Or, more likely, he could have been overthrown and his policy reversed by a group of opposing hard-liners. Indeed, in 1991, there was a coup effort against him by such Communists and, had they been successful, it is possible that they would have reestablished Cold War hostilities. Actually, the coup conspirators, during their fifteen minutes of fame, seemed to indicate that while planning to undo some of Gorbachev's domestic reforms and to adopt a tougher line about the potential breakup of the Soviet Union, they did not intend to amend, alter, or reverse the basic changes Gorbachev had made to the Cold War situation. But, of course, it is possible that they eventually would have done so. Therefore, the "ending" of the Cold War could have proved to be something less than a terminal experience.

However, this concern holds for *any* supposed ending point for the Cold War. Indeed, we are not completely out of the woods yet. The Communist Party remains strong in Russia, and some of its core supporters are quite hard-line. It is conceivable that if those characters managed to get into office in Russia, they might seek to reinstitute the Cold War, albeit with a somewhat smaller geographic base than the Soviet Union enjoyed at its imperial peak. This seems pretty unlikely, but given the tumultuousness of Russian politics, it is surely not impossible. Hence, any proposed ending date for the Cold War is potentially reversible.

In addition, the argument here deals with when the Cold War ended and with what it was about, but not with *why* the Soviet Union changed its ideology. Some analysts, like Robert English, stress intellectual factors and argue that the ideological change was in the works for well over a decade before 1989, while others, like Stephen Brooks and William Wohlforth, contend that material factors essentially impelled the change.[1] Although I have distinct views on this debate, I am concerned here with the consequences of the ideological shift, not with its causes.

Dating the ending of the Cold War

Although later events were to prove more striking and dramatic, there is quite a bit of evidence to suggest that by the spring of 1989, many key people in the West had already substantially accepted the proposition that the Cold War was essentially over.

Thatcher, Reagan, and the Reagan administration

Perhaps the earliest proclamation by an important policy maker that the Cold War was over was made by British Prime Minister Margaret Thatcher in an interview published on the front page of the *Washington Post* on 18 November 1988. "We're not in a Cold War now," she noted, but in a "new relationship much wider than the Cold War ever was." At the same time, she was entirely sensitive to the possibility that progress could be reversed, suggesting that the West be prepared to make a reassessment and return to confrontation should Gorbachev be toppled or become stymied.[2]

Three weeks later, on 8 December 1988, in his last press conference as president, Ronald Reagan was asked a remarkable question by *Washington Post* reporter Lou Cannon: did he think the Soviets might once again become allies with the United States as they had been during World War II. At the time, Reagan was not quite willing to admit the Soviet Union into NATO, perhaps, but he did take the rather startling question quite seriously, and he substantially, if a bit equivocally, suggested that the Cold War was just about over. Moreover, he explained his reasoning:

If it can be definitely established that they no longer are following the expansionary policy that was instituted in the Communist revolution, that their goal must be a one-world Communist state ... [then] they might want to join the family of nations and join them with the idea of bringing about or establishing peace.[3]

The reporter's question and Reagan's answer were likely influenced by an important speech Soviet leader Mikhail Gorbachev had given at the United Nations the day before. In this speech, he had announced that he planned to reduce Soviet arms unilaterally and, in addition, he made a striking declaration about ideology and its role:

The new phase also requires de-ideologizing relations among states. We are not abandoning our convictions, our philosophy or traditions, nor do we urge anyone to abandon theirs.

But neither do we have any intention to be hemmed in by our values. That would result in intellectual impoverishment, for it would mean rejecting a powerful source of development—the exchange of everything original that each nation has independently created.

In the course of such exchange, let everyone show the advantage of their social system, way of life or values—and not just by words or propaganda, but by real deeds. That would be a fair rivalry of ideologies. But it should not be extended to relations among states.[4]

In many respects, this declaration was the culmination of a development that had begun shortly after Gorbachev came to office in 1985, in which the Soviet Union came to abandon its once-central devotion to the international class struggle.[5] As part of the process, Gorbachev promised in 1987 to withdraw from Afghanistan, where the country was bogged down in a costly war. Reagan administration officials had at first felt that this was "too good to be true,"[6] but Gorbachev fulfilled the promise, and the pullout was completed by 15 February 1989. This, of course, was a clear indication that despite the pronouncements of the Brezhnev Doctrine of 1968, the Soviet Union was willing not only to cease expansion but also to withdraw, at least from areas where it had become overextended, even though a Communist government would likely be replaced by a non-Communist one in these areas. There were also passages in Gorbachev's UN speech that could be taken to suggest that the Soviet Union would not use force to maintain its control over the countries of Eastern Europe.[7]

Reagan was not the only member of his administration to be impressed by such words and deeds. His Secretary of State, George Shultz, entitles the final chapter of his memoirs, "Turning Point." In it, he concludes that "Margaret Thatcher had it right ... it was all over but the shouting," and notes that the "Cold War was over" when he stepped down in January 1989 and that his main apprehension was that the new foreign policy team being assembled by the incoming president, George H.W. Bush, might not understand or accept this fact.[8] Referring to

Gorbachev's UN appearance, Shultz has said, "If anybody declared the end of the Cold War, he did in that speech." And Soviet foreign policy spokesman Anatoly Chernyaev called it "a turning point—he publicly renounced Marxism-Leninism."[9]

The New York Times

Impressed by the developments, the *New York Times* published a series of op-ed pieces under the theme, "Is the Cold War Over?" during the first months of 1989. Then, on Sunday, 2 April 1989, it ran a long editorial summarizing the discussion, under the title, "The Cold War Is Over."

The editorial actually tended to extrapolate beyond what most of its comparatively tentative commentators had indicated, and it was perhaps intended to be rather provocative. But it was a pronounced declaration by a source with a reputation for sober judgement.

The Washington Post *and the views of major foreign policy figures*

A month later, in early May, the *Washington Post* ran a two-part series on its front page, pointedly entitled, "Beyond the Cold War." In one of these articles, Don Oberdorfer surveyed various foreign policy figures outside of government and found that "nearly all of them said that the vast changes under way in the world are bringing an end to the post-World War II era."[10]

Thus, former Secretary of Defense Robert S. McNamara noted that "for 40 years U.S. foreign policy and defense programs have been shaped largely by one major force: fear of and opposition to the spread of Soviet-backed communism," but now, he argued, new organizing principles for governing international life must be found: "We face an opportunity—the greatest in 40 years—to bring an end to the Cold War." Former Secretary of State Cyrus Vance concluded that "we are entering a new era" in which "we will find ourselves very often on the same side with the Soviet Union," and William Hyland, editor of *Foreign Affairs*, indicated that "what began in 1943–45 is ending, and something else is taking its place." Former Secretary of State Henry A. Kissinger found that "international factors have rarely been so fluid. The one thing that cannot occur is a continuation of the status quo."

According to former National Security Council Director Zbigniew Brzezinski, "We are quite literally in the early phases of what might be called the post-communist era. This is a massive, monumental transformation." Conflicts in the Third World, he observed, "will be deprived of the extra ideological fuel which often contributed to igniting even greater passions and tensions than the conflicts were capable of generating in themselves." Brzezinski recalled that Winston Churchill's famous "Iron Curtain" speech of 1946 had "closed the gap between public consciousness and a reality that already existed" and, in the process, had essentially announced the Cold War. A similar gap-closing declaration, Brzezinski argued, was now needed to inaugurate the new era.

Public opinion

Actually, the public may not have needed the reminder. It already seems to have been aware that a new era was dawning (or had dawned).

Figure 5.1 displays the results from a pair of questions that crudely, but clearly, pose the central Cold War question: Was the Soviet Union, after all, actually out to take over the world, or was it mainly just interested in its own security? In the early years of the Cold War, and reaching a high at the time of the Communist Chinese entry into the Korean War at the end of 1950, the public strongly opted for the former interpretation of Soviet behavior. Once Gorbachev had established himself, however, the public reversed itself. Although the amazing changes of 1989 certainly enhanced the benign interpretation of Soviet behavior, it is impressive how positive it already was at the end of 1988.

Figure 5.2 supplies data concerning the degree to which the public found the Soviet Union to be a threat. By the time of Gorbachev's United Nations speech in December 1988, over half of the public was already willing to find that country to be only a minor threat (44 percent) or no threat at all (10 percent), and by mid-June of 1989, still well before the dramatic fall of the Berlin Wall, these numbers had increased to 45 percent and 14 percent, respectively. For comparison, the figure also includes data from a somewhat similar question concerning the alarming new "threat" to national security perceived at the time to be presented by economically impressive, if demilitarized, Japan. By the spring of 1989, the Japanese threat was seen to be nearly comparable to the one posed by the Soviet Union.

The Wall Street Journal

The *Wall Street Journal* also picked up the message and joined the journalistic chorus. In a 24 May 1989 editorial ebulliently entitled, "Bulletin: We won!" the publication noted that Gorbachev was "repudiating 70 years of his country's history," and declared that "containment plus the Reagan doctrine worked. If the Cold War is over, the West has won."[11]

The Bush Doctrine

Partly impelled, perhaps, by the series in the *Times* and the *Post*, the new Bush administration engaged in an extensive review of Cold War policy in the spring of 1989. The administration appears to have been groping for the gap-closing phraseology that Brzezinski, the press, and the public were calling for, and Condoleezza Rice, a member of the National Security Council staff, came up with the phrase "beyond containment," something, as Oberdorfer notes, that was "almost the reverse of containment" in its "encouragement of Soviet integration into the Western economic and political community."[12] Working with Robert Blackwill, she produced a secret seven-page National Security Directive, NSD-23, which included the key phrasing: "containment was never an end in itself. It was a strategy born of the condition of the postwar world. [But] a new era may now be upon us.

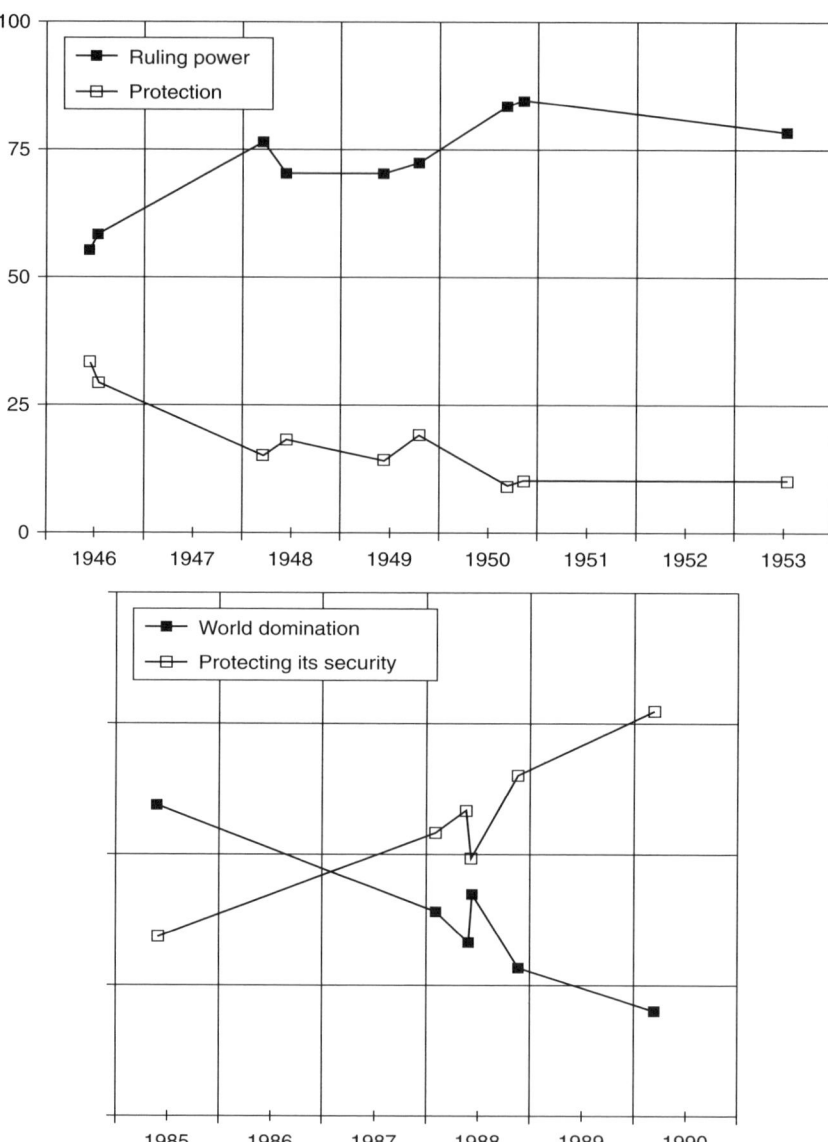

Figure 5.1 Public opinion on Soviet motives.

Upper graph: Subjects were asked: "As you hear and read about Russia these days, do you believe Russia is trying to build herself up to be *the* ruling power of the world, or do you think Russia is just building up protection against being attacked in another war?"

   Lower graph: Subjects were asked: "Do you believe the Soviet Union is mainly interested in world domination or mainly interested in protecting its own national security?"

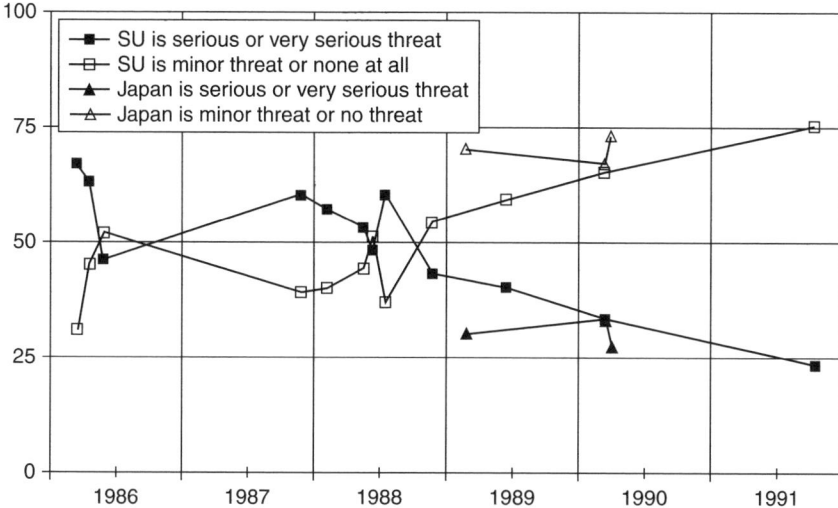

Figure 5.2 Public opinion on the Soviet and Japanese threats.

Subjects were asked, "How much of a threat would you say the Soviet Union is to the United States these days: a very serious threat, a serious threat, a minor threat, or not a threat at all?" "Do you feel the national security of the United States is threatened because Japan has become so strong economically? If yes, is the threat to U.S. national security a very serious threat, a serious threat, or only a minor threat?"

We may be able to move beyond containment to a new U.S. policy that actively promotes the integration of the Soviet Union into the international system."[13]

National Security adviser Brent Scowcroft was taken with the phrase and with the policy change. There was even talk of labeling it the "Bush Doctrine," but Scowcroft rejected this idea on the grounds that the press, not presidents themselves, are supposed to confer such labels.[14] There was also consideration of declaring the Cold War over, but the cautious Scowcroft vetoed that phraseology, not because he necessarily thought it invalid, but because of concerns about reversibility: "That's the kind of line that once you've said it, it can never be unsaid."[15] The "beyond containment" idea was presented to Bush and he quickly embraced it.

The phrase was first used in a major address at Texas A&M University on 12 May 1989. Bush began this important speech by placing the policy of containment quite clearly in the past tense:

> Wise men—Truman and Eisenhower, Vandenberg and Rayburn, Marshall, Acheson, and Kennan—crafted the strategy of containment. They believed that the Soviet Union, denied the easy course of expansion, would turn inward and address the contradictions of its inefficient, repressive, and inhumane system. And they were right—the Soviet Union is now publicly facing this hard reality. Containment worked.

Now, Bush continued, it was time to move on to a bold new policy:

> We are approaching the conclusion of an historic postwar struggle between two visions: one of tyranny and conflict and one of democracy and freedom. The review of U.S.–Soviet relations that my administration has just completed outlines a new path toward resolving this struggle. Our goal is bold, more ambitious than any of my predecessors could have thought possible. Our review indicates that 40 years of perseverance have brought us to a precious opportunity, and now it is time to move beyond containment to a new policy for the 1990s—one that recognizes the full scope of change taking place around the world and in the Soviet Union itself.

And, Bush extrapolated, that meant essentially reversing containment:

> In sum, the United States now has as its goal much more than simply containing Soviet expansionism. We seek the integration of the Soviet Union into the community of nations. . . . Ultimately, our objective is to welcome the Soviet Union back into the world order.

At the end of the speech, he noted that a Texas A&M graduate had been the first American soldier to shake hands with the Soviets when the forces met at the Elbe River at the conclusion of World War II. Making use of this rhetorical convenience, Bush made a clear comparison between the end of World War II and the end of the Cold War: "Once again, we are ready for a hand in return. And once again, it is a time for peace."[16]

This was not simply a momentary reflection, but a major policy declaration, and Bush hammered it home in speeches over the weeks that followed. The next day he went out of his way in two separate speeches to point out that "yesterday I announced a new policy for the 1990s" that "seeks to bring the Soviet Union into the family of nations, a policy, if you will, of reintegration." On 24 May, he repeated the notion at a major speech at the Coast Guard Academy, again employing the past tense when dealing with containment: "We now have a precious opportunity to move beyond containment. . . . Our goal, integrating the Soviet Union into the community of nations, is every bit as ambitious as containment was at its time."[17] These sentiments were stressed in additional statements over the next several days.[18]

Although these pronouncements did not declare the Cold War to be over in so many words—as someone like Shultz might have preferred—they strongly carried this implication in their call not simply to go beyond containment, but effectively to reverse it. Bush and Scowcroft reflect that although they were trying to be appropriately "cautious and prudent" in these speeches, they were consciously "shifting policy" and presenting a "new strategy toward the cockpit of East–West confrontation."[19]

Bush's important policy shift garnered little notice at the time, perhaps because it was too atmospheric (or too "cautious and prudent"), because Bush was not very good at handling what he called "the vision thing," because the Texas A&M speech was belabored with a distracting, dead-on-arrival policy proposal that was mostly a warmed-over rephrasing of the "Open Skies" idea from the Eisenhower administration,[20] because of Scowcroft's unwillingness to engage in explicit hype, and because "beyond containment" as a phrase simply doesn't have the same vivid ring or resonance as "iron curtain." At any rate, some in the administration were disappointed in their hopes that the press would grasp the importance of the message Bush was trying to deliver and dub it the "Bush Doctrine."[21]

Earlier rhetoric

At various points, there were "thaws" in the Cold War, accompanied by suggestions that things were notably improving. There was, for example, the "Spirit of Geneva" in 1955, following the death of Stalin and the rise of new, more moderate Soviet leadership. Or there was the development of what came to be called "detente" after 1963, as the United States and the USSR mostly put crisis aside as a diplomatic technique and focused on engineering arms control agreements designed to reduce the likelihood of nuclear war between them. Some also saw notable improvement when the Helsinki Agreement was signed in 1975.

However, none of these mellowings inspired the kind of direct and repeated "beyond containment" or "the Cold War is over" rhetoric of early 1989. Nor did they lead to a significant and often unilateral dampening of the arms race of the sort that followed the changes of 1988–1989 (to be discussed more fully below).

One indication of the differences was the conversion of the conservative American commentator, Francis Fukuyama. In the fall of 1987, he published an article suspiciously suggesting that Gorbachev's mellowing could simply be a temporary tactical maneuver akin to some that the Communists had employed in the past.[22] By May 1989, however, when his famous article, "The End of History?" went to press for the summer issue of *National Interest*, he was triumphally proclaiming the irreversible ascendance of liberalism.

Ideology versus deeds

Fukuyama's 1987 analysis also can be used to sort out the role of ideological declaration from other factors—particularly from the effects of deeds or acts of policy such as the Soviet withdrawal from Afghanistan. Fukuyama points to the rightward, accomodationist shifts in Soviet policy during the New Economic Policy period of 1921–1928, during the popular front period of 1935–1939, during the wartime alliance period of 1941–1947, and variously during the Khrushchev and immediate post-Khrushchev period of 1954–1972, and he notes that once these tactical actions had served their purposes, policy once again shifted sharply to the left.

Following this approach, it seems clear that many of the policy acts of the Gorbachev era had resonances with earlier periods. In particular, Nikita Khrushchev, like Gorbachev, sought to dampen Cold War tensions that could lead to direct conflict between the Soviet Union and the West, and, due in large part to economic strains, he unilaterally cut back on military expenditures, reduced repressive internal policies, accepted notable arms control arrangements, and established more businesslike economic relations with Western capitalist countries.

However, while it could be held that these changes ended the most directly confrontational period of the Cold War (there were few, if any, direct crises between East and West after the Cuban missile crisis of 1962), Western policy makers and commentators had not prominently and repeatedly declared the Cold War to be over or suggested that the time had now come to move "beyond containment." The difference, it seems to me, was that Khrushchev still retained his ideological commitment. He termed his policy one of "peaceful coexistence," but he precisely defined at the time what he meant by that: "intense economic, political, and ideological struggle between the proletariat and the aggressive forces of imperialism in the world arena." In fact, he ebulliently assured the world that "the victory of socialism on a world scale, inevitable by virtue of the laws of history, is no longer far off."[23] And he continued to keep the faith even after he had been drummed humiliatingly and unceremoniously out of office. In the memoirs secretly dictated during his induced retirement, he declared, "Both history and the future are on the side of the proletariat's ultimate victory. . . . We Communists must hasten this process. . . . There's a battle going on in the world to decide who will prevail over whom. . . . To speak of ideological compromise would be to betray our Party's first principles."[24] And "peaceful coexistence among different systems of government is possible, but peaceful coexistence among different ideologies is not."[25]

Like Khrushchev, Gorbachev instituted policy actions that led to accommodation, arms reduction, and a relaxation of tensions. Unlike Khrushchev, however, he was also willing to betray his party's first principles. And that made all the difference. For example, the Soviet withdrawal from Afghanistan by early 1989 is properly taken as a "costly signal" of Gorbachev's sincerity.[26] But if that is so, it is because the signal was costly ideologically—a tangible admission that Gorbachev had abandoned Communist expansionary ideas.[27] That is, had such deeds not been accompanied by indications of an ideological shift, they, like those of Khrushchev, would have been seen to be signaling simply that the Soviet Union was capable of pragmatic retreat from an overextended position—rather like the Israeli withdrawal from southern Lebanon in 2000 or that of America from Vietnam in the 1970s.

What the Cold War was not about

Not everyone considered the Cold War to be over by the spring of 1989.[28] But by then, a considerable array of important decision makers, foreign policy experts, opinion leaders, and leading newspapers in the West had strongly suggested, and sometimes explicitly declared, its demise. If the Cold War essentially did come to an end in the spring of 1989, this would suggest that it could not have been about a number of issues and themes.

Nuclear weapons and the military balance

If the Cold War was centrally about nuclear weapons, and the "bipolarity" they have been said to produce, it would still be going on: the United States and Russia continue to retain enormous nuclear arsenals. In fact, about the only thing that didn't change at the Cold War's end was the size of the nuclear arsenals that the East and West had pointed, or potentially pointed, at one another.

Nor was the Cold War about the military balance or the "distribution of capabilities" more generally.[29] Later events, particularly those surrounding Russia's muddled effort to deal militarily with the secessionist movement in Chechnya in the mid-1990s, have led to the realization that the Soviet "military machine" may well have been much less enormous and, especially, much less capable than anyone really imagined in 1989. At the end of the Cold War, however, Soviet military might and potential still inspired awe. In its 2 April 1989 declaration of the Cold War's end, the *New York Times* readily acknowledged that "two enormous military machines still face each other around the world." This view was widely shared. As one of its series essayists, hard-liner Frank Carlucci, stressed, "At present, and in spite of actual and announced reform initiatives, the Soviet Union is in sheer military terms more formidable than ever before. This is a fact that has not changed under the leadership of Mikhail S. Gorbachev, and one that will persist even, for instance, after Gorbachev's promised reductions in the Soviet military."[30] And even as he announced his "beyond containment" policy, George Bush pointed out that "we must not forget that the Soviet Union has acquired awesome military capabilities. . . . That is a fact of life for me today as President of the United States."[31] Yet the *Times* and, it appears, Bush concluded that the Cold War was essentially over, even though the military balance seemed to be as monumental and as potentially dangerous as ever.

The Soviet Union had impressively agreed to the Intermediate-range Nuclear Force (INF) treaty in 1987, and in his 8 December 1988 UN speech, Gorbachev announced his unilateral arms cuts. But these measures, as Carlucci noted, still left the country with a massive military force. Although they could be treated as "costly signals" of his sincerity, they could also, by themselves, be dismissed as temporary and readily reversible measures to reduce military costs, with the long-run intention, as the *Economist* magazine put it in 1988, of making the country a "more formidable adversary for the West, not a partner with it."[32]

To be sure, the Soviet Union's military capabilities were at all times factored into the risk calculation during the Cold War; the threat was particularly alarming because it was linked to an impressive military arsenal. But it was the threat that was principally motivating, not the size of the arsenal. North Korea and Iraq have been seen as threatening and dangerous because they have sometimes acted or talked threateningly, even though their military capabilities pale in comparison with those of, say, unthreatening France or Britain. And of late, the United States has become deeply alarmed about the dangers presented by tiny bands of fanatical and suicidal terrorists, whose ability to kill Americans, even in the most apocalyptic scenarios, is dwarfed by the damage that could have been inflicted upon the

United States by the Soviet Union in the 1980s—or for that matter, by Russia today.[33]

This suggests that the arms balance was more nearly an indicator of international Cold War tensions than the cause of them. Hans J. Morgenthau once proclaimed that "men do not fight because they have arms"; rather "they have arms because they deem it necessary to fight."[34] It follows, then, that when countries no longer deem it necessary to fight, they will get rid of their arms. And that is exactly what happened as the Cold War came to an end: once the ideological struggle had begun to wane, something resembling a negative arms race evolved because the weapons built to wage it began to seem burdensome and even parodic. Indeed, within days of Gorbachev's 7 December 1988 speech, press reports observed that there was a "new reluctance to spend for defense." In a month, reports were noting that Gorbachev's pronouncements "make it harder for Western governments to justify large sums for military machines. . . . The Soviet bear seems less threatening to Western publics these days, so that they want to do less on the weapons front. . . . Western perceptions [are] that the Soviet threat is receding and that big armies are expensive and inconvenient—perhaps even irrelevant." A few months later, as more proposals and counterproposals were spun out by both sides, the *Wall Street Journal* was calling the process a "race to demobilize."[35]

The arms buildup, of course, had not been accomplished through written agreement; instead, there had been a sort of free market, in which each side, keeping a wary eye on the other, sought security by purchasing varying amounts of weapons and troops. With the demise of the Cold War, a similar reactive arms policy continued between West and East, except that now it was focused on arms reduction. Jerimi Suri argues that "a race to disarm dominated the end of the Cold War."[36] It seems, rather, that this "race" naturally followed it.

Communism in the Soviet Union

Neither in his 7 December 1988 speech nor in his later pronouncements did Gorbachev indicate that he intended to abandon Communism or Communist Party control in the Soviet Union. Indeed, even after the failed coup attempt against him in 1991 by members of that party, he continued to contend that while some bad elements needed to be removed from the party and while his policy of *glasnost* should be further advanced, he still deeply believed in Communism as a system and felt that it needed to be reformed, not abandoned: he pledged to "work for the renewal of the party."[37]

Consequently, if the Cold War essentially ended in the spring of 1989 (or even in late 1991), it could not have been about the fact that the Soviet Union had happened to adopt Communism as its domestic economic and governmental form. As the quintessential Cold Warrior, John Foster Dulles, once put it, "The basic change we need to look forward to isn't necessarily a change from Communism to another form of government. The question is whether you can have Communism in one country or whether it has to be for the world. If the Soviets had national Communism we could do business with their government."[38] In 1962, President John Kennedy made the same point:

> The real problem is the Soviet desire to expand their power and influence. If Mr. Khrushchev would concern himself with the real interests of the people of the Soviet Union—that they have a higher standard of living, to protect his own security—there is no real reason why the United States and the Soviet Union . . . should not be able to live in peace. But it is this constant determination . . . that they will not settle for a peaceful world, but must settle for a Communist world . . . [that] makes the sixties so dangerous.[39]

In his proclamations, including the 7 December 1988 speech, Gorbachev essentially indicated that he only wanted Communism in his country and was not interested in forcibly exporting it: "In the course of such exchange, let everyone show the advantage of their social system, way of life or values—and not just by words or propaganda, but by real deeds. That would be a fair rivalry of ideologies. But it should not be extended to relations among states."[40]

When it became clear that Gorbachev meant it, Bush and other Western leaders moved to accommodate. They certainly hoped for further economic and political liberalization in the Soviet Union. But that liberalization, however desirable, does not seem to have been an essential condition for calling an end to the Cold War.

The need for the world to be democratic and/or capitalist

If the Cold War was not about the fact that certain major countries had domestic processes built around Communism, neither was it about the fact that those countries, and others, were neither democratic nor capitalist. The United States has been a champion of both institutions, of course, and has long tried to promote them and continues to do so. But it has generally been willing to adopt a live-and-let-live policy toward various kinds of dictatorships, whether dominated by Fascist parties (as with Franco's Spain), by Communist ones (as with today's China), or by militaristic groups (as in dozens of places in Latin America), as long as those dictatorships do not threaten their neighbors or, particularly, the United States and its core interests.

The existence of the Soviet Union

Dating the demise of the Cold War to coincide with the collapse of the Soviet Union at the end of 1991 makes little sense. Not only does that seem far too late, following the reasoning above, but the United States actually made considerable efforts to keep the country from collapsing, fearing the kind of violent chaos that was to erupt in Yugoslavia in the 1990s. Most notably, earlier in the year, Bush had gone to Kiev in the Ukraine to give a speech in which he essentially urged the various Soviet Republics to work it out and to remain within the country.[41] If there was a Cold War raging at that time, the United States and the Soviet Union were on the same side.

Soviet control over Eastern Europe

The pronouncements noted above about the end of the Cold War all came while the Soviet Union still controlled Eastern Europe. Although there were signs of liberalization in Hungary and although Poland was going to hold semi-open elections in June 1989, Soviet control of the area seemed quite firm. Indeed, several of the countries—particularly East Germany, Bulgaria, Romania, and Albania— were under the domination of Communist hard-liners, who greeted Gorbachev's reforms with utter dismay and even open contempt.

In its 2 April 1989 declaration of the end of the Cold War, the *New York Times* readily acknowledged this issue, noting that "Europe remains torn in two" and that "No one seems to have a good answer about the division of Europe, always the most dangerous East–West question." It called for "super-power talks to bring about sovereign nations in Eastern Europe and special arrangements for the two Germanys."[42] Indeed, Philip Zelikow and Condoleezza Rice argue that whatever the implications of the "beyond containment" speeches (which they helped write), Bush essentially felt that the Cold War could not be over until Europe was "whole and free," a phrase he used a few times both before and after the set of "beyond containment" speeches.[43]

Consideration of this issue is confused somewhat by the incredible speed with which Soviet control over Eastern Europe was terminated. De-Sovietization there substantially took place over a few months at the end of 1989, and the peaceful unification of Germany was accomplished over the following year. But no one had really envisioned the astonishing speed with which these massive changes would come about. The editors of the *Times* almost certainly felt that working out viable arrangements in Europe would take many years of careful diplomacy with a Soviet Union that was now clearly willing to negotiate in good faith on the issue. Once the remarkable revolutions in Eastern Europe began, of course, the possibility of rapid change began to be more accepted. However, even on 12 November 1989—even after the Berlin Wall had crumbled—George Kennan published an article in the *Washington Post* noting, accurately, that "the changes now sweeping over Central and Eastern Europe are momentous, irreversible, and truly epoch making," but then going on to argue that the process of designing a new Europe was very complex and profound and would "take years, not months. We will be lucky if the task is substantially accomplished before the end of the century."[44] As Zelikow and Rice recall, "For weeks after the Berlin Wall fell on the night of November 9–10, 1989, even those who dared think about [the] unification [of Germany] laid out timetables in years, not months."[45]

Essentially, these comments suggest that the expectations at the time were that the Soviet Union would retain overall control over Eastern Europe for some considerable period, but would work, over the years, in a businesslike manner to negotiate relative autonomy for individual states and to develop an accommodation on the division of Germany, allowing much-increased contacts and perhaps even a kind of confederation. At the same time, it would presumably continue to dampen East–West military tensions through arms control agreements, in the manner of the important 1987 INF treaty, and it would assist in the rise of Gorbachev-style reformers in places like East Germany, Czechoslovakia, Bulgaria, and, insofar as it could, Romania and Albania.

In this process, it was to be expected that the Soviets—or indeed any regime in that geographical location—would proceed with great caution to make sure its security was not compromised. The country had, of course, been invaded twice in the century through Eastern Europe, and Western policy makers were fully sensitive to this understandable security concern. Any armed Soviet suppression of independence movements in Eastern Europe (of the sort Gorbachev had earlier instituted in Lithuania) would likely have been condemned by the West. But even these would probably not have fatally derailed the process or led to major claims that the Cold War was still on—any more than the later Russian wars in Chechnya have. Most likely, of course, was that the Eastern Europeans, as sensitive as anybody to historical realities, would be content to participate in a gradual process of liberation. Indeed, this approach was urged upon them by Thatcher. In her 1988 interview, she anticipated progress toward solving the Eastern European problem, but warned those still behind the Iron Curtain about being too impatient: "They can get their increasing liberty if they handle it well."[46] If the Cold War could only end when Europe became "whole and free," its demise—from the perspective of early 1989—was years, possibly even decades off. The 1989 rhetoric and declarations of Bush and others detailed above suggest, by contrast, that the Cold War could end long before that event took place.

The issue, then, is whether settlement in Eastern Europe was crucial to ending the Cold War or whether it was more nearly the first really important item on the post-Cold War agenda, one that, as it happens, was resolved with astonishing and utterly unexpected speed. The evidence seems to point more toward the latter interpretation. As the American ambassador to the Soviet Union, Jack Matlock, recalls, "There was a change—it was rather gradual, but *very* perceptible after [Gorbachev's 1988 UN speech] in that it was no longer a zero sum game in terms of Soviet negotiating. We disagreed on a lot of things. But we all agreed the new Europe should be united. . . . And that was not characteristic of Cold War negotiations."[47] That is, well before the tumultuous events took place in Eastern Europe, the key leaders in the East and West had reached a crucial agreement: that, in Matlock's words, "Europe should be united." The rest was detail—highly significant detail to be sure, but detail nonetheless.

An important element in the institution of the Cold War was doubtless Western reaction to Soviet control over the areas it happened to occupy in Eastern Europe after World War II. But the containment policy, formulated after that accomplished fact, essentially accepted that control and was designed mainly to stop any expansion. Thus, although Soviet domination of Eastern Europe was not acceptable to the West, Cold War policy essentially acknowledged that reality. The Cold War could logically end even while such domination continued, particularly if the former contestants were determined to resolve the issue in an orderly fashion. And it did.

Previous endings: Yugoslavia and China

This argument can, I think, be strengthened by looking at two earlier, if partial, endings in the Cold War.

Shortly after World War II, the version of Communism in Yugoslavia under Josip Tito was perhaps the most dynamically ideological and confrontational in the world. This condition changed after the Tito–Stalin split of 1948, when Tito and his party were excommunicated from the international Communist movement led by Moscow. In desperation, Yugoslavia largely abandoned its ideologically confrontational approach and sought accommodation with the West. Even though the country was still a Communist dictatorship and was to remain one for decades, the West responded almost immediately, supplying aid year after year, and it was soon declaring that Yugoslavia was "of direct importance to the defense of the North Atlantic area" and that its ability to defend itself "was important to the security of the United States." For a while Yugoslavia was close to becoming an informal participant in NATO.[48]

Similarly, when China abandoned its commitment to worldwide anticapitalist revolution in the 1970s, it was gradually embraced by the capitalist world and eventually came into something like an alliance with the United States: if the Soviet Union contemplated invading China in the 1960s, it would not have had to wonder much about the possibility that the United States would come to China's defense; by the 1980s, it would have. As early as 1980, there were official discussions between China and the United States about the possible transfer of American defense technology to China and about "limited strategic cooperation on matters of common concern."[49] All this even though the Communist Party remained (and remains) fully in control in China (as well as in colonized contiguous Tibet), even though democracy has never really been allowed to flower there, and even though (although later considerably reformed) the domestic economy remained strongly controlled from the center.[50]

The process was summarized in 1985 by Reagan adviser Richard Pipes: "China has turned inward and ceased being aggressive, and so we are friendly toward China, just as we are toward Yugoslavia. We may deplore their Communist regimes, but these countries are not trying to export their systems and therefore do not represent a threat to our national security."[51]

What the Cold War was about

By the spring of 1989, Gorbachev had been able to convince a broad array of important Western leaders and analysts as well as, it seems, the American public that the USSR was giving up on Leninist notions about the international class struggle. It no longer yearned for the demise of capitalism and, certainly, it was no longer interested in using violence in any form to accomplish that goal.[52] Once the West became convinced that this ideological reversal had taken place, the Cold War came to an end.

As noted, in his last presidential press conference, Reagan was quite clear about what the Cold War was about: "the expansionary policy that was instituted in the

Communist revolution, that their goal must be a one-world Communist state."[53] And in his "beyond containment" speeches of 1989, Bush expressed a similar understanding. Containment involved denying the Soviet Union "the easy course of expansion" until it "turned inward" to address its own "contradictions." Or it required "checking the Soviet Union's expansionist aims, in the hope that the Soviet system itself would one day be forced to confront its internal contradictions." This happy consequence, Bush felt, had now come about.[54]

The quintessential and seminal declaration of U.S. policy toward international Communism remains George Kennan's "The Sources of Soviet Conduct," published in *Foreign Affairs* in 1947. Kennan expresses concern about Soviet military strength, but argues that what makes that strength threatening is an ideology that is fundamentally expansionist. In the first paragraphs of the article, he argues that "the outstanding features of Communist thought" are: "the capitalist system of production is a nefarious one which inevitably leads to the exploitation of the working class by the capital-owning class"; "capitalism contains the seeds of its own destruction" which must "result inevitably and inescapably in a revolutionary transfer of power to the working class"; countries where revolutions have been successful will "rise against the remaining capitalist world"; capitalism will not "perish without proletarian revolution"; and "a final push" is "needed from a revolutionary proletariat movement in order to tip over the tottering structure."[55]

There has been considerable debate about the degree to which ideology actually impelled Soviet policy.[56] However, over the decades, prominent Soviet leaders have repeatedly made statements such as the following:

> The existence of the Soviet Republic side by side with the imperialist states for a long time is unthinkable. One or the other must triumph in the end. And before that end supervenes, a series of frightful collisions between the Soviet Republic and the bourgeois states will be inevitable.[57]
>
> (Lenin)

> As soon as we are strong enough to fight the whole of capitalism, we shall at once take it by the neck.[58]
>
> (Lenin)

> The goal is to consolidate the dictatorship of the proletariat in one country, using it as a base for the overthrow of imperialism in all countries.[59]
>
> (Stalin)

> To eliminate the inevitability of war, it is necessary to destroy imperialism.[60]
>
> (Stalin)

> All the socialist countries and the international working-class and Communist movement recognize their duty to render the fullest moral and material

assistance to the peoples fighting to free themselves from imperialist and colonial tyranny.[61]

(Khrushchev)

Of course, there is some possibility that pronouncements like these and slogans like "Workers of the World, Unite!" are simply philosophical boilerplate.[62] And it could certainly be suggested that Western policy makers often exaggerated the degree to which the Communists had the daring, will, and capacity to carry them out.[63] However, after they have been recited millions of times in speeches, books, leaflets, brochures, letterhead, tracts, training manuals, banners, pamphlets, proclamations, announcements, billboards, handbooks, bumper stickers, and T-shirts, one might begin to suspect that the sentiments could just possibly actually reflect true thought processes.

At any rate, because such sentiments are explicitly and lethally threatening, responsible leaders of capitalist countries ought, at least out of simple prudence, to take them seriously. And it seems clear that Western leaders and analysts like Kennan, Churchill, Dulles, Kennedy, Thatcher, Reagan, Shultz, and Bush did so. Moreover, it rather appears that these ideological threats were absolutely crucial to the Cold War. Once Gorbachev was able to convince Western leaders that the Soviet Union no longer subscribed to such notions, the Cold War came to an end, even though other aspects of the international environment remained substantially unchanged.

John Gaddis has observed that "Moscow's commitment to the overthrow of capitalism throughout the world had been the chief unsettling element in its relations with the West since the Russian revolution."[64] The ending of the Cold War suggests that that commitment comes close to being the only cause of the Cold War. As Jack Matlock puts it, "The cold war could not end, truly and definitively, until the Soviet Union abandoned its system's ideological linchpin, the class struggle concept."[65] That is, even if the Soviet Union had retrenched geographically and militarily, it would have continued to be seen as an adversary—although a somewhat less-potent one—if it had continued to embrace its threatening ideology.

The Cold War, in essence, was not about Communism per se, about Soviet control over Eastern Europe, about Communist control in the Soviet Union, or about arms and power balances. It was about something else: the Soviet Union's attraction to, and support of, an ideology that threatened the West. Once that changed, the Cold War came to an end. Other developments, however important historically, were essentially ancillary. And by the spring of 1989, the necessary and sufficient condition for the ending of the Cold War was in place. Nothing more was required.

Notes

1 Robert D. English, *Russia and the Idea of the West: Gorbachev, Intellectuals, and the End of the Cold War* (New York: Columbia University Press, 2001); Robert D. English,

"Power, Ideas, and New Evidence on the Cold War's End," *International Security* 26 (Spring 2002): 70–92; Stephen G. Brooks and William C. Wohlforth, "Power, Globalization, and the End of the Cold War," *International Security* 25 (Winter 2000/01): 5–53; Stephen G. Brooks and William C. Wohlforth, "From Old Thinking to New Thinking in Qualitative Research," *International Security* 26 (Spring 2002): 93–111; see also Mark Kramer, "Ideology and the Cold War," *Review of International Studies* 25 (October 1999): 539–576.

2 Don Oberdorfer, "Thatcher Says Cold War Has Come to an End: Briton Calls for Support of Gorbachev," *Washington Post*, 18 November 1988.

3 See *New York Times*, 9 December 1988. Reagan had actually strongly signaled this perspective earlier in 1988 on a trip to Moscow. Asked whether he still believed the Soviet Union to be an evil empire, he responded firmly in the negative and explained, "I was talking about another time, another era"; Don Oberdorfer, *The Turn: From the Cold War to a New Era, The United States and the Soviet Union 1983–1990* (New York: Simon and Schuster, 1991), 299.

4 "In Gorbachev's Words," *New York Times*, 8 December 1988.

5 By 1986, Gorbachev had begun forcefully to undercut Communist ideology about the "class struggle" and about the Soviet Union's "internationalist duty" as the leader of world socialism. Oberdorfer, *The Turn*, 158–164; see also 141–142. By mid-1988, the Soviets were admitting the "inadequacy of the thesis that peaceful coexistence is a form of class struggle," and began to refer to the "world socialist system" or the "socialist community of nations" rather than to the "socialist camp." David Binder, "Soviet and Allies Shift on Doctrine: Guiding Terminology Changes—'Class Struggle' Is Out, 'Struggle for Peace' In," *New York Times*, 25 May 1988. And by October, the Kremlin's chief ideologist was explicitly rejecting the notion that a world struggle was going on between capitalism and Communism. Bill Keller, "New Soviet Ideologist Rejects Idea of World Struggle Against West," *New York Times*, 6 October 1988. There is a very substantial literature on the origins and development of this important ideological change and on Gorbachev's internal struggles. In addition to the references above and to those in note 1, see, for example, Jack Snyder, "The Gorbachev Revolution: A Waning of Soviet Expansionism?" *International Security* 12 (Winter 1987/88): 93–131; John Mueller, *Retreat from Doomsday: The Obsolescence of Major War* (New York: Basic Books, 1989), ch. 9; William G. Hyland, *The Cold War Is Over* (New York: Times Books, 1990), ch. 14; Raymond L. Garthoff, *The Great Transition: American–Soviet Relations and the End of the Cold War* (Washington, DC: Brookings, 1994), 255–265, 358–368, 753–757, 769–778; Philip Zelikow and Condoleezza Rice, *Germany Unified and Europe Transformed* (Cambridge, MA: Harvard University Press, 1995), ch. 1; Jeffrey T. Checkel, *Ideas and International Political Change: Soviet/Russian Behavior and the End of the Cold War* (New Haven, CT: Yale University Press, 1997); John Lewis Gaddis, *We Now Know* (New York: Oxford University Press, 1997); John A. Vasquez, *The Power of Power Politics* (Cambridge, UK: Cambridge University Press, 1998), ch. 13; Jeremi Suri, "Explaining the End of the Cold War: A New Historical Consensus?" *Journal of Cold War Studies* 4 (Fall 2002): 60–92.

6 Oberdorfer, *The Turn*, 243.

7 George P. Shultz, *Turmoil and Triumph: My Years as Secretary of State* (New York: Scribner's, 1993), 1107; Zelikow and Rice, *Germany Unified*, 16; Jack F. Matlock, Jr., *Autopsy on an Empire: The American Ambassador's Account of the Collapse of the Soviet Union* (New York: Random House, 1995), 154, 192. Additionally, on a trip to Cuba in April 1989, Gorbachev publicly denounced the "export of revolution and counterrevolution" and had begun to cut off aid to the Sandinistas in Nicaragua and to other like-minded forces—though not yet to a degree that made the new Bush administration fully comfortable. Michael R. Beschloss and Strobe Talbott, *At the Highest Levels: The Inside Story of the End of the Cold War* (Boston, MA: Little, Brown, 1993),

58–59, 105; George Bush and Brent Scowcroft, *A World Transformed* (New York: Knopf, 1998), 135. He also worked to extricate the Soviet Union from Angola and to secure the withdrawal of Communist Vietnam from Cambodia.

8 Shultz, *Turmoil and Triumph*, 1131, 1138; see also Matlock, *Autopsy*, 197.

9 Cold War Retrospective, panel discussion, School of International Affairs, Princeton University, 26 February 1993, as recorded by C-SPAN.

10 Don Oberdorfer, "Eased East–West Tension Offers Chances, Dangers," *Washington Post*, 7 May 1989; see also Oberdorfer, *The Turn*, 346.

11 See also the editorial, "The Empire Pulls Back," *Wall Street Journal*, 10 February 1989.

12 Oberdorfer, *The Turn*, 347.

13 Beschloss and Talbott, *At the Highest Levels*, 69.

14 Ibid., 70.

15 Quoted by Philip Zelikow at the Annual Conference of the Society for Historians of American Foreign Relations, Princeton University, 25 June 1999; see also Zelikow and Rice, *Germany Unified*, 20. On Scowcroft's continuing "reservations" about Gorbachev even after the spring of 1989, see Bush and Scowcroft, *World Transformed*, 135.

16 *Public Papers of the Presidents of the United States: George Bush, 1989* (Washington, DC: United States Government Printing Office, 1990), 541, 543.

17 Ibid., 546, 553, 602.

18 Ibid., 606, 617, 667–668.

19 Bush and Scowcroft, *World Transformed*, 55.

20 Although Bush rather liked the Open Skies idea, Scowcroft says he found that it "smacked of gimmickry, and would wrongly give the impression that we did not have the brain power to think of something innovative and had to reach back thirty years for an idea." Bush and Scowcroft, *World Transformed*, 54.

21 In an effort to jigger things along, Blackwill promised an excellent dinner to anyone in the administration who used the phrase "beyond containment" on television after the Texas A&M speech: Beschloss and Talbott, *At the Highest Levels*, 70.

22 Francis Fukuyama, "Patterns of Soviet Third World Policy," *Problems of Communism* 36 (September–October 1987): 1–13.

23 G.F. Hudson, Richard Lowenthal, and Roderick MacFarquhar, eds., *The Sino–Soviet Dispute* (New York: Praeger, 1961), 214. Similarly, his successor, Leonid Breznhev, declared in 1976, "Detente does not in the slightest way abolish, and cannot abolish or change the laws of the class struggle. We do not conceal the fact that we see detente as a way to create more favorable conditions for peaceful socialist and communist construction." Geir Lundestad, *East, West, North, South*, 4th ed. (New York: Oxford University Press, 1999), 111.

24 Strobe Talbott, ed., *Khrushchev Remembers: The Last Testament* (Boston, MA: Little, Brown, 1974), 530–531.

25 Edward Crankshaw and Strobe Talbott, eds., *Khrushchev Remembers* (Boston, MA: Little, Brown, 1970), 512.

26 Andrew Kydd, "Trust, Reassurance, and Cooperation," *International Organization* 54 (Spring 2000): 346.

27 In his 1987 essay, Fukuyama pointedly suggested that Soviet behavior in Afghanistan would "provide a good test of how far-reaching the changes in Soviet Third World policy are." Fukuyama, "Patterns of Soviet Third World Policy," 11.

28 For an assessment of conservative analysts who wanted more evidence and who waited for the Eastern European revolutions of late 1989 to relax, see Kydd, "Trust, Reassurance, and Cooperation," 349–350.

29 See Kenneth Waltz, *Theory of International Politics* (Reading, MA: Addison-Wesley, 1979), 98, 170.

30 Frank C. Carlucci, "Is the Cold War Over: No Time to Change U.S. Defense Policy," *New York Times*, 27 January 1989.

31 *Public Papers of the Presidents: Bush*, 541; see also Vasquez, *Power of Power Politics*, 330; Owen Harries, "Is the Cold War Really Over?" *National Review*, 10 November 1989, 45.

32 See Kydd, "Trust, Reassurance, and Cooperation," 345–348, 350. With its later withdrawal from Eastern Europe, the Soviet ability to invade Western Europe was, of course, vastly reduced, but it still retained a huge army and nuclear capacity. The failure of the Soviet economic and administrative system clearly encouraged Gorbachev and others to reexamine their basic ideology. However, as Myron Rush notes, these problems by no means required a doctrinal change: had the Soviet Union done nothing about them, "its survival to the end of the century would have been likely," and "by cutting defense spending sharply . . . a prudent conservative leader in 1985 could have improved the Soviet economy markedly." Myron Rush, "Fortune and Fate," *National Interest* (Spring 1993): 21.

33 In a parallel to the Cold War discussion, if terrorists led by Osama bin Laden were to credibly give up their anti-American ideological zeal, concerns about them would diminish markedly, even though their physical capacity to commit damaging acts of terror would be unchanged.

34 Hans J. Morgenthau, *Politics Among Nations: The Struggle for Power and Peace* (New York: Knopf, 1948), 327; see also James Lee Ray and Bruce Russett, "The Future as Arbiter of Theoretical Controversies: Predictions, Explanations and the End of the Cold War," *British Journal of Political Science* 26 (October 1996): 457.

35 Amity Shlaes, "Talk Turns to Triple Zero in West Germany," *Wall Street Journal*, 9 December 1988; Robert Keatley, "Gorbachev Peace Offensive Jars the West," *Wall Street Journal*, 20 January 1989; editorial, *Wall Street Journal*, 31 May 1989; see also R. Jeffrey Smith, "Arms Cuts Gain Favor as Anxieties Ebb," *Washington Post*, 8 May 1989. On the phenomenon of the negative arms race, see John Mueller, *Quiet Cataclysm: Reflections on the Recent Transformation of World Politics* (New York: HarperCollins, 1995), ch. 3.

36 Suri, "Explaining the End of the Cold War," 84.

37 Beschloss and Talbott, *At the Highest Levels*, 437.

38 John Lewis Gaddis, *Strategies of Containment* (New York: Oxford UP, 1982), 143.

39 *Public Papers of the Presidents of the United States: John F. Kennedy, 1962* (Washington, DC: United States Government Printing Office, 1963), 551.

40 "In Gorbachev's Words," *New York Times*, 8 December 1988.

41 Beschloss and Talbott, *At the Highest Levels*, 417–418; Bush and Scowcroft, *World Transformed*, 515–516; Matlock, *Autopsy*, 565–566.

42 On this issue, see also Michael Mandelbaum, "Ending Where It Began," *New York Times*, 27 February 1989. By mid-1988, some analysts were noting that the Soviet position in burdensome Eastern Europe had become negotiable and might lead to some sort of Finlandization of the Soviet colonies there. Irving Kristol, "The Soviets' Albatross States," *Wall Street Journal*, 22 July 1988. See also Garthoff, *Great Transition*, 377–378.

43 *Public Papers of the Presidents: Bush*, 431. Zelikow and Rice, *Germany Unified*, 24, 31. Zelikow and Rice date the end of the Cold War with the unification of Germany. Ibid., 3.

44 George F. Kennan, "This Is No Time for Talk Of German Reunification," *Washington Post*, 12 November 1989. Similarly, Henry Kissinger anticipated at the time that it would take three or four years even for a de facto unification of Germany to take place. Michael R. Gordon, "Kissinger Expects a United Germany: Declares Changes in the East Set in Motion Forces That Cannot Be Reversed," *New York Times*, 16 November 1989. In a spring 1989 memo, Scowcroft noted that "virtually no West German expects German unification to happen in this century." Zelikow and Rice, *Germany Unified*, 28. A personal note may be of interest in this regard. In 1986, I presented a paper at the International Studies Association meetings arguing that because the Cold War was

about ideology (a theme continued in the present article) and because Gorbachev was already in the process of dismembering this crucial element, the Cold War might well be in terminal demise—that we might be coming to the end of the world as we knew it (the paper can be found at http://psweb.sbs.ohio-state.edu/faculty/jmueller/isa 1986. pdf). In 1985 and 1986, I tried to get the unfashionable argument published, in various versions, in *Foreign Policy, National Interest, Washington Post, New York Times, Wall Street Journal, Los Angeles Times,* and *New Republic* to no avail. I then gave up and blended the argument into a book that came out in February 1989 (*Retreat from Doomsday,* see especially 211–214). While I think I got the basic mechanism for the demise of the Cold War right, I was as flabbergasted as anybody by the speed with which events in Eastern Europe took place. At the 1986 meeting, someone asked me when I thought the Soviet Union might decide to leave Eastern Europe. The paper suggests that this might happen "eventually" and "in the long term," and I tried to take refuge behind such crafty vapidities. But he kept badgering me, and I finally blurted out, "Maybe by 1995," with what I felt was amazing heroism. If I had heard myself saying "1989" I would have had myself committed.

45 Zelikow and Rice, *Germany Unified,* 2.
46 Oberdorfer, "Thatcher Says Cold War Has Come to an End."
47 Comment at the Annual Conference of the Society for Historians of American Foreign Relations, Princeton University, 26 June 1999.
48 John C. Campbell, *Tito's Separate Road: America and Yugoslavia in World Politics* (New York: Harper and Row, 1967), 24–27.
49 Jonathan D. Pollack, "China and the Global Strategic Balance" in Harry Harding, ed., *China's Foreign Relations in the 1980s* (New Haven, CT: Yale University Press, 1984), 159. On the potential for alliance, see also Strobe Talbott, "The Strategic Dimension of the Sino–American Relationship" in Richard H. Solomon, ed., *The China Factor* (Englewood Cliffs, NJ: Prentice-Hall, 1981), 81–113. On China's abandonment of threatening ideology, see Mueller, *Retreat from Doomsday,* 184–186.
50 In his assessment of the end of the Cold War, Andrew Kydd ignores ideological change and seeks to explain the development by stressing instead various tangible signals and reassurances put forward by Gorbachev. But as he notes in passing, China abandoned the Cold War, and was accepted by the West, even without such tangible signals. The experience serves, he suggests, "as a reminder that a transition path from communism exists that does not provide a great deal of reassurance to the outside world." Kydd, "Trust, Reassurance, and Cooperation," 350.
51 *Policy Review* (Winter 1985): 33. An interesting comparson can be made with Cuba. Although there is little concern that that tiny nation can do much to harm the United States, a great deal of hostility toward the regime lingers in part at least because, however materially impotent, it still subscribes to a hostile ideology.
52 An important Soviet official observed in 1987, "Previously we reasoned: the worse for the adversary, the better for us. . . . But today this is no longer true. . . . The better things are going in the European world economy, the higher the stability and the better the prospects for our development." Snyder, "Gorbachev Revolution," 115. See also Harries, "Is the Cold War Really Over?" 40–42.
53 *New York Times,* 9 December 1988.
54 *Public Papers of the Presidents: Bush,* 541, 602.
55 X [George F. Kennan], "The Sources of Soviet Conduct," *Foreign Affairs* 25 (July 1947): 566–567.
56 For an able analysis and discussion, see Nigel Gould-Davies, "Rethinking the Role of Ideology in International Politics During the Cold War," *Journal of Cold War Studies* 1 (Winter 1999): 90–109.
57 Frederic S. Burin, "The Communist Doctrine of the Inevitability of War," *American Political Science Review* 57 (June 1963): 337.

58 Melvyn P. Leffler, *The Specter of Communism* (New York: Hill and Wang, 1994), 17.

59 Historicus [George Allen Morgan], "Stalin on Revolution," *Foreign Affairs* 27 (January 1949): 198.

60 William Taubman, *Stalin's American Policy* (New York: Norton, 1982), 224. As Taubman points out, Stalin was referring to wars *between* capitalist states, something often neglected when the West examined this statement. Nevertheless, even taking that into account, the declaration clearly remains profoundly threatening to capitalist states. On this issue more generally, see Burin, "Communist Doctrine."

61 Hudson et al., *Sino–Soviet Dispute*, 196.

62 This is essentially the position taken in the waning months of the Cold War by Gorbachev adviser Giorgi Arbatov, who argued that Gorbachev was in the process of destroying "anti-Soviet stereotypes." He concluded, "Something very serious is happening: The beginning of the demise of the entire political infrastructure of the Cold War. The Western press is already saying that Gorbachev's destruction of the stereo-type of the 'enemy' is his 'secret weapon.' The arms race, power politics in the Third World, and military blocs are unthinkable without the 'Soviet threat.' " "Is America No Longer Exceptional?" *New Perspectives Quarterly* 5 (Summer 1988): 31. For the forceful argument that the sentiments reflected real ideological zeal and importantly affected policy during the Cold War, see Douglas J. Macdonald, "Communist Bloc Expansion in the Early Cold War: Challenging Realism, Refuting Revisionism," *International Security* 20 (Winter 1995/96): 152–188.

63 See Robert H. Johnson, *Improbable Dangers: U.S. Conceptions of Threat in the Cold War and After* (New York: St. Martin's, 1994).

64 John Lewis Gaddis, "Was the Truman Doctrine a Real Turning Point?" *Foreign Affairs* 52 (January 1974): 388; see also Garthoff, *Great Transition*, ch. 16.

65 Matlock, *Autopsy*, 649.

REFLECTIONS

Massive extrapolation

According to the ideology on which the Soviet regime had been founded in 1917—the chief motor of the Cold War in my view—world history is a vast, continuing process of progressive revolution. Steadily, in country after country, the oppressed working classes will violently revolt, destroying the oppressing capitalist classes and aligning their new regimes with other like-minded countries, eventually transforming the world. But the Soviets, however dynamic and threatening their ideology, never subscribed to a Hitler-style theory of direct, Armageddon-risking conquest to move history along, and the tactical sense of regime founder Vladimir Lenin was decidedly cautious. The notion, then, was that while holding the capitalist world at bay by defensive military preparations and ingenious political maneuvers, the Soviets would nudge inevitable historical processes along by aiding and inspiring subversive revolutionary movements around the globe. As Josef Stalin put it in 1945, they envisioned that the USSR, where "the dictatorship of the proletariat" would be consolidated, would be used "as a base for the overthrow of imperialism in all countries."

Western policymakers were aware that the Soviet expansionist threat was likely to be expressed primarily in what they called "indirect aggression": subversion, diplomatic and military pressure, revolution, and armed uprising—all inspired, partly funded, and heavily influenced by Moscow. To deal with this challenge, the policy of containment was formally set in motion. In the long run, it was hoped, the Soviets, frustrated in their drive for territory and expanded authority, would become less hostile and more accommodating.

The issue of direct military aggression by the Soviets, however, was more problematic. Many people, like George Kennan, one of containment's chief architects, felt its likelihood was exceedingly small. But no one, of course, could be sure.

In 1950, Stalin was led to experiment with outright warfare—albeit in a seemingly safe corner of the world. In late 1949 his close ally, Kim Il-sung, the leader of Communist North Korea, insisted that, in Nikita Khrushchev's reflection, if prodded with the "point of a bayonet," an "internal explosion" in South Korea would be touched off. Although Stalin had misgivings, Kim was "absolutely certain of success," promising that South Korea would quickly fall into the Communist camp before the West even had much of a chance to react. Eventually, both Stalin and the Chinese Communists accepted the scheme. What Stalin approved, as William Stueck had documented, was a distant war of expansion not by the Soviet Union but by a faithful ally, a war that was expected to be quick, risk-free, and cheap. And, in allowing Kim to proceed, he made it clear that if things went badly, Kim would have to depend on China to help, not on the Soviet Union. There was no evidence at the time that Stalin actually had anything broader in mind, nor has any come to light since. From the perspective of the Communists, the event was a unique opportunity and an extreme one in terms of risk. Thus, it seems unlikely that, even if successful, such a venture would have been attempted elsewhere, much less one even more risky such as a direct attack on Western Europe or the United States.

The Communist venture in Korea, then, was a limited, opportunistic, and quite cautious military probe at a point of perceived vulnerability in a peripheral area, and it proved to be an aberration, not a harbinger, and to be counterproductive to the goals of the perpetrators. Nonetheless, the victims of the attack insisted on placing the Communist venture, or adventure, in the most cosmic of contexts, with extravagant and essentially dire consequences for policy and expenditure. It importantly reinforced (or created) a tendency to envision international Communism not simply as a subversive threat, but as a direct military threat. The result was a truly massive emphasis on exquisite theorizing and on defense expenditures. All this, primarily to confront, to deter, and to make glowering and menacing faces at a threat of direct military aggression that, essentially, didn't exist.

Western policymakers were correct to see expunging capitalism and Western-style democracy as the ultimate goals of international Communism, but they massively extrapolated from the Korean experience to conclude that the Soviets were willing to apply direct military action to advance that goal. Almost everyone simply assumed that the war was being directed from Moscow and was part of a broad, militarized quest for "world domination" and a direct analogy with Hitlerian aggression in Europe was readily applied: as Truman recalled later, "If this was allowed to go unchallenged it would mean a third world war, just as similar incidents had brought on the second world war." A few people at the time challenged this interpretation, but they were ignored even though their interpretation was plausible and could not be rejected on the basis of the evidence available at the time (or, as it happens, since).

Bernard Brodie, one of the few defense analysts of the time seriously to consider the premises of such policies, came to the conclusion by 1966 that it was "difficult to discover what meaningful incentives the Russians might have for attempting to conquer Western Europe—especially incentives that are even remotely commensurate with the risks." After it was all over a great amount of documentary evidence became available, but as Robert Jervis notes, "the Soviet archives have yet to reveal any serious plans for unprovoked aggression against Western Europe, not to mention a first strike against the United States."

But deterring the essentially non-existent threat of direct military aggression became a central, even overwhelming, preoccupation. As Robert Johnson puts it, the process (which he aptly labels "nuclear metaphysics") involved "making the most pessimistic assumptions possible about Soviet intentions and capabilities" and then assuming that the capabilities (which turned out almost always to have been substantially exaggerated) would be used "to the adversary's maximum possible advantage." I have explored this costly absurdity further in my *Atomic Obsession*.

The enemy within

The Korean War also escalated American concerns about domestic Communists. If Communists could subvert countries abroad, many after World War II increasingly worried about the danger of subversion at home and envisioned even the small domestic Communist Party to be a potential threat. Fears rose when a respected former State Department official, Alger Hiss, was accused of having sent huge quantities of classified documents to the Soviets before World War II. Then a former Communist, British physicist Klaus Fuchs, admitted that he had sent atomic secrets to the Soviets. The trail from Fuchs soon led to the arrests of various co-conspirators and ultimately to the celebrated trial of two Americans, Julius and Ethel Rosenberg, who were convicted as atomic spies.

Accordingly, fears about the dangers presented by "the enemy within" became greatly heightened and then fully internalized, and politicians scurried to spend billions upon billions to surveil, to screen, to protect, and to spy on an ever-expanding array of individuals who had come to seem suspicious. For example, a group of German emigré writers living in the United States and Mexico were under FBI surveillance for decades. None was ever found to pose much of a subversive threat, and what impresses Alexander Stephan is the essential absurdity of the situation: the "high efficiency and gross overkill" as hundreds of agents were paid to intercept and catalogue communications, to endlessly record goings and comings, and to sift enterprisingly through trash bins, all at taxpayers' expense.

In fact, despite huge anxieties about it at the time, there seem to have been few, if any, instances in which domestic Communists engaged in anything that could be considered espionage after World War II. Moreover, at no time did any domestic Communist ever commit anything that could be considered violence in support of the cause—this, despite deep apprehensions at the time about that form of terrorism then dubbed "sabotage."

Yet, as far as I can see, at no point during all this did anyone say in public "many domestic Communists adhere to a foreign ideology that ultimately has as its goal the destruction of capitalism and democracy, and by violence if necessary. However, they do not present much of a danger, are actually quite a pathetic bunch, and couldn't subvert their way out of a wet paper bag. Why are we expending so much time, effort, and treasure on this?" It is astounding to me that this plausible, if arguable, point of view seems never to have been publicly expressed by anyone—politician, pundit, professor, editorialist—during the Cold War.

Reflections references

Bernard Brodie, *Escalation and the Nuclear Option*. Princeton, NJ: Princeton University Press, 1966.

Robert Jervis, Was the Cold War a Security Dilemma? *Journal of Cold War Studies*, Winter 2001.

Robert H. Johnson, *Improbable Dangers: U.S. Conceptions of Threat in the Cold War and After*. New York: St. Martin's, 1994.

Nikita Khrushchev, *Khrushchev Remembers*. Boston: Little, Brown, 1970.

Alexander Stephan, *"Communazis": FBI Surveillance of German Emigré Writers*. New Haven, CT: Yale University Press, 2000.

William Stueck, *Rethinking the Korean War: A New Diplomatic and Strategic History*. Princeton, NJ: Princeton University Press, 2002.

Harry S. Truman, *Years of Trial and Hope*. Garden City: Doubleday, 1956.

6   Simplicity and spook

Terrorism and the dynamics of threat exaggeration

"At the summit of foreign policy," Warner Schilling once observed, "one always finds simplicity and spook." This observation was triggered by a consideration of the process by which Japan and the United States managed to go to war with each other in 1941. Japan, he notes, launched war on the vague, unexamined hope that the United States would seek a compromise peace after being attacked, "a hope nourished in their despair at the alternatives." Meanwhile, "the American opposition to Japan rested on the dubious proposition that the loss of Southeast Asia could prove disastrous for Britain's war effort and for the commitment to maintain the territorial integrity of China—a commitment as mysterious in its logic as anything the Japanese ever conceived." And at no time, he notes, did American leaders "perplex themselves with the question of just how much American blood and treasure the defense of China and Southeast Asia was worth" (Schilling, 1965:389; see also Russett, 1972; Mueller, 1995:101–110).

It has been common, at least since 1945, for the United States to exaggerate foreign threats, and then to overreact to them, something that seems to be continuing with current concerns over international terrorism. Some of this proclivity may derive from the experience with Japan before World War II: there may have been a tendency to underestimate its capacity and its willingness to take risks, and the traumatic experience of Pearl Harbor led to embracing the over-learned lesson never to do that again.[1] It may also have derived from underestimates of Hitler in the 1930s—underestimates, however, that were inspired in part and in turn by the exaggerated assumption that the next war would lead to human annihilation, an assumption that led to the logical conclusion that Hitler could not possibly be willing to risk one (see Mueller, 1989:ch.3). There is danger in overlearning, and as Robert Jervis has suggested, "those who remember the past are condemned to making the opposite mistakes" (1976:275).

This article sketches threat exaggeration during the Cold War and extends that experience to the current era.

Threat exaggeration during the Cold War

During the Cold War, it seems clear in hindsight, the United States and sometimes its allies persistently and often vastly exaggerated both the capacity of international Communism to inflict damage in carrying out its threatening revolutionary goals and its willingness to accept risk to do so.

The results of the exaggeration—or proclivity to err on the safe side—were economically and occasionally militarily costly, and they were often emotionally draining.

The threat

None of this is to deny that Communism, a coordinated, conspiratorial, subversive, revolutionary, and state-based international movement, did pose a threat. According to its core ideology, it was out to destroy capitalism and democracy. Moreover, it explicitly and repeatedly declared that violence—in particular, revolutionary violence—would be required to accomplish this central goal. There has been a considerable debate about the degree to which ideology actually impelled Soviet policy.[2] However, over the decades prominent Soviet leaders repeatedly made statements like the following:

> Lenin: "The existence of the Soviet Republic side by side with the imperialist states for a long time is unthinkable. One or the other must triumph in the end. And before that end supervenes, a series of frightful collisions between the Soviet Republic and the bourgeois states will be inevitable".
>
> (Burin, 1963:337)

> Lenin: "As soon as we are strong enough to fight the whole of capitalism, we shall at once take it by the neck".
>
> (Leffler, 1994:17)

> Stalin: "The goal is to consolidate the dictatorship of the proletariat in one country, using it as a base for the overthrow of imperialism in all countries".
>
> (Historicus, 1949:198)

> Stalin: "To eliminate the inevitability of war, it is necessary to destroy imperialism".[3]
>
> (Taubman, 1982:224)

> Khrushchev: "peaceful coexistence" means "intense economic, political, and ideological struggle between the proletariat and the aggressive forces of imperialism in the world arena".
>
> (Hudson, Lowenthal, and MacFarquhar, 1961:214)

> Khrushchev: "All the socialist countries and the international working-class and Communist movement recognize their duty to render the fullest moral and material assistance to the peoples fighting to free themselves from imperialist and colonial tyranny".
>
> (Hudson et al., 1961:196)

There is some possibility, of course, that pronouncements like these are simply theological boilerplate. However, after they have been recited millions of times in speeches, books, leaflets, brochures, letterhead, tracts, training manuals, banners, pamphlets, proclamations, announcements, billboards, handbooks, bumper stickers, and T shirts, one might begin to suspect that the sentiments could just possibly actually reflect true thought processes.[4]

At any rate, as they are explicitly and lethally threatening, responsible leaders of capitalist countries ought, at least out of simple prudence, to take them seriously. And it seems clear that they did. For example, the ideological threat was stressed in the quintessential and seminal declaration of U.S. policy toward international Communism: George Kennan's "The Sources of Soviet Conduct," published in *Foreign Affairs* in 1947. The article is concerned about Soviet military strength, but it argues that what makes that strength threatening is an essentially expansionist ideology. In the first paragraphs of the article, Kennan outlines "the outstanding features of Communist thought." According to Kennan, these include the following notions: (1) "the capitalist system of production is a nefarious one which inevitably leads to the exploitation of the working class by the capital-owning class"; (2) "capitalism contains the seeds of its own destruction" that must "result inevitably and inescapably in a revolutionary transfer of power to the working class"; (3) countries where revolutions have been successful will "rise against the remaining capitalist world"; (4) capitalism will not "perish without proletarian revolution"; and (5) "a final push" is "needed from a revolutionary proletariat movement in order to tip over the tottering structure" (1947:566–567).

And others readily accepted that characterization. For example, in his last presidential press conference, Ronald Reagan was quite clear about what he felt the Cold War was about: "the expansionary policy that was instituted in the Communist revolution, that their goal must be a one-world Communist state."[5] And in speeches in 1989, George H. W. Bush noted that the policy of containment required "checking the Soviet Union's expansionist aims, in the hope that the Soviet system itself would one day be forced to confront its internal contradictions."[6] Similar statements were frequently made by such leading Cold Warriors as Winston Churchill, John Foster Dulles, John F. Kennedy, Lyndon Johnson, Margaret Thatcher, and George Shultz (see Mueller, 2004–2005).

The reality

But to say that international Communism was threatening is not to say that it had the capacity to carry the threat out.[7] For the most part it proved, as Kennan noted, to carry the seeds of its own destruction. Although there were times in which it seemed to be, in Nikita Khruschev's phrase, "the wave of the future," it eventually collapsed of its own weight and lack of appeal and of the failure of its misguided, even romantic, world view. In retrospect, it seems clear that although policies designed to contain and counter this threat may have sometimes speeded this process along, the fears the policies were based on were often excessive and overwrought and sometimes counterproductive. This is suggested by a brief sketch of some of the Cold War experience.

When the Communists successfully fomented a coup in democratic Czechoslovakia in 1948, there were great fears that this would soon be followed by further Communist takeovers in Europe, especially in Italy and France. But it was not. No coups took place, and, in fact, by that time, the appeal of Communism in Western Europe was already declining markedly, and it continued to do so. The threat of internal subversion and of revolution in the developed world proved to be minor.

Communist aggression in Korea in 1950 was deeply alarming. President Harry Truman immediately concluded that "The attack upon Korea makes it plain beyond all doubt that Communism has passed beyond the use of subversion to conquer independent nations and will now use armed invasion and war" (Shulman, 1963:150). As Bernard Brodie recalls, the Joint Chiefs "were utterly convinced that the Russians were using Korea as a feint to cause us to deploy our forces there while they prepared to a launch a 'general' (total) war against the United States through a major attack on Europe" (1973:63). They were not. In fact, the invasion seems to have been a limited probe at a point of perceived vulnerability. It is possible that a Communist success there might have encouraged further such ventures (Mueller, 1989: 130–131). However, the episode does seem to have been something of an outlier, and there have been no Koreas since Korea.

Or there was the almost hysterical reaction to the Soviet Union's dramatic launch in 1957 of Sputnik, the first artificial space satellite. Deeply alarmed by that development and by the Soviet Union's apparent economic progress, the hastily assembled, if august and authoritative, President's Commission on National Goals declared the democratic world to be in "grave danger" from Communism's "great capacity for political organization and propaganda" and from the "specious appeal of Communist doctrine to peoples eager for rapid escape from poverty" (1960:1–2). And the CIA helpfully extrapolated in 1960 that the Soviet Union's Gross National Product might be triple that of the United States by the year 2000 (Reeves, 1993:54).[8] In time, such fears, to say the least, proved absurd.

It was feared that Castro's 1959 victory in Cuba and his subsequent embrace of Soviet Communism would be repeated all over Latin America. It was not: over time, Communism in Latin America lost its appeal.

When the United States massively escalated its efforts in Vietnam in 1965, there was widespread agreement with the views of David Halberstam, a future war critic, who argued that Vietnam was a "strategic country in a key area . . . perhaps one of only five or six nations in the world that is truly vital to U.S. interests," and that if America failed there "the pressure of Communism on the rest of Southeast Asia will intensify" and "throughout the world the enemies of the West will be encouraged to try insurgencies like the one in Vietnam" (Halberstam, 1965:315, 319; oddly, these passages are not included in the 1988 reprint edition of the book). Or as reporter Neil Sheehan, another future critic of American policy in Vietnam, put it in 1964, "The fall of Southeast Asia to China or its denial to the West over the next decade because of the repercussions from an American defeat in Vietnam would amount to a strategic disaster of the first magnitude." Only the United States, he argued, could meet "the Chinese Communist challenge for hegemony in Asia." These fears, so deadly in their consequences, proved to be exaggerated.[9]

When the Soviet Union invaded neighboring Afghanistan in 1979, many saw it as an aggressive ploy relevant to the entire Middle East and South Asia. Alarmed that the Soviet probe might merely be a prologue to further adventures in the oil-rich Persian Gulf area, President Jimmy Carter sternly threatened to use "any means necessary" to counter a further Soviet military move in the area, a threat basically reiterated by his replacement, Ronald Reagan, the next year (Halperin, 1987:45). It was the first time that Soviet forces had been sent directly into a country outside their empire since 1945; it was also the last and proved to be a disaster for the international Communist movement.

Under Carter, and even more so under his successor, Ronald Reagan, the defense budget was escalated under the popular assumption, pushed, among others, by a group of august doomsayers who ominously called themselves the Committee on the Present Danger that somehow the Soviet Union's military capacity had vastly and threateningly increased, and there were extravagant claims that the Soviet Union was willing to accept massive casualties to acquire world domination (Johnson, 1994:ch. 6). Events were to prove this budgetarily costly fear, based on what Brodie at the time labeled "worst case fantasies" (1978:68), to be much exaggerated.

Evaluating the success of containment

In the 1980s, under the leadership of Mikhail Gorbachev, the Soviets did mellow their foreign policy decisively, and shortly after that the whole country imploded. It is natural to conclude from this experience that the wisdom of the containment strategy and of the defense buildup has been affirmed. But while those policies *intended* a certain desirable effect, it does not follow that they *caused* it.

In fact, the policy of containment is logically flawed. If the Soviet system really was as rotten as Kennan and others more or less accurately surmised, then the best policy would not have been to contain it, but to give it enough rope—to let it expand until it reached the point of terminal overstretch. Indeed, one of Kennan's favorite quotes comes from Gibbon: "there is nothing more contrary to nature than the attempt to hold in obedience distant provinces" (Gaddis, 1982:47; Gellman, 1984:53). If that is true, an expansive country will discover this lesson faster if it is allowed to gather in new distant provinces than if it is contained. That is, if the goal was to speed the Soviet Union's inevitable rendezvous with its decadent destiny, it might have been wiser—logically, at least—to let it expand to the rotting point.

In fact, what ultimately helped to bring about the mellowing of Soviet expansionism was not containment's success, but its failure. Wherever they expanded, the Soviets sought, often brutally, to suppress religions, nationalisms, and freedoms. In 1947, Kennan, found it "unlikely" that the 100 million Soviets could permanently hold down not only their own minorities, but "some 90 millions of Europeans with a higher cultural level and with long experience in resistance to foreign rule" (Gaddis, 1982:43; Taubman, 1982:170). By the 1980s, the Soviets' empire in Eastern Europe had indeed become a severe economic drain and a psychic problem—although this, of course, cannot be credited to Western policy, which strenuously opposed the occupation from the beginning.

Then in 1975 three countries—Cambodia, South Vietnam, and Laos—toppled into the Communist camp. Partly out of fear of repeating the Vietnam experience, the United States went into a sort of containment funk and watched from the sidelines as the Soviet Union, in what seems in retrospect to have been remarkably like a fit of absent mindedness, opportunistically gathered a set of Third World countries into its imperial embrace: Angola in 1976, Mozambique and Ethiopia in 1977, South Yemen and Afghanistan in 1978, and Grenada and Nicaragua in 1979. The Soviets at first were quite gleeful about these acquisitions—the "correlation of forces," they concluded, had magically and decisively shifted in their direction (Breslauer, 1987:436–437).

However, far from whetting their appetite for more, these gains ultimately not only satiated their appetite for expansion but, given the special properties of the morsels they happened to consume, the process served to give the ravenous expanders a troubling case of indigestion. For almost all the new acquisitions soon became economic and political basket cases, fraught with dissension, financial mismanagement, and civil warfare. In 1979, the situation in neighboring Afghanistan had so deteriorated that the Soviets found it necessary to send in troops, and they then descended into a long period of enervating warfare there. As each member of their newly expanded empire turned toward the Soviet Union for maternal warmth and sustenance, many Soviets began to wonder about the wisdom of the venture. Perhaps, it began to seem, they would have been better off contained.[10]

The "internal contradictions" that the Soviets came to confront, then, were a direct result of misguided domestic and foreign policies, and these contradictions would have come about no matter what policy the West chose to pursue. Soviet domestic problems derived from decades of mismanagement, mindless brutality, and fundamental misconceptions about basic economic and social realities. Their defense dilemmas came from a conspiratorial world view that created external enemies and then exaggerated the degree to which the enemies would use war to destroy them. And their foreign policy failures stemmed from a fundamentally flawed, and often highly romantic, conception of the imperatives of history and of the degree to which foreign peoples would find appeal in Communism. It took 40 years but, plagued by economic and social disasters and changes, the Soviets were finally able to rise above ideology, embrace grim reality, and adopt serious reform.[11]

The Western policy of containment may have helped to keep some countries free from Communism, and it may have further reduced the already low danger of major war. But insofar as it was devised to force the Soviets to confront their inherent contradictions, the history of the Cold War suggests a curious paradox. Kennan and the other early containment theorists were correct to conclude that Soviet Communism is a singularly undesirable and fundamentally flawed form of government, and they were right to anticipate that it would inevitably have to mellow when it could no longer avoid confronting its inherent contradictions. But Soviet Communism might have reached this point somewhat earlier if its natural propensity to expand had been tolerated rather than contained.

Nuclear anxieties

Another fear that proved exaggerated during the Cold War concerned the prospects for World War III. Throughout most of the time, there was great concern that somehow a new world war was all but inevitable due to the depth of the hostility between nuclear East and nuclear West. As the doomsday clock on the cover of the *Bulletin of Atomic Scientists* kept suggesting, many thought calamity was imminent and/or nearly certain. The common images were of the sword of Damocles and of two scorpions in a bottle.

Thus historian Arnold Toynbee confidently proclaimed, "In our recent Western history war has been following war in an ascending order of intensity; and today it is already apparent that the War of 1939–1945 was not the climax of this crescendo movement" (1950:4). In 1945, Ambassador Joseph Grew, one of America's most perceptive diplomats, concluded that "a future war with the Soviet Union is as certain as anything in this world" (quoted, Gaddis, 1987:218n). Soviet dictator Josif Stalin concurred: "We shall recover in fifteen or twenty years and then we'll have another go at it" (quoted, Djilas, 1962:114–115). Public opinion polls conducted in the United States in the mid-1940s characteristically found very substantial percentages opining that the next world war would occur within 25 years (Mueller, 1979:303–307), and Albert Einstein was certain that "Unless we are able, in the near future, to abolish the mutual fear of military aggression, we are doomed" (1960:417). In 1960, strategist and futurist Herman Kahn wrote, "I have a firm belief that unless we have more serious and sober thought on various aspects of the strategic problem . . . we are not going to reach the year 2000—and maybe not even the year 1965—without a cataclysm" (1960:x), and C. P. Snow (1961) assured his listeners that unless nuclear weapons were restricted, it was a "certainty" that within "at the most, ten years, some of those bombs are going off." In 1979, realist Hans J. Morgenthau concluded that "the world is moving ineluctably towards a third world war—a strategic nuclear war. I do not believe that anything can be done to prevent it. The international system is simply too unstable to survive for long" (Boyle, 1985:73). Three years later, historian William McNeill advocated that a "global sovereign power willing and able to enforce a monopoly of atomic weaponry" be fabricated because the "alternative appears to be sudden and total annihilation of the human species" (1982:383–384), and Jonathan Schell proclaimed, "One day—and it is hard to believe that it will not be soon—we will make our choice. Either we will sink into the final coma and end it all or, as I trust and believe, we will awaken to the truth of our peril . . . and rise up to cleanse the earth of nuclear weapons" (1982:231). "Nuclear war," observed Bruce Russett in 1983, "is the central terror of our time" (1983:1). As late as the mid-1980s, polls found that 20–37 percent of the American population considered the fear of war to be the most important problem facing the country (Mueller, 1994:211; see also Mueller, 2002a:151–152).

World War III never happened, and, it seems, never even got close.[12] Huge numbers of nuclear weapons continue to exist in the arsenals of East and West, but fears that they will be massively slung at each other have vanished. We have neither cleansed the earth of nuclear weapons nor descended into Schell's "final coma."

Threat exaggeration at the end of the Cold War

Although the central focus remained on Communism, other threats rose in concern toward the end of the Cold War.

When some 50 American diplomats were taken hostage by an unstable and ill-directed regime in Iran in 1979, the United States went through over a year of official and popular angst until the hostages were returned safely. The slogan of the time, "America Held Hostage," suggests the degree to which a relatively minor incident was exaggerated.

Similarly, in the 1980s, the Reagan administration became fixated on a handful of American hostages held by terrorists in Lebanon. At the time, Reagan's normally judicious Secretary of State, George Shultz, was proclaiming that we needed desperately to blast somebody somewhere "on a moment's notice" even without adequate evidence in order to avoid looking like the indecisive "Hamlet of nations" (Gwertzman, 1984). He apparently preferred the King Lear approach. Normally, however, only lunatics and children rail at storms; sensible people invest in umbrellas and lightning rods (Simon, 2001:180–186; see also Mueller, 1987).

As the Cold War was dissipating, there emerged a dangerous new enemy on the economic front: insidiously peaceful Japan. Those of the America-in-decline and of the FLASH! JAPAN BUYS PEARL HARBOR! schools argued that a need had suddenly arisen to fear not "missile vulnerability" but "semiconductor vulnerability." And "economics," they apparently seriously warned us, "is the continuation of war by other means" (Huntington, 1991:8, 10).[13] Danger signals arise because Japan had become the largest provider of foreign aid and because it shockingly endowed professorships at Harvard and MIT (Huntington, 1993a:77, 80). This concern soon evaporated, of course, as Japan's "threatening" economy stagnated.

Threat exaggeration after the Cold War

When the Cold War ended and the Soviet Union and China ceased to appear threatening (or in the former case vanished altogether), the focus of alarm was fully freed to shift to other perceived threats. For example, the notion quickly took hold that international affairs had somehow become especially tumultuous, unstable, and complex, an idea repeated so often that it soon began to sound like a mantra. Thus, Bill Clinton proclaimed in his 1993 Presidential inaugural address that "the new world is more free but less stable." And a few days later, his nominee to become the head of the Central Intelligence Agency, James Woolsey, testified darkly that "we have slain a large dragon, but we live now in a jungle filled with a bewildering variety of poisonous snakes." His predecessor at the CIA, Robert Gates, fully agreed: "The events of the last two years have led to a far more unstable, turbulent, unpredictable and violent world" (1993), or as Stanley

Hoffmann put it, "the problem of order has become even more complex than before" (1992:37).

Ethnic warfare

One of Woolsey's primary snakes was ethnic war that alarmingly broke out in Yugoslavia in the early 1990s. He and many others feared that it would metastasize all over Eastern Europe, perhaps even leading to a nuclear war between Russia and Ukraine. Some analysts were soon given to arguing that "conflicts among nations and ethnic groups are escalating" (Huntington, 1993a:71), that such conflicts are "now engulfing the world" (Kober, 1993:82), that "there is a virtual epidemic of armed civil or intranational conflict" (Hamburg, 1993), and that the "breakdown of restraints" seen in Yugoslavia is part of "a global trend" (Job, 1993:71; see also Kaplan, 1991, 1993a, b; Mearsheimer, 1990; Moynihan, 1993; Huntington, 1993b, c; Brzezinski, 1993; Van Evera, 1994:36).

However, most such wars, particularly those in Europe, eventually fizzled away, and did not spread (see Mueller, 1996:113–114). Moreover, the murderous dynamic of these wars was perpetrated more by bands of thugs than by ideologues or by neighbors out to get neighbors in some sort of frenzied Hobbesian state of nature (see Collier, 2000; Mueller, 2000a, b, 2004, ch. 6; Fearon and Laitin, 2003). In fact, by 2002 the number of wars in the world had dwindled considerably (Eriksson, Wallensteen, and Stollenberg, 2003), and that trend may be continuing: the number of armed conflicts inflicting over 1,000 battle or battle-related deaths per year (a standard requirement for a conflict to be designated a "war") is now very small.

Rogue states

When big problems go away, small problems tend to be elevated in perceived importance, and in the post-Cold War era, special status was given to something called "rogue states" as if this were a new problem in international affairs. Yet there were plenty of such states—devils du jour, one might call them—during the Cold War, and some of these were variously in devious complicity with the big, threatening rogues: the Soviet Union and China. Sukarno's Indonesia, for example, was a problem for years as it engaged in a policy of military "confrontation" with some neighboring states, and it often obtained support and encouragement from one major Communist country or another (see Hilsman, 1967, part 8). Something similar was true of Nasser's Egypt, Castro's Cuba, Qaddafi's Libya, and Iran's Khomeini to say nothing of the trouble and potential danger stirred by egomaniacal and sometimes deranged leaders in far more potent states like Stalin's Soviet Union and Mao's China.

The post-Cold War problems posed by such enfeebled, impoverished, and friendless states as Iraq and North Korea pale in comparison (indeed, North Korea is far less significant a threat than during the Cold War when it was variously backed by China and the USSR). Moreover, the "rogue state" label implies that they are too irrational to be deterred by policies designed to deal with "normal" countries, and it therefore leads to an extreme version of the security dilemma as weaponry that might be obtained by such states to deter an attack is almost automatically assumed to be designed for offensive purposes even though such use would be patently suicidal for the rogues and their regimes.

Thus, despite considerable evidence to the contrary (see Sigal, 1998; Harrison, 2002; Kang, 2003; also Fallows, 1994/95), the United States has consistently viewed North Korea as a continuing threat even though its neighbors, especially South Korea, do not. Having worked themselves up to a lather during the 1990s, the Americans and the British even went to war against Saddam Hussein's pathetic regime in Iraq in 2003 because, unlike all of Iraq's neighbors except Israel, their leaders imagined a "grave and gathering" threat to lurk there. Prominent fear-mongers, many of whom had previously been active in exaggerating the Soviet threat,[14] asserted that Saddam was planning to dominate the Middle East. When war broke out, his military—with which that domination was presumably to be carried out—crumbled pathetically, incoherently, and predictably.[15] Departing from the advice of John Quincy Adams in an 1821 Fourth of July speech in the House of Representatives, the United States has actively gone abroad "in search of monsters to destroy."

Weapons of mass destruction

During the Cold War, the phrase "weapons of mass destruction" was used only infrequently and then almost always to apply to nuclear weapons. After the Cold War, the phrase has been systematically and extensively embellished to embrace biological and chemical weapons as well. This escalation of language is highly questionable.[16]

Nuclear weapons, most decidedly, can indeed inflict massive destruction, and it is certainly reasonable to point out that an atomic bomb in the hands of a terrorist or rogue state could kill tens of thousands of people. But it may also be worthwhile to note that making such a bomb is an extraordinarily difficult task and that warnings about the possibility that small groups, terrorists, and errant states could fabricate nuclear weapons have been repeatedly uttered at least since 1947 (Allison, 2004:104) and especially since the 1950s when the "suitcase bomb" appeared to become a practical possibility. Interestingly, to generate alarm about such dangers, a recent book opens by grimly (and irrelevantly) recycling Einstein's failed half-century-old prediction about nuclear war: "Since the advent of the Nuclear Age, everything has changed except our modes of thinking and we thus drift toward unparalleled catastrophe" (Allison, 2004:1).

Moreover, proliferation of these weapons has been remarkably slow. During the Cold War, there were many dire predictions about nuclear proliferation that proved to be greatly exaggerated. Among these are the nearly unanimous expectations in the 1950s and 1960s that dozens of countries would have nuclear weapons by now. For example, in 1958, the National Planning Association predicted "a rapid rise in the number of atomic powers . . . by the mid-1960s" (1958:42). A couple of years later, C. P. Snow sagely predicted that, "Within, at the most, six years, China and several other states [will] have a stock of nuclear bombs" (1961:259); and John Kennedy observed that there might be "ten, fifteen, twenty" countries with a nuclear capacity by 1964 (Kraus, 1962:394). This position continued after the Cold War. Over a decade ago, Christopher Layne confidently insisted that Japan by natural impulse would soon come to yearn for nuclear weapons (1993:37) while John Mearsheimer equally confidently argued that "Germany will feel insecure without nuclear weapons" (1990:38). The Japanese and the Germans themselves continue uncooperatively to seem viscerally uninterested, although problems with North Korea could alter that perspective for Japan.[17]

Properly developed and deployed, biological weapons could indeed, if thus far only in theory, kill hundreds of thousands, perhaps even millions, of people. The discussion remains theoretical because biological weapons have scarcely ever been used even though the knowledge about their destructive potential as weapons goes back decades, even centuries in some respects (the English, e.g., made some efforts to spread smallpox among American Indians in the French and Indian War) (Christopher, Cieslak, Pavlin, and Eitzen, 1997:412).

Belligerents have eschewed such weapons with good reason: biological weapons are extremely difficult to deploy and to control. Terrorist groups or rogue states may be able to solve such problems in the future with advances in technology and knowledge, but the record thus far is unlikely to be very encouraging to them. For example, Japan reportedly infected wells in Manchuria and bombed several Chinese cities with plague-infested fleas before and during World War II. These ventures may have killed thousands of Chinese, but they apparently also caused thousands of unintended casualties among Japanese troops and seem to have had little military impact.[18] In the 1990s, Aum Shinrikyo, a Japanese cult that had some 300 scientists in its employ and an estimated budget of $1 billion, reportedly tried at least nine times over five years to set off biological weapons by spraying pathogens from trucks and wafting them from rooftops, hoping fancifully to ignite an apocalyptic war. These efforts failed to create a single fatality— in fact, nobody even noticed that the attacks had taken place (Broad, 1998; Rapoport, 1999:57).

For the most destructive results, biological weapons need to be dispersed in very low-altitude aerosol clouds: aerosols do not appreciably settle, and anthrax (which is not easy to spread or catch and is not contagious) would probably have to be sprayed near nose level (Meselson, 1995; Panofsky, 1998; Terry, 1998). Explosive methods of dispersion may destroy the organisms. Moreover, except for anthrax spores, long-term storage of lethal organisms in bombs or warheads is difficult, and, even if refrigerated, most of the organisms have a limited lifetime. The effects of such weapons can take days or weeks to have full effect, during which time they can be countered with civil defense measures. And their impact is very difficult to predict and in combat situations may spread back on the attacker (OTA, 1993:48–49, 62; Broad and Miller, 1998; Easterbrook, 2002).

Chemical arms do have the potential, under appropriate circumstances, for panicking people; killing masses of them in open areas, however, is beyond their modest capabilities.[19] Although they obviously can be hugely lethal when released in gas chambers, their effectiveness as weapons has been unimpressive, and their inclusion in the weapons-of-mass-destruction category is highly dubious unless the concept is so diluted that bullets or machetes can also be included.[20]

Biologist Matthew Meselson calculates that it would take a ton of nerve gas or five tons of mustard gas to produce heavy casualties among unprotected people in an open area of 1 km^2. Even for nerve gas this would take the concentrated delivery into a rather small area of about 300 heavy artillery shells or seven 500-lb bombs (1991:13). And, this would usually require a considerable amount of time, allowing many people to evacuate the targeted area (McNaugher, 1990:31). A 1993 analysis by the Office of Technology Assessment of the U.S. Congress finds that a ton of Sarin nerve gas perfectly delivered under absolutely ideal conditions over a heavily populated area against unprotected people could cause between 3,000 and 8,000 deaths. Under slightly less ideal circumstances—if there was a moderate wind or if the sun was out, for example—the death rate would be only 1/10th as great.[21] Nuclear weapons are considered weapons of mass destruction because a single bomb can generate great devastation. For chemical weapons to cause extensive damage, by contrast, many of them must be used, just like conventional ones.

Discussions of chemical weapons often stress their ability to cause casualties— both dead and wounded (e.g., Roberts, 1992:75–84). This glosses over the fact that historically most of those incapacitated by chemical weapons have not actually died. But clearly, to be classified as "weapons of mass destruction" they must destroy, not simply incapacitate. In World War I, only some 2 or 3 percent of those gassed on the western front died while, by contrast, wounds caused by traditional weapons were some 10 or 12 times more likely to prove fatal.[22] Chemical weapons were used against substantially unprotected Iranians by Iraq in their 1980–1988 war, but of the 27,000 gassed through March 1987, Iran reported that only 262 died (McNaugher, 1990:19n). Similarly, when Aum Shinrikyo abandoned its biological efforts in frustration and instead released "deadly" Sarin nerve gas into a Japanese subway in 1995, the attack caused thousands of casual- ties, but only 12 deaths (although a more skillful attack could have killed more) (Broad, 1998). Moreover, troops wounded by gas tend to return to combat more quickly than those wounded by bullets or shrapnel (McNaugher, 1990:20n) and to suffer less (Gilchrist, 1928:47). Against well-protected troops, gas is almost wholly ineffective except as an inconvenience (Meselson, 1991:13; Roberts, 1992:81; OTA, 1993:8, 58).

Although gas was used extensively in World War I, it accounted for less than 1 percent of the battle deaths (Gilchrist, 1928:7). In fact, on average it took over a ton of gas to produce a single fatality (Fetter, 1991:15). In the conclusion to the official British history of the war, chemical weapons are accordingly relegated to a footnote that asserts that gas "made war uncomfortable . . . to no purpose" (Edmonds and Maxwell-Hyslop, 1947:606). Defense analyst Thomas McNaugher considers this conclusion to be "overly glib," but goes on to suggest that "it is closer to the truth than the contention that chemical weapons are nearly magical devices that invariably cause large casualties and inspire panic" (1990:21).[23]

International terrorism

Like international Communism, international terrorism is explicitly threatening. Some groups of terrorists focus on Israel (and therefore on U.S. policy in the Middle East), while others, as seen on September 11, 2001, feel they must target the United States itself. As with the Communist threat during the Cold War, concern is certainly justified, but alarm, hysteria, and panic are not.

That is, it makes great sense to heighten security and policing measures, and to ask people to maintain awareness—as with crime, to report any suspicious behavior to authorities. But it is important that this be done without inducing hysteria. In the extreme foreign policy events noted above, the creation of panic and hysteria was only a by-product of the concern; in the case of terrorism, it is a central objective. Thus, alarmism can be harmful, particularly economically, and it can help create the damaging consequences that the terrorists seek but are unable to perpetrate on their own.

Capacity

The capacity for small bands of terrorists to do harm is far less than was the case for the great countries behind international Communism who possessed a very impressive military (and nuclear) capacity and had, in addition, shown great skill at political subversion.

By contrast, for all the attention it evokes, terrorism, in reasonable context, actually causes rather little damage and the likelihood that any individual will become a victim in most places is microscopic. Those adept at hyperbole like to proclaim that we live in "the age of terror" (Hoagland, 2004). However, the number of people worldwide who die as a result of international terrorism is generally only a few hundred a year, tiny compared with the numbers who die in most civil wars or from automobile accidents. In fact, until 2001 far fewer Americans were killed in any grouping of years by all forms of international terrorism than were killed by lightning. And except for 2001, virtually none of these terrorist deaths occurred within the United States itself. Indeed, outside of 2001, fewer people have died in America from international terrorism than have drowned in toilets.[24]

Even with the September 11 attacks included in the count, however, the number of Americans killed by international terrorism since the late 1960s (which is when the State Department began its accounting) is about the same as the number killed over the same period by lightning—or by accident-causing deer or by severe allergic reaction to peanuts. In almost all years, the total number of people world-wide who die at the hands of international terrorists is not much more than the number who drown in bathtubs in the United States.

Some of this is definitional. When terrorism becomes really extensive, we generally no longer call it terrorism, but war. But people are mainly concerned about random terror, not sustained warfare. Moreover, even using an expansive definition of terrorism and including domestic terrorism in the mix, it is likely that far fewer people were killed by terrorists in the entire world over the last hundred years than died in any number of unnoticed civil wars during that century.

Obviously, this could change if international terrorists are able to assemble sufficient weaponry or devise new tactics to kill masses of people and if they come to do so routinely—and this, of course, is the central fear. Nonetheless, it should be kept in mind that 9/11 was an extreme event: until then, no more than 329 had ever been killed in a single terrorist attack (in a 1985 Air India explosion), and during the entire twentieth century fewer than 20 terrorist attacks resulted in the deaths of more than 100 people. The economic destruction on September 11 was also unprecedented, of course. However, extreme events often remain exactly that—aberrations, rather than harbingers.[25] A bomb planted in a piece of checked luggage was responsible for the explosion that caused a PanAm jet to crash into Lockerbie Scotland in 1988. Since that time, hundreds of billions of pieces of luggage have been transported on American carriers and none has exploded to down an aircraft.[26] This does not mean that one should cease worrying about luggage on airlines, but it does suggest that extreme events do not necessarily assure repetition—any more than Timothy McVeigh's Oklahoma City bombing of 1995 has. Since its alarming release of poison gas in the Tokyo subway in 1995, the apocalyptic group, Aum Shinrikyo, appears to have abandoned the terrorism business and its example has not been followed. Some sort of terrorist inoculated Tylenol capsules with cyanide in 1982 killing seven people; however, this frightening and much publicized event (which generated 125,000 stories in the print media alone and cost the manufacturer more than $1 billion) failed to inspire much in the way of imitation (Mitchell, 2002). Moreover, although there have been many terrorist incidents in the world since 2001, all (thus far, at least) have relied on conventional methods.[27]

Interestingly, if chemical and biological attacks are so easy and attractive to terrorists, it is impressive that none have so far been used in Israel. Although there have been plenty of terrorist attacks there, all have used conventional explosives. The science with respect to chemical and biological weaponry has been known with considerable sophistication for more than a century, and that science has become massively more developed over the last hundred years. Yet, the difficulties of controlling and dispersing such substances seem to have persisted.

Actually, it is somewhat strange that so much emphasis has been put on the dangers of high-tech weapons. Some of the anxiety may derive from the post-September 11 anthrax scare even though that terrorist event killed only a few people. The bombings of September 11 by contrast were remarkably low tech, and could have happened long ago: both skyscrapers and airplanes have been around for a century now.

Responding to terrorism

Contrary to the common wisdom, then, it appears that the 9/11 tragedy has changed little except our modes of thinking—to update, and reverse, Einstein's famous dictum. And it is this development, not terrorism itself, that is having the most substantial consequences. People have been led, or have led themselves, to develop what Leif Wenar of the University of Sheffield has aptly labeled a false sense of insecurity. Filmmaker Michael Moore happened to remark on CBS' popular *60 Minutes* on February 16, 2003, that "the chances of any of us dying in a terrorist incident is very, very, very small." His interviewer, Bob Simon, promptly admonished, "But no one sees the world like that." Both statements, remarkably, are true—the first only a bit more so than the second.

As noted, the creation of insecurity, fear, and hysteria was not particularly a goal of Communism, but it is for terrorists. That is, anything that enhances fear effectively gives in to them. Indeed, very often the costs of terrorism come much more from hasty, ill-considered, and overwrought reactions, or overreactions, to it than from anything the terrorists have done. For example, responding to several vicious acts of terrorism apparently perpetrated by Chechens, the Russian government in 1999 reinstituted a war against the breakaway republic that has resulted in far more destruction of Russian (and, of course, Chechen) lives and property than the terrorists ever brought about. Ronald Reagan bombed Libya in 1986 after terrorists linked to that country had blown up a Berlin discotheque, killing two people, a raid that then apparently led to the blowing up of an airliner, killing 270 and toppling the airline company into bankruptcy (Simon, 2001:197–200). When two American embassies in Africa were bombed in 1998, killing over 200 (including a few Americans), Bill Clinton retaliated by bombing a suspect pharmaceutical factory in Sudan, the loss of which may have led to the deaths of tens of thousands of Sudanese over time (Daum, 2001:19). Also bombed were some of Osama bin Laden's terrorist training camps in Afghanistan that caused the Afghan government, the Taliban, to renege on pledges to extradite the troublesome and egoistic bin Laden to Saudi Arabia, made him into an international celebrity, essentially created his al Qaeda organization by turning it into a magnet for funds and recruits, and converted the Taliban from reluctant hosts to allies and partners (Cullison and Higgins, 2002; Burke, 2003:167–168; Coll, 2004:400–402, 414–415; on this process more generally, see Lake, 2002).[28]

The revolutionary, Frantz Fanon, reportedly held that "the aim of terrorism is to terrify." And the inspiration of consequent overreaction seems central to bin Laden's strategy. As it put it mockingly in a videotaped message in 2004, it is "easy for us to provoke and bait. . . . All that we have to do is to send two mujahidin . . . to raise a piece of cloth on which is written al Qaeda in order to make the generals race there to cause America to suffer human, economic, and political losses." His policy, he extravagantly believes, is one of "bleeding America to the point of bankruptcy," and it is one that depends on overreaction by the target: he triumphally points to the fact that the 9/11 terrorist attacks cost al Qaeda $500,000 while the attack and its aftermath inflicted, he claims, a cost of more than $500 billion on the United States.[29]

If this is the plan, terrorists can be defeated simply by not becoming terrified and by resisting the temptation to overreact. The shock and tragedy of 9/11 does demand a focused and dedicated program to confront international terrorism and to attempt to prevent a repetition, of course. But it seems sensible to suggest that part of this reaction should include an effort by politicians, officials, and the media to inform the public reasonably and realistically about the terrorist context instead of playing into the hands of terrorists by effectively seeking to terrify the public. What is needed, then, as one statistician suggests, is some sort of convincing, coherent, informed, and nuanced answer to a central question: "How worried should I be?" Instead, the message, as one concerned Homeland Security official puts it, is "Be scared. Be very, very scared. But go on with your lives" (Gorman, 2003a:1461–1462).

There is at present a great and understandable concern about what would happen if terrorists are able to shoot down an American airliner or two, perhaps with shoulder-fired missiles. Obviously, this would be a major tragedy in the first instance. But the ensuing public reaction to it, many fear, could come close to destroying the industry. It would seem to be reasonable for those with that fear to consider the following: how many airliners would have to crash before flying becomes as dangerous as driving the same distance in an automobile? It turns out that someone has made that calculation. The conclusion is that there would have to be one set of 9/11 crashes a month for the risks to balance out. More generally, they calculate that an American's chance of being killed in one non-stop airline flight is about one in 13 million (even taking the September 11 crashes into account), while to reach that same level of risk when driving on America's safest roads, rural interstate highways, one would have to travel a mere 11.2 miles (Sivak and Flannagan, 2003).[30]

Or there ought to be at least some discussion of the almost completely unaddressed, but seemingly obvious, observation that, in the words of another risk analyst, David Banks, "it seems impossible that the United States will ever again experience takeovers of commercial flights that are then turned into weapons—no pilot will relinquish control, and passengers will fight." The scheme worked in 2001 because the hijackers had the element of surprise working for them: previous airline hijackings had mostly been fairly harmless as hijackers generally landed the planes someplace and released the passengers. The passengers and crew on the fourth plane on September 11 had fragmentary knowledge about what the earlier hijackings that day had led to, and they prevented the plane from reaching its target. This is likely to hold even more for any later attempted hijackings. Nonetheless, notes Banks, "enormous resources are being invested to prevent this remote contingency." There is a distinction, he argues, "between realistic reactions to plausible threats and hyperbolic overreaction to improbable contingencies" (2002:10).

Moreover, any problems caused by radiological, chemical, and perhaps biological weapons are likely to stem far more from the fear and panic they may cause than from the weapons themselves. While a "dirty bomb" might raise radiation 25 percent over background levels in an area and therefore into a range the Environmental Protection Agency officially considers undesirable, there ought to be some discussion about whether that really constitutes "contamination" or indeed much of a danger given the somewhat arbitrary and exceedingly cautious levels declared to be acceptable by the EPA. The potential use of such bombs apparently formed the main concern during the Orange Alert at the end of 2003 (Allison, 2004:56–57; "Dirty Bombs", 2004). But since all the bombs do is raise radiation levels somewhat above normal background levels in a small area, a common recommendation from nuclear scientists and engineers is that those exposed should calmly walk away. But this bit of advice has not been advanced prominently (or even, perhaps, at all) by those in charge. Effectively, therefore, they encourage panic, and, as one nuclear engineer points out, "if you keep telling them you expect them to panic, they will oblige you. And that's what we're doing" (Allison, 2004:8, 59, 220; see also Glanz and Revkin, 2002; Rockwell, 2003).

It seems to me that the efforts against terrorism should be considered more like a campaign against crime than like a war, however much the war imagery may get the juices flowing (see also Howard, 2002). Wars end, but as they are carried out by isolated individuals or by tiny groups at times of their own choosing, terrorism and crime never do. One cannot, therefore, "conquer" terrorism or "bring it to an end." Like crime, one can at best seek to reduce its frequency and destructiveness so that people feel reasonably—but never perfectly—safe from it. Of course, military measures may sometimes be useful in the campaign, as they have proved to be in Afghanistan. But to frame the campaign against terror as a "war" risks the danger of raising unreasonable expectations.[31]

Opportunity costs

At least so far, terrorism is a rather rare and, in appropriate context, not a very destructive phenomenon as argued above. However, the enormous sums of money being spent to deal with this threat have in part been diverted from other, possibly more worthy, endeavors. The budget for the Office of Homeland Security, for example, has now reached nearly $30 billion while state and local governments spend additional billions (see Gorman, 2004a). Some of that money doubtless would have been spent on similar ventures under earlier budgets, and much of it likely has wider benefits than simply securing the country against a rather limited threat. But much of it, as well, has very likely been pulled away from programs that do much good.

Accordingly, three key issues set out by risk analyst Howard Kunreuther require careful discussion (2002:662–663):

> How much should we be willing to pay for a small reduction in probabilities that are already extremely low?
> How much should we be willing to pay for actions that are primarily reassuring, but do little to change the actual risk?
> How can certain measures, such as strengthening the public health system, which provide much broader protection than terrorism, get the attention they deserve?

Or as Banks puts it, "If terrorists force us to redirect resources away from sensible programs and future growth, in order to pursue unachievable but politically popular levels of domestic security, then they have won an important victory that mortgages our future" (2002:10).[32]

Hysteria versus absorption

It would thus seem to be reasonable for someone in authority sometime to do something to explore the probabilities and to explain them to the public—in Kunreuther's words, "More attention needs to be devoted to giving people perspective on the remote likelihood of the terrible consequences they imagine" (2002:663). That would seem to be at least as important as boosting the sale of duct tape, issuing repeated and costly color-coded alerts based on vague and unspecific intelligence, and warning people to beware of Greeks, or just about anybody, bearing almanacs.[33] But we get plenty of official alarmism and almost nothing—*nothing*—about realistic risks and probabilities.

What we need is more pronouncements like the one in a recent book by Senator John McCain and Salter: "Get on the damn elevator! Fly on the damn plane! Calculate the odds of being harmed by a terrorist! It's still about as likely as being swept out to sea by a tidal wave. . . . Suck it up, for crying out loud. You're almost certainly going to be okay. And in the unlikely event you're not, do you really want to spend your last days cowering behind plastic sheets and duct tape? That's not a life worth living, is it?" (2004:35–36).[34]

But admonitions like that are exceedingly rare, almost non-existent. By contrast, what we mostly get is fear-mongering, some of it bordering on hysteria. Some prominent commentators, like David Gergen (2002), argue that the United States has become "vulnerable," even "fragile." Others, like Indiana senator Richard Lugar are given to proclaiming that terrorists armed with weapons of mass destruction present an "existential" threat to the United States,[35] or even, in columnist Charles Krauthammer's view, to "civilization itself" (2004).[36] A recent best-selling book by an anonymous CIA official repeatedly assures us that our "survival" is at stake and that we are engaged in a "war to the death" (Anonymous, 2004:160, 177, 226, 241, 242, 250, 252, 263).[37]

Alarmism reached a kind of pinnacle during the Orange Alert at the end of 2003. At the time Homeland Security czar Tom Ridge was given bravely to declaring that "America is a country that will not be bent by terror. America is a country that will not be broken by fear." Meanwhile, however, General Richard Myers, chairman of the Joint Chiefs of Staff, was assuring a television audience that if terrorists were able to engineer a catastrophic event that killed 10,000 people, they would successfully "do away with our way of life" (Kerr, 2003). The sudden deaths of that many Americans—although representing less than 4/1000ths of 1 percent of the population—would indeed be horrifying and tragic, the greatest one-day disaster the country has suffered since the Civil War. But the only way it could "do away with our way of life" would be if we did that to ourselves in reaction. The process would presumably involve repealing the bill of rights, boarding up all churches, closing down all newspapers and media outlets, burning all books, abandoning English for North Korean, and refusing evermore to consume hamburgers. By such accountings, it is not only the most-feared terrorists who are suicidal—the enemy, in fact, is us.

All societies are "vulnerable" to tiny bands of suicidal fanatics in the sense that it is impossible to prevent every terrorist act. But the United States is hardly "vulnerable" in the sense that it can be toppled by dramatic acts of terrorist destruction, even extreme ones. In fact, the country can readily, if grimly, absorb that kind of damage—as it "absorbs" some 40,000 deaths each year from automobile accidents. As RAND's Bruce Hoffman puts it, "Unfortunately, terrorism is just another fact of modern life. It's something we have to live with" (Gorman, 2003a:1463).

Thus, rather than inducing hysteria, a sensible policy approach to the problem might be to stress that any damage terrorists are able to accomplish likely can be absorbed, and that, while judicious protective and policing measures are sensible, extensive fear and anxiety over what at base could well prove to be a rather limited problem is misplaced, unjustified, and counterproductive.

The role of politicians and the media

This is a difficult challenge, and a problem with getting coherent thinking on the issue is that reporters and politicians mostly find extreme and alarmist possibilities so much more appealing than discussions of broader context, much less of statistical reality. That is, although hysteria and alarmism rarely make much sense, politicians and the media are often naturally drawn to them.

There is no reason to suspect that George W. Bush's concern about terrorism is anything but genuine. However, his approval rating did receive the greatest boost for any president in history in September 2001, and it would be politically unnatural for him not to notice. His chief political adviser, Karl Rove, in fact declared in 2003 that the "war" against terrorism would be central to Bush's reelection campaign the next year (Clines, 2003; Gorman, 2003b:2781). The Democrats, scurrying to keep up, have stumbled all over each other with plans to expend even more of the federal budget on the terrorist threat, such as it is, than President Bush.

This process is hardly new. The preoccupation of the media and of Jimmy Carter's presidency with the hostages taken by Iran in 1979 to the exclusion of almost everything else may look foolish in retrospect, as Carter's Secretary of State, Cyrus Vance, reflects in his memoirs (1983:380; see also Mueller, 1984). But it doubtless appeared to be good politics at the time—Carter's dismal approval rating soared when the hostages were seized.

Since 9/11, the American public has been treated to endless yammering about terrorism on the media. Politicians may feel, correctly, that, given the public concern on the issue, they will lose votes if they appear insensitively to be downplaying the dangers of terrorism (although this fear does not seem to have infected Senator McCain). But the media like to tout that they are devoted to presenting fair and balanced coverage of important public issues. I may have missed it, but I have never heard anyone on the media point out that in every year except 2001 only a few hundred people in the entire world have died as a result of international terrorism.

As has often been noted, the media appear to have a congenital incapacity for dealing with issues of risk and comparative probabilities—except, of course, in the sports and financial sections. But even in their amazingly rare efforts to try, the issue—one that would seem to be absolutely central to any sensible discussion of terrorism and terrorism policy—never goes very far. For example, in 2001 the *Washington Post* published an article by a University of Wisconsin economist that attempted quantitatively to point out how much safer it was to travel by air than by automobile even under the heightened atmosphere of concern inspired by the September attacks. He reports that the article generated a couple of media inquiries, but nothing more. Gregg Easterbrook's cover story in the October 7, 2002 *New Republic* forcefully argued that biological and especially chemical weapons are hardly capable of creating "mass destruction," a perspective relevant not only to concerns about terrorism but also to the drive for war against Iraq that was going on at the time. The *New York Times* asked him to fashion the article into an op-ed piece, but that was the only interest the article generated in the media.

In addition, it should be pointed out that the monied response to 9/11 has created a vast and often well-funded terrorism industry. Its members would be out of business if terrorism were to be back-burnered, and accordingly they have every competitive incentive (and they are nothing if not competitive) to conclude it to be their civic duty to keep the pot boiling.

Moreover, there is more reputational danger in underplaying risks than in exaggerating them. People routinely ridicule futurist H.G. Wells' prediction that the conflict beginning in 1914 would be "the war that will end war," but not his equally confident declaration at the end of World War II that "the end of everything we call life is close at hand" (1968:67). Disproved doomsayers can always claim that caution induced by their warnings prevented the predicted calamity from occurring. (Call it the Y2K effect.) Disproved pollyannas have no such convenient refuge (see also Gorman, 2003a:1464).

Not only are failed predictors of doomsday rarely held to account, but they have proved remarkably agile at creative nuance and extrapolation after failure. Thus, in 2004, the terrorism industry repeatedly insisted that some Big Terrorist Event was likely in connection with (a) the Athens Olympics, (b) the Democratic Party convention in Boston, (c) the Republican convention in New York, (d) the election campaign, and/or (e) the presidential vote in November. When nothing happened (a terrorist wearing kilts did show up to disrupt the marathon in Athens briefly, but this, apparently, did not count), the argument was floated that a taped encyclical issued by bin Laden in late October somehow demonstrated that he was too weak to attack before the election. However, the tape was further taken to suggest that bin Laden was marshalling his resources and that, accordingly, the several months *after* the election had now become especially dangerous (Gorman, 2004b:3534). A notable terrorist attack during that interval would generate hundreds of thousands of news items not to mention a veritable paroxysm of breast-beating by the terrorism industry. The absence of an attack during the same time would likely scarcely be noticed.

It seems sensible to suggest that officials and the media should responsibly assess probabilities and put them in some sort of context (as they do routinely on the sports pages) rather than simply to stress extreme possibilities so much and so exclusively. But that seems unlikely to happen.

Public perceptions

It is easy to blame politicians and the media for the distorted and context-free condition under which terrorism is so often discussed. In many respects, however, that circumstance arises not so much from their own proclivities, but rather from those of their customers. Hysteria and alarmism often sell.

The record with respect to fear about crime, for example, suggests that efforts to deal responsibly with the risks of terrorism will prove difficult. Fear of crime rose notably in the mid-1990s even as statistics were showing it to be in pronounced decline. When David Dinkins, running for reelection as Mayor of New York, pointed to such numbers, he was accused by A.M. Rosenthal of the *New York Times* of hiding behind "trivializing statistics" that "are supposed to convince us that crime is going down" (1993).[38] New Yorkers did eventually come to feel safer from crime, but this was probably less because crime rates actually declined than because of atmospherics such as graffiti, panhandlers, aggressive windshield washers, and the homeless were banished or hidden from view. So it may have made sense in the months after the September 11 attacks to have armed reservists parading menacingly around in airports. It is doubtful that they prevented any terrorist attacks, and pulling them from productive jobs hardly helped the economy. But if they provided people with a sense of security, their presence may have been worth it.

In the end, it is not clear how one can deal with the public's often irrational fears about remote dangers. Some people say they prefer dangerous forms of transportation like the private passenger automobile (the necessary cause of over three million American deaths during the twentieth century) to safe ones like commercial airliners because they feel they have more "control" (see also Applebaum, 2003). But they seem to feel no fear on buses and trains—which actually are a bit more dangerous than airplanes—even without having that sense of control and even though derailing a speeding train or crashing a speeding bus are likely to be much easier than downing an airliner. And people tend to be more alarmed by dramatic fatalities—which the September 11 crashes certainly provided—than by ones that cumulate statistically. Thus, in the United States the 3,000 deaths of September 11 inspire far more grief and fear than the 150,000 deaths from auto accidents that have taken place there since then.

In some respects, fear of terror may be something like playing the lottery except in reverse. The chances of winning the lottery or of dying from terrorism may be microscopic, but for monumental events that are, or seem, random, one can irrelevantly conclude that one's chances are just as good, or bad, as those of anyone else.

The communication of risk, then, is no easy task. There have been many attempts. Some analysts, for example, have calculated the chances that an individual could die over a 50-year period from an astroid impact (1 in 6,000) and used that as a benchmark to compare other risks: tornado (1 in 50,000), airplane crash (1 in 20,000), auto accident (1 in 100) (see also Chapman and Morrison, 1989:ch. 19; Broad, 1991).[39] Whether exercises like that will work is not at all clear, however. Risk analyst Paul Slovic points out that people tend greatly to overestimate the chances of dramatic or sensational causes of death, that realistically informing people about risks sometimes only makes them more frightened, that strong beliefs in this area are very difficult to modify, that a new sort of calamity tends to be taken as a harbinger of future mishaps, that a disaster tends to increase fears not only about that kind of danger but of all kinds, and that people, even professionals, are susceptible to the way risks are expressed—far less likely, for example, to choose radiation therapy if told the chances of death are 32 percent rather than that the chances of survival are 68 percent (1986).[40]

But risk assessment and communication should at least be part of the policy discussion over terrorism, something that may well prove to be a far smaller danger than is popularly portrayed. The public does not seem to be constantly on edge about the threat of terrorism (Gorman, 2003b) any more than it was during the McCarthy era about the threat of internal Communism (Stouffer, 1955: ch. 3). However, the constant unnuanced stoking of fear by politicians and the media is costly, enervating, potentially counterproductive, and unjustified by the facts.

Caveats and conclusions

This discussion should not be taken to suggest that all extreme events prove to be the last in their line or that nothing bad ever happens, of course. At the time, World War I, called the Great War for decades, was the worst war of its type. Yet an even more destructive one followed.

Nor is it to suggest that deep concern about extreme events is unreasonable or necessarily harmful. Although I have expressed some skepticism about their necessity or efficacy, it could be argued that aid and alliances in Western Europe helped to keep the area out of Communist hands, the forceful response in Korea to dissuade the Communists from further direct military probes, anti-Castro efforts in Latin America to prevent further Communist gains there, intervention in the Balkans to contain the conflicts. Thus, efforts to confront rogue states and to reduce the incidence and destructiveness of terrorism are sensible and may be justified.

Moreover, while Aum Shinrikyo and Qaddafi may be under control, al Qaeda and like-minded terrorist groups are unlikely to die out any time soon. Like the Communists, they appear to be in it for the long haul: September 11 marked, after all, their second attempt to destroy the World Trade Center. Much of the current alarm is generated from the knowledge that many of today's terrorists simply want to kill, and kill more or less randomly, for revenge or as an act of what they take to be war. At one time, it was probably safe to conclude that terrorism was committed principally for specific political demands or as a form of political expression, and therefore in the oft-repeated observation of terrorism expert Brian

Jenkins that "terrorists want a lot of people watching, not a lot of people dead" (1975:15). Moreover, the suicidal nature of many attacks, while not new, can be very unsettling because deterring by threatening punishment to the would-be perpetrator becomes impossible. And, of course, terrorism itself will never go away: it has always existed and always will.

A central issue, however, is whether such spectacularly destructive terrorist acts will become commonplace. The record suggests that terrorists will find it difficult to match or top them and that terrorism's destructiveness, despite the creative visions of worst-case scenarioists, may well fail to escalate dramatically. Moreover, the extreme destruction of September 11 has raised the bar, possibly reducing the impact of less damaging attacks.

In the meantime, hysteria and hysterical overreaction about terrorism and rogue states are hardly required and can be costly and counterproductive. As during the Cold War, there are uncertainties and risks out there, and, as then, plenty of dangers and threats. But none of these is existential. The sky, as it happens, never actually fell during the Cold War, and it is unlikely to do so now.

Notes

1 Thus, Albert Wohlstetter's highly influential thesis that the balance of power was "delicate" rested on the assumption that the Soviet enemy could potentially come to be as clever, lucky, diabolical, and desperate as Japan was in 1941, a thesis conveniently embellished by recommendations for his wife's excellent book on Pearl Harbor (Wohlstetter (1959), and seminars conducted by him at UCLA in the early 1960s; Wohlstetter (1962)).

2 For an able analysis and discussion, see Gould-Davies (1999).

3 As Taubman points out, Stalin was referring to wars *between* capitalist states, something often neglected when the West examined this statement. Nevertheless, even taking that into account, the declaration clearly remains profoundly threatening to capitalist states. On this issue more generally, see Burin (1963).

4 For the forceful argument that the sentiments reflected real ideological zeal and importantly affected policy during the Cold War, see Macdonald (1995/96).

5 *New York Times*, December 9, 1988:A18.

6 *Public Papers of the Presidents of the United States: George Bush, 1989* (Washington, DC: United States Government Printing Office, 1990):602; see also p. 541.

7 On this issue, see in particular Johnson (1994).

8 On the Soviet Union's apparent economic strength at the time, see Yergin and Stanislaw (1998:22, 272).

9 There was also a recurring pessimism that democracy was doomed or at least stagnated. In 1975, the usually ebullient Daniel Patrick Moynihan proclaimed that democracy "increasingly tends to the condition of monarchy in the nineteenth century: a holdover form of government, one which persists in isolated or peculiar places here and there" but "which has simply no relevance to the future" (1975:6). In a similar mood, Germany's Willy Brandt was reported to believe at the time that "Western Europe has only 20 or 30 more years of democracy left in it; after that it will slide, engineless and rudderless, under the surrounding sea of dictatorship" (quoted, Crozier, Huntington, and Watanuki, 1975:2). In 1984, in the midst of what he was later to label the "third wave" of democratization, Samuel Huntington looked to the future and essentially concluded that democracy could only emerge through economic development or through force: "with a few exceptions, the prospects for the extension of democracy to

other societies are not great. These prospects would improve significantly *only* if there were major discontinuities in current trends—such as if, for instance, the economic development of the Third World were to proceed at a much faster rate and to have a far more positive impact on democratic development than it has had so far, or if the United States reestablished a hegemonic position in the world comparable to that which it had in the 1940s and 1950s. In the absence of developments such as these, a significant increase in the number of democratic regimes in the world is unlikely" (1984:218, emphasis added). Similarly, Robert Dahl concluded in 1971 that, "In the future as in the past," democracy is "more likely to result from rather slow evolutionary processes" and "the transformation of hegemonic regimes" into democracies "is likely to remain a slow process, measured in generations" (1971:45, 47). In early 1989, on the brink of a major expansion of democracy as the Soviet empire collapsed, he concluded that "it would be surprising" if the proportion of the countries in the world that are democratic "were to change greatly over the next twenty years" (1989:264). And in late 1993, economist Robert Barro crisply applied an economic model of democratic development to South Africa and came to a decisive conclusion: "Considering the country's level and distribution of income, the ethnic divisions, and the political and economic experiences of most of the countries of Sub-Sahara Africa, this event would perhaps be the greatest political accomplishment in human history. To put it another way, it's not going to happen." When that country unobligingly became a democracy a few months later, an unbent Barro predicted that "The political changes in South Africa in 1994 have probably already overshot the mark, and a substantial decline of political freedom is likely after this year."

10 Charles Wolf and his colleagues at the RAND Corporation (1983) estimated that the cost of the Soviet empire (excluding the costs of maintaining troops in East Europe, but including the costs of the war in Afghanistan) rose enormously between 1971 and 1980 from about 1 percent of its Gross National Product to nearly 3 percent when measured in dollars, or from under 2 percent to about 7 percent when measured in rubles. (By comparison, insofar as the United States could be said to have had a comparable empire, the costs were less than one half of 1 percent of its Gross National Product.)

11 However, it does not follow that economic and social travail necessarily lead to a mellowing of ideology. Leaders, in this case Gorbachev, had to *choose* that policy route. Faced with the same dilemmas, a conservative leader might have stuck to the faith while suffering gradual decline (like the Ottoman empire) or one might have adopted more modest reforms to maintain the essential quality of the system and the privileges of its well-entrenched elite (Rush, 1993; see also Checkel, 1997; English, 2000; Mueller, 2004–05).

12 For the argument that the world was not at all on the "brink" during the Cuban Missile Crisis, see Mueller (1989:152–155). See also Taubman (2003:563, 566–567, 573).

13 The concept of economic war comes close to being oxymoronic. There are times when it may make some sense (as when the world coordinated to embargo Iraq in 1990), but war is substantially zero (or negative) sum while economic exchange, although not always fully fair or equal, is generally positive sum—both parties gain. See Jervis (1993:57–58).

14 On this issue, see Halper and Clarke (2004). See also Johnson (1994:ch. 6).

15 Saddam was so afraid of his own army that he would not allow it to bring heavy weapons anywhere near Baghdad out of fear that regular troops might turn and use it against his government (O'Kane, 1998). On the monumental inadequacy and incompetence of the Iraq military and its leadership during the 2003 war, see Wilson (2003); Zucchino (2003); Shanker (2004). For the pre-war argument that Iraq presented little threat, see Mearsheimer and Walt (2003); Mueller (with Lindsey) (2003). On threat exaggeration in the runup to the Iraq War, see Kaufmann (2004). Although Haiti was never elevated to "rogue state" status, President George H. W. Bush did assert that an anti-democratic coup there in 1991 somehow managed to pose "an unusual and

extraordinary threat to the national security, foreign policy and economy of the United States," a phrase his successor Bill Clinton chose to repeat when sending troops to set things right there in 1994 (*Washington Post*, September 16, 1994:A31). When what passed for democracy crumbled again in Haiti a decade later, however, the administration of Bush's son scarcely noticed.

16 For an excellent overview of these issues, see Easterbrook (2002). See also Panofsky (1998); Mueller and Mueller (1999:45–47); Mueller and Mueller (2000:166–168).

17 On the slowness of the proliferation process more generally, see Mueller (1967, 1998); Meyer (1984); Graham (1991); Reiss (1995); Paul (2000).

18 OTA (1993:60); Williams and Wallace (1989:ch. 6); Christopher et al. (1997:413); Blumenthal and Miller (1999:A10). In 1979, there was an accidental release of biological agents in the Soviet Union that killed under 100 people, and also an anthrax outbreak in Rhodesia that killed 79 and may have been deliberately caused: "Plague War," Frontline (PBS television), 13 October 1998.

19 On the rise of the sentiment that killing by gas is peculiarly wicked and immoral (as opposed to killing by bullets and shrapnel), see Brown (1968); Price (1997).

20 For a recognition of this point, see OTA (1993:9); also 46. See also Betts (1998: 30–31); Panofsky (1998).

21 OTA (1993:54). Another estimate is that some 300 kg of Sarin delivered under ideal circumstances might kill between 200 and 3,000, a figure that drops by 90 percent if there is civil defense: Fetter (1991:22).

22 McNaugher (1990:19n). For the United States, 2 percent of gas casualties died while 24 percent of those wounded by other weapons died. The rates for Germany were 2.9 and 43 percent, and for the British they were 3.3 and 36.6 percent. Overall, the estimates are that there were 1,009,038 gas casualties in the war, of whom 78,390 (7.7 percent) died. Gas fatalities were suffered very disproportionately by the Russians who were ill-protected against gas. However, even taking that into consideration, their ratio of gas deaths to total gas casualties, 11.7 percent, is so out of line with those found on the western front that it seems likely that the number of gas fatalities is exaggerated (Gilchrist, 1928:7–8, 48).

23 Since that war, gas was apparently used in rather limited amounts in the 1930s by Italy in Ethiopia and by Japan in China, as well as by Egypt in the civil war in Yemen in the mid-1960s and during the Iran–Iraq War of 1980–1988 (Brown, 1968:185n; Price, 1997:ch.5, 6; McNaugher, 1990; Fetter, 1991:15). In 1988, during the Iran–Iraq War, there was a chemical attack, apparently by Iraqi forces, on Halabja, an Iraqi town that had been the site of considerable battles between Iranians, Kurds working on their side, and Iraqis. It is said that 5,000 people were killed by chemical munitions dropped from a single airplane during a single pass in daylight (see, for example, Mackey, 2002:262). There are a number of problems with this assessment. To begin with, attacks on the city took place over several days and involved explosive munitions as well, and there is a possible confusion over deaths caused by chemical weapons and those caused by other means. Additionally, all the reports from journalists who were taken to the town by the Iranians shortly after the attack indicate that they saw at most "hundreds" of bodies, and, although some of them report the 5,000 figure, this number is consistently identified as coming from Iranian authorities who obviously had a great incentive to exaggerate. Moreover, the Iranians apparently said that an additional 5,000 were wounded by the chemical weapons when one would expect that an attack killing 5,000 would have injured far more than that. A Human Rights Watch report on the events has an appendix in which other Iraqi chemical attacks in Kurdish areas are evaluated; in two of these attacks it is suggested that 300 or 400 might have been killed, while all the other estimates are under 100, most under 20 (1995:262–264).

24 Toilet figures: Stossel (2004:77). More generally, see Chapman and Harris (2002).

25 See also Mueller (2002b, c, 2003). By contrast, in 2004 Charles Krauthammer characterized the post-9/11 period as "three years in which, contrary to every expectation and

prediction, the second shoe never dropped" (2004) and Allison noted that "in the weeks and months following 9/11, the American national security community focused on what was called the question of the 'second shoe.' No one believed that the attacks on the World Trade Center and the Pentagon were an isolated occurrence" (2004:6).

26 And millions of passengers who checked bags at hotels and retrieved them before heading to the airport have routinely lied to an airline agent when answering the point-lessly obligatory question about whether their luggage had at all times been in their possession.

27 On the preference of terrorists for weapons that they know and understand, see Rapoport (1999:51).

28 Reactions to terrorism have also often led to massive persecution. The Jewish pogroms in Russia at the end of the nineteenth century, for instance, were impelled in major part because Jews were notable in terrorist movements at the time (Rapoport, 2004:68). On the often deadly and indiscriminant overreaction to anarchist terrorism in the United States and elsewhere, see Jensen (2002).

29 Richard Betts estimates the costs at under $1 million and more than $100 billion, respectively (2002:27).

30 Three years after September 2001, domestic airline flights in the United States were still 7 percent below their pre-9/11 levels (*Financial Times*, September 14, 2004:8). During that period, some 120,000 Americans died in automobile accidents. If a small percentage of these deaths occurred to people who were driving because they feared to fly, the number of Americans who died in overreaction to 9/11 could well surpass the number who were killed by the terrorists on that terrible day. One study, in fact, has concluded that over 1,000 people died this way in 2001 between September 11 and December 31 (Sivak and Flannagan, 2004).

31 The war imagery also suggests that people should be asked somehow to make sacri-fices. This popular conclusion is at least partly fanciful. Few Americans except those directly involved in the wars in Korea or Vietnam really made much of a sacrifice, and, although there were inconveniences on the homefront during World War II, consumer spending by the Greatest Generation generally surged (Mueller, 1989:83). A goal of terrorism presumably is to hamper the economy, and therefore the best response to it, hardly much of a "sacrifice," would be to go out and buy a refrigerator or to take an airplane to a vacation resort. The war imagery suggests we should be cutting back; but cutting back actually helps the terrorists.

32 Roger Congleton calculates that measures that effectively require people to spend an additional half-hour in airports cost the economy $15 billion per year; by contrast, total airline profits in the 1990s never exceeded $5.5 billion per year (2002:62).

33 On the almanac menace, see Eggen (2003).

34 The imperatives of full disclosure require me to report that the ellipses in that statement conceal the following remarkable assertion: "Watch the terrorist alert and go outside again when it falls below yellow." Since the ever-watchful and ever-cautious Depart-ment of Homeland Security seems unlikely *ever* to lower the threat level below yellow, McCain's admonition seems effectively to contradict the spirit in the rest of the passage by encouraging everyone to cower inside for the rest of their lives. An email inquiring about this curiosity was sent to Senator McCain's office in August, 2004, but it has yet to generate a reply.

35 *Fox News Sunday*, June 15, 2003; see also Krauthammer (2002/03:9).

36 The threat to Israel from terrorism and from its reaction (or overreaction) to the internal terrorist challenge, however, could conceivably be existential, and this is perhaps what Krauthammer means by "civilization." See Fukuyama (2004:65).

37 One of the book's many hysterical passages runs: "To secure as much of our way of life as possible, we will have to use military force in the way Americans used it on the fields of Virginia and Georgia, in France and on the Pacific islands, and from skies over Tokyo

and Dresden. Progress will be measured by the pace of killing and, yes, by body counts. Not the fatuous body counts of Vietnam, but precise counts that will run to extremely large numbers. The piles of dead will include as many or more civilians as combatants because our enemies wear no uniforms. Killing in large number is not enough to defeat our Muslim foes. With killing must come a Sherman-like razing of infrastructure. Roads and irrigation systems; bridges, power plants, and crops in the field; fertilizer plants and grain mills—all these and more will need to be destroyed to deny the enemy its support base. Land mines, moreover, will be massively reintroduced to seal borders and mountain passes too long, high, or numerous to close with U.S. soldiers. As noted, such actions will yield large civilian casualties, displaced populations, and refugee flows." In the acknowledgments, the author thanks Ms. Christina Davidson, his editor, "who labored mightily to delete from the text excess vitriol" (Anonymous, 2004: xiii, 241–242). Perhaps Ms. Davidson should have labored just a bit more mightily.

38 For data showing that crime peaked in New York in 1990 and declined steadily thereafter, see *New York Times*, February 19, 1998:A16. For a discussion of the fear of crime, see Warr (2000).

39 In recent correspondence, astronomer Alan W. Harris suggests that on further consideration a number around one in 50,000 or so is probably more appropriate than one in 6,000. On the issue, see also Easterbrook (2003).

40 It has also been found that even health professionals are considerably less likely to recommend discharging a mental patient when the odds the patient will commit violence are expressed as 20 out of 100 than when they are expressed as 20 percent or two chances in 10 (Slovic, Monahan, and MacGregor, 2000:288).

References

Allison, G. (2004) *Nuclear Terrorism: The Ultimate Preventable Catastrophe*. New York: Times Books.

Anonymous. (2004) *Imperial Hubris: Why the West Is Losing the War on Terror*. Dulles, VA: Brassey's.

Applebaum, A. (2003) "Finding Things to Fear." *Washington Post*, September 24.

Banks, D. L. (2002) "Statistics for Homeland Defense." *Chance* 15(1):8–10.

Barro, R. J. (1993) "Pushing Democracy Is No Key to Prosperity." *Wall Street Journal*, December 14.

Barro, R. J. (1994) "Democracy: A Recipe for Growth?" *Wall Street Journal*, December 1.

Betts, R. K. (1998) "The New Threat of Mass Destruction." *Foreign Affairs* 77(1):6–41.

Betts, R. K. (2002) "The Soft Underbelly of American Primacy: Tactical Advantages of Terror." *Political Science Quarterly* 117:19–36.

bin Laden, O. (2004) Full transcript of bin Laden's speech. ⟨http://english.aljazeera.net/NR/exeres/79C6AF22-98FB-4A1C-B21F-2BC36E87F61F.html⟩ (November 2, 2004).

Blumenthal, R., and J. Miller (1999) "Japanese Germ-War Atrocities: A Half-Century of Stonewalling the World." *New York Times*, March 4.

Boyle, F. A. (1985) *World Politics and International Law*. Durham, NC: Duke University Press.

Breslauer, G. W. (1987) "Ideology and Learning in Soviet Third World Policy." *World Politics* 39:429–448.

Brezinski, Z. (1993) *Out of Control: Global Turmoil on the Eve of the 21st Century*. New York: Scribner's.

Broad, W. J. (1991) "Asteroids, a Menace to Early Life, Could Still Strike the Earth." *New York Times*, June 18.

Broad, W. J. (1998) "How Japan Germ Terror Alerted World." *New York Times*, May 26.

Broad, W. J., and J. Miller (1998) "Iraq's Deadliest Arms: Puzzles Breed Fears." *New York Times*, February 16.

Brodie, B. (1973) *War and Politics*. New York: Macmillan.

Brodie, B. (1978) "The Development of Nuclear Strategy." *International Security* **2**(4):65–83.

Brown, F. J. (1968) *Chemical Warfare: A Study in Restraints*. Princeton, NJ: Princeton University Press.

Burin, F. S. (1963) "The Communist Doctrine of the Inevitability of War." *American Political Science Review* **57**(2):334–354.

Burke, J. (2003) *Al-Qaeda: Casting a Shadow of Terror*. New York: Tauris.

Chapman, C., and A. W. Harris (2002) "A Skeptical Look at September 11th." *Skeptical Inquirer* (September/October):29–34.

Chapman, C., and D. Morrison (1989) *Cosmic Catastrophes*. New York: Plenum Press.

Checkel, J. T. (1997) *Ideas and International Political Change: Soviet/Russian Behavior and the End of the Cold War*. New Haven, CT: Yale University Press.

Christopher, G. W., T. J. Cieslak, J. A. Pavlin, and E. M. Eitzen Jr. (1997) "Biological Warfare: A Historical Perspective." *JAMA* **278**(5):412–417.

Clines, F. X. (2003) "Karl Rove's Campaign Strategy Seems Evident: It's the Terror, Stupid." *New York Times*, May 10.

Coll, S. (2004) *Ghost Wars: The Secret History of the CIA, Afghanistan, and bin Laden, from the Soviet Invasion to September 10, 2001*. New York: Penguin.

Collier, P. (2000) "Doing Well out of War: An Economic Perspective." In *Greed and Grievance: Economic Agendas in Civil Wars*, edited by M. Berdal and D. M. Malone, pp. 91–111. Boulder, CO: Lynne Rienner.

Congleton, R. D. (2002) "Terrorism, Interest—Group Politics, and Public Policy." *Independent Review* (Summer):47–67.

Crozier, M., S. P. Huntington, and J. Watanuki, eds. (1975) *The Crisis of Democracy*. New York: York University Press.

Cullison, A., and A. Higgins (2002) "Strained Alliance: Al Qaeda's Sour Days in Afghanistan." *Wall Street Journal*, August 2.

Dahl, R. A. (1971) *Polyarchy*. New Haven, CT: Yale University Press.

Dahl, R. A. (1989) *Democracy and Its Critics*. New Haven, CT: Yale University Press.

Daum, W. (2001) "Universalism and the West: An Agenda for Understanding." *Harvard International Review* (Summer):19–23.

"Dirty Bombs" (2004) " 'Dirty Bombs' were New Year's Worry." *USA Today*, January 8.

Djilas, M. (1962) *Conversations with Stalin*. New York: Harcourt Brace.

Easterbook, G. (2002) "Term Limits: The Meaninglessness of WMD." *New Republic*, October 7.

Easterbook, G. (2003) "We're All Gonna Die." *Wired*, July.

Edmonds, J. E., and R. Maxwell-Hyslop, eds. (1947) *Military Operations: France and Belgium, 1918*, Vol. 5. London: HMSO.

Eggen, D. (2003) "Almanacs May Be Tool For Terrorists, FBI Says." *Washington Post*, December 30.

Einstein, A. (1960) *Einstein on Peace*, edited by O. Nathan and H. Norden. New York: Simon and Schuster.

English, R. D. (2000) *Russia and the Idea of the West: Gorbachev, Intellectuals, and the End of the Cold War*. New York: Columbia University Press.

Eriksson, M., P. Wallensteen, and M. Stollenberg (2003) "Armed Conflict." *Journal of Peace Research* **40**:593–607.

Fallows, J. (1994/95) "The Panic Gap: Reactions to North Korea's Bomb." *National Interest* (Winter): 40–45.

Fearon, J. D., and D. Laitin (2003) "Ethnicity, Insurgency, and Civil War." *American Political Science Review* **97**:75–90.

Fetter, S. (1991) "Ballistic Missiles and Weapons of Mass Destruction: What is the Threat?" *International Security* **16**(1):5–42.

Fukuyama, F. (2004) "The Neoconservative Moment." *National Interest* (Summer): 57–68.

Gaddis, J. L. (1982) *Strategies of Containment*. New York: Oxford University Press.

Gaddis, J. L. (1987) *The Long Peace: Inquiries Into the History of the Cold War*. New York: Oxford University Press.

Gates, R. M. (1993) "No Time to Disarm." *Wall Street Journal*, August 23.

Gellman, B. (1984) *Contending with Kennan: Toward a Philosophy of American Power*. New York: Praeger.

Gergen, D. (2002) "A Fragile Time for Globalism." *U.S. News and World Report*, February 11.

Gilchrist, H. L. (1928) *A Comparative Study of World War Casualties from Gas and Other Weapons*. Edgewood Arsenal, MD: Chemical Warfare School.

Glanz, J., and A. C. Revkin (2002) "Some See Panic As Main Effect Of Dirty Bombs." *New York Times*, March 7.

Gorman, S. (2003a) "Fear Factor." *National Journal*, May 10.

Gorman, S. (2003b) "Shaken, Not Stirred." *National Journal*, September 13.

Gorman, S. (2004a) "On Guard, But How Well?" *National Journal*, March 5.

Gorman, S. (2004b) "War on Terror, Phase Two." *National Journal*, November 20.

Gould-Davies, N. (1999) "Rethinking the Role of Ideology in International Politics during the Cold War." *Journal of Cold War Studies* **1**(1):90–109.

Graham, T. W. (1991) "Winning the Nonproliferation Battle." *Arms Control Today* (September):8–13.

Gwertzman, B. (1984) "Tougher Policy Against Terror Is Seen Gaining." *New York Times*, October 28.

Halberstam, D. (1965) *The Making of a Quagmire*. New York: Random House.

Halberstam, D. (1988) *The Making of a Quagmire*, revised ed. New York: Knopf.

Halper, S., and J. Clarke (2004) *America Alone: The Neo-Conservatives and the Global Order*. New York: Cambridge University Press.

Halperin, M. H. (1987) *Nuclear Fallacy: Dispelling the Myth of Nuclear Strategy*. Cambridge, MA: Ballinger.

Hamburg, D. A. (1993) *Preventing Contemporary Intergroup Violence*. New York: Carnegie Corporation of New York.

Harrison, S. S. (2002) *Korean Endgame: A Strategy for Reunification and U.S. Disengagement*. Princeton, NJ: Princeton University Press.

Hilsman, R. (1967) *To Move a Nation: The Politics of Foreign Policy in the Administration of John F. Kennedy*. New York: Delta.

Historicus [G. A. Morgan] (1949) "Stalin on Revolution." *Foreign Affairs* **27**(2):175–214.

Hoagland, J. (2004) "In Europe, The Enemy Within." *Washington Post*, February 26.

Hoffmann, S. (1992) "Delusions of World Order." *New York Review of Books*, April 9.

Howard, M. (2002) "What's in a Name?" *Foreign Affairs* **81**(1):8–13.

Hudson, G. F., R. Lowenthal, and R. MacFarquhar, eds. (1961) *The Sino–Soviet Dispute*. New York: Praeger.

Human Rights Watch/Middle East. (1995) *Iraq's Crime of Genocide: The Anfal Campaign Against the Kurds*. New Haven, CT: Yale University Press.

Huntington, S. P. (1984) "Will More Countries Become Democratic?" *Political Science Quarterly* **99**:193–218.

Huntington, S. P. (1991) "America's Changing Strategic Interests." *Survival* (January/ February): 3–17.

Huntington, S. P. (1993a) "Why International Primacy Matters." *International Security* **17**(4):68–83.

Huntington, S. P. (1993b) "The Clash of Civilizations?" *Foreign Affairs* **72**(3):22–49.

Huntington, S. P. (1993c) "If Not Civilizations, What?" *Foreign Affairs* **72**(5):186–194.

Jenkins, B. M. (1975) "International Terrorism: A New Mode of Conflict." In *International Terrorism and World Security*, edited by D. Carlton and C. Schaerf, pp. 13–49. New York: Wiley.

Jensen, R. B. (2002) "The United States, International Policing and the War against Anarchist Terrorism, 1900–1991." *Terrorism and Political Violence* **13**(1):15–46.

Jervis, R. (1976) *Perception and Misperception in International Politics*. Princeton, NJ: Princeton University Press.

Jervis, R. (1993) "International Primacy: Is the Game Worth the Candle?" *International Security* **17**(4):52–67.

Job, C. (1993) "Yugoslavia's Ethnic Furies." *Foreign Policy* (June):52–74.

Johnson, R. H. (1994) *Improbable Dangers: U.S. Conceptions of Threat in the Cold War and After*. New York: St. Martin's.

Kahn, H. (1960) *On Thermonuclear War*. Princeton, NJ: Princeton University Press.

Kang, D. C. (2003) "International Relations Theory and the Second Korean War." *International Studies Quarterly* **47**:301–324.

Kaplan, R. D. (1991) "History's Cauldron." *Atlantic* (June):93–104.

Kaplan, R. D. (1993a) *Balkan Ghosts: A Journey Through History*. New York: St. Martin's.

Kaplan, R. D. (1993b) "A Reader's Guide to the Balkans." *New York Times Book Review*, April 18.

Kaufmann, C. (2004) "Threat Inflation and the Failure of the Marketplace of Ideas: The Selling of the Iraq War." *International Security* **29**(1):5–48.

Kennan, G. F. [X]. (1947) "The Sources of Soviet Conduct." *Foreign Affairs* **25**(4):566–582.

Kerr, J. C. (2003) "Terror Threat Level Raised to Orange." *Associated Press*, December 21.

Kober, S. (1993) "Revolutions Gone Bad." *Foreign Policy* (Summer):63–83.

Kraus, S., ed. (1962) *The Great Debates: Kennedy vs. Nixon, 1960*. Bloomington: University of Indiana Press.

Krauthammer, C. (2002/03) "The Unipolar Moment Revisited." *National Interest* (Winter):5–17.

Krauthammer, C. (2004) "Blixful Amnesia." *Washington Post*, July 9.

Kunreuther, H. (2002) "Risk Analysis and Risk Management in an Uncertain World." *Risk Analysis* **22**:655–664.

Lake, D. A. (2002) "Rational Extremism: Understanding Terrorism in the Twenty-first Century." *Dialog–IO* (Spring):15–29.

Layne, C. (1993) "The Unipolar Illusion: Why New Great Powers Will Rise." *International Security* **17**(4):5–51.

Leffler, M. P. (1994) *The Specter of Communism: The United States and the Origins of the Cold War, 1917–1953*. New York, NY: Hill and Wang.

Macdonald, D. J. (1995/96) "Communist Bloc Expansion in the Early Cold War: Challenging Realism, Refuting Revisionism." *International Security* **20**(3):152–188.

Mackey, S. (2002) *The Reckoning: Iraq and the Legacy of Saddam Hussein.* New York: Norton.

McCain, J., and M. Salter (2004) *Why Courage Matters: The Way to a Braver Life.* New York: Random House.

McNaugher, T. L. (1990) "Ballistic Missiles and Chemical Weapons: The Legacy of the Iran–Iraq War." *International Security* **15**(2):5–34.

McNeill, W. H. (1982) *The Pursuit of Power: Technology, Armed Force, and Society since A.D. 1000.* Chicago: University of Chicago Press.

Mearsheimer, J. J. (1990) "Back to the Future: Instability in Europe after the Cold War." *International Security* **15**(1):5–56.

Mearsheimer, J. J., and S. M. Walt (2003) "Iraq: An Unnecessary War." *Foreign Policy* (January/ February):50–59.

Meselson, M. (1991) "The Myth of Chemical Superweapons." *Bulletin of the Atomic Scientists* (April):12–15.

Meselson, M. (1995) "How Serious is the Biological Weapons Threat?" Massachusetts Institute of Technology: Defense & Arms Control Studies Program Seminar, November 29.

Meyer, S. M. (1984) *The Dynamics of Nuclear Proliferation.* Chicago: University of Chicago Press.

Mitchell, M. L. (2002) "The Impact of External Parties on Brand-Name Capital: The 1982 Tylenol Poisonings and Subsequent Cases." In *Risk, Media and Stigma: Understanding Public Challenges to Modern Science and Technology*, edited by J. Flynn, P. Slovic, and H. Kunreuther, pp. 203–217. London: Earthscan.

Moynihan, D. P. (1975) "The American Experiment." *Public Interest* (Fall):4–8.

Moynihan, D. P. (1993) *Pandaemonium: Ethnicity in International Politics.* New York: Oxford University Press.

Mueller, J. (1967) "Incentives for Restraint: Canada as a Nonnuclear Power." *Orbis* **11**:864–884.

Mueller, J. (1979) "Public Expectations of War During the Cold War." *American Journal of Political Science* **23**:301–329.

Mueller, J. (1984) "Lessons Learned Five Years After the Hostage Nightmare." *Wall Street Journal*, November 6.

Mueller, J. (1987) "Presidents and Terrorists Should Not Mix." *Wall Street Journal*, March 31.

Mueller, J. (1989) *Retreat from Doomsday: The Obsolescence of Major War.* New York: Basic Books.

Mueller, J. (1994) *Policy and Opinion in the Gulf War.* Chicago: University of Chicago Press.

Mueller, J. (1995) *Quiet Cataclysm: Reflections on the Recent Transformation of World Politics.* New York: HarperCollins.

Mueller, J. (1996) "Democracy, Capitalism and the End of Transition." In *Post-Communism: Four Views*, edited by M. Mandelbaum, pp. 102–167. New York: Council on Foreign Relations.

Mueller, J. (1998) "The Escalating Irrelevance of Nuclear Weapons." In *The Absolute Weapon Revisited: Nuclear Arms and the Emerging International Order*, edited by T. V. Paul, R. J. Harknett, and J. J. Wirtz, pp. 73–98. Ann Arbor: University of Michigan Press.

Mueller, J. (2000a) "The Banality of 'Ethnic War.' " *International Security* **25**(1):42–70.

Mueller, J. (2000b) *The Banality of "Ethnic War": Yugoslavia and Rwanda*, Paper presented at the Annual Meeting of the American Political Science Association, Washington, DC, September 2. Available at ⟨http://psweb.sbs.ohio-state.edu/faculty/jmueller/links⟩.

Mueller, J. (2002a) "American Foreign Policy and Public Opinion in a New Era: Eleven Propositions." In *Understanding Public Opinion*, edited by B. Norrander and C. Wilcox, pp. 49–72. Washington, DC: CQ Press.

Mueller, J. (2002b) "Harbinger or Aberration? A 9/11 Provocation." *National Interest* (Fall): 45–50.

Mueller, J. (2002c) "False Alarms." *Washington Post*, September 22.

Mueller, J. (2003) "Blip or Step Function?" Paper presented at the Annual Convention of the International Studies Association, Portland, OR, February 27. Available at ⟨http://psweb.sbs.ohio-state.edu/faculty/jmueller/links⟩.

Mueller, J. (2004) *The Remnants of War*. Ithaca, NY: Cornell University Press.

Mueller, J. (2004–05) "What Was the Cold War About? Evidence from Its Ending." *Political Science Quarterly* **119**(4):609–631.

Mueller, J. (with B. Lindsey) (2003) "Should We Invade Iraq?" *Reason* (January):40–48. Available at ⟨http://www.reason.com/0301/fe.jm.should.shtml⟩.

Mueller, J., and K. Mueller (1999) "Sanctions of Mass Destruction." *Foreign Affairs* **78**(3): 43–53.

Mueller, J., and K. Mueller (2000) "The Methodology of Mass Destruction: Assessing Threats in the New World Order." In *Preventing the Use of Weapons of Mass Destruction*, edited by E. Herring, pp. 163–187. London: Frank Cass.

National Planning Association. (1958) *1970 Without Arms Control*. Washington, DC: National Planning Association.

Office of Technology Assessment, United States Congress. (1993) *Proliferation of Weapons of Mass Destruction: Assessing the Risks, OTA-559, August*. Washington, DC: U.S. Government Printing Office.

O'Kane, M. (1998) "Saddam Wields Terror—and Feigns Respect." *Guardian*, November 25.

Panofsky, W. K. H. (1998) "Dismantling the Concept of 'Weapons of Mass Destruction'." *Arms Control Today*, April.

Paul, T. V. (2000) *Power Versus Prudence: Why Nationals Forgo Nuclear Weapons*. Montreal: McGill-Queen's University Press.

President's Commission on National Goals. (1960) *Goals for Americans*. New York: Prentice-Hall.

Price, R. M. (1997) *The Chemical Weapons Taboo*. Ithaca, NY: Cornell University Press.

Rapoport, D. C. (1999) "Terrorists and Weapons of the Apocalypse." *National Security Studies Quarterly* **5**(1):49–67.

Rapoport, D. C. (2004) "The Four Waves of Modern Terrorism." In *Attacking Terrorism: Elements of a Grand Strategy*, edited by A. Kurth Cronin and J. M. Ludes, pp. 46–73. Washington, DC: Georgetown University Press.

Reeves, R. (1993) *President Kennedy: Profile of Power*. New York: Simon & Schuster.

Reiss, M. (1995) *Bridled Ambition: Why Countries Constrain Their Nuclear Capabilities*. Washington, DC: Woodrow Wilson Center Press.

Roberts, B. (1992) *Chemical Disarmament and International Security. Adelphi Paper 267*. London: International Institute for Strategic Studies.

Rockwell, T. (2003) "Radiation Chicken Little." *Washington Post*, September 16.

Rosenthal, A. M. (1993) "New York to Clinton." *New York Times*, October 1.

Rush, M. (1993) "Fortune and Fate." *National Interest* (Spring):19–25.

Russett, B. (1972) *No Clear and Present Danger: A Skeptical View of the United States' Entry into World War II*. New York: Harper and Row.

Russett, B. (1983) *The Prisoners of Insecurity*. San Francisco: Freeman.

Schell, J. (1982) *The Fate of the Earth*. New York: Knopf.

Schilling, W. R. (1965) "Surprise Attack, Death, and War." *Journal of Conflict Resolution* **9**:285–290.

Shanker, T. (2004) "Regime Thought War Unlikely Iraqis Tell U.S." *New York Times*, February 12.

Sheehan, N. (1964) "Much Is At Stake in Southeast Asian Struggle." *New York Times*, August 16.

Shulman, M. D. (1963) *Stalin's Foreign Policy Reappraised*. New York: Atheneum.

Sigal, L. V. (1998) *Disarming Strangers: Nuclear Diplomacy with North Korea*. Princeton, NJ: Princeton University Press.

Simon, J. D. (2001) *The Terrorist Trap: America's Experience with Terrorism*, 2nd ed. Bloomington: Indiana University Press.

Sivak, M., and M. J. Flannagan (2003) "Flying and Driving after the September 11 Attacks." *American Scientist* **91**(1):6–9.

Sivak, M., and M. J. Flannagan (2004) "Consequences for Road Traffic Fatalities of the Reduction in Flying Following September 11." *Transportation Research Part F*: 301–305.

Slovic, P. (1986) "Informing and Educating the Public about Risk." *Risk Analysis* **6**:403–415.

Slovic, P., J. Monahan, and D. G. MacGregor (2000) "Violence Risk Assessment and Risk Communication: The Effects of Using Actual Cases, Providing Instruction, and Employing Probability Versus Frequency Formats." *Law and Human Behavior* **24**(3):271–296.

Snow, C. P. (1961) "The Moral Un-Neutrality of Science." *Science*, January 27.

Stossel, J. (2004) *Give Me a Break*. New York: HarperCollins.

Stouffer, S. A. (1955) *Communism, Conformity, and Civil Liberties*. Garden City, NY: Doubleday.

Taubman, W. (1982) *Stalin's American Policy*. New York: Norton.

Taubman, W. (2003) *Khrushchev: The Man and His Era*. New York: Norton.

Terry, D. (1998) "Treating Anthrax Hoaxes With Costly Rubber Gloves." *New York Times*, December 29.

Toynbee, A. J. (1950) *War and Civilization*. New York: Oxford University Press.

Van Evera, S. (1994) "Hypotheses on Nationalism and War." *International Security* **18**(4):5–39.

Vance, C. (1983) *Hard Choices: Critical Years in America's Foreign Policy*. New York: Simon & Schuster.

Warr, M. (2000) "Fear of Crime in the United States: Avenues for Research and Policy." *Criminal Justice* **4**:451–489.

Wells, H. G. (1914) *The War That Will End War*. New York: Duffield.

Wells, H. G. (1968) *The Last Books of H. G. Wells*. London: H. G. Wells Society.

Williams, P., and D. Wallace (1989) *Unit 731: Japan's Secret Biological Warfare in World War II*. New York: Free Press.

Wilson, G. C. (2003) "Why Didn't Saddam Defend His Country?" *National Journal*, April 19.

Wohlstetter, A. (1959) "The Delicate Balance of Terror." *Foreign Affairs* **27**(2):211–234.

Wohlstetter, R. (1962) *Pearl Harbor: Warning and Decision*. Stanford, CA: Stanford University Press.

Wolf, C. Jr., K. C. Yeh, E. Brunner Jr., A. Gurwitz, and M. Lawrence (1983) *The Costs of Soviet Empire*. Santa Monica, CA: Rand Corporation.

Woolsey, R. J. Jr. (1993) Testimony before the Senate Intelligence Committee, February 2.

Yergin, D., and J. Stanislaw (1998) *The Commanding Heights: The Battle Between Government and the Marketplace That Is Remaking the Modern World*. New York: Simon & Schuster.

Zucchino, D. (2003) "Iraq's Swift Defeat Blamed on Leaders." *Los Angeles Times*, August 11.

REFLECTIONS

Sales resistance to the Hitler threat

As this article argues, there has been since the Second World War a tendency to exaggerate threats. However, this process requires that the threat be accepted as a notable one to begin with. The exaggeration begins in the salesmanship that leads up to the acceptance and then is further applied if acceptance is established.

In an important book, Stephen Walt has stressed that countries tend to balance not so much against power as against apparent threat. The next question, however, is how is it exactly that they decide what those threats are? It is a key concern that is far too little discussed in the literature. I have tried to explore the issue in this article and in my book *Overblown*, and a 2009 book edited by Trevor Thrall and Jane Cramer assembles a set of essays (including one by me) dealing with the question.

However, for all its patent importance, it remains a tricky issue. It is comparatively easy to explain after the fact why some threats are embraced, but often difficult to predict beforehand. Why is an oil slick emotionally embraced as a threat, but not fatty food? Why is illegal immigration from Mexico seen to be a threat in some years, but not in others? Why was America held hostage when Americans were kidnapped in Iran in 1979 or in Lebanon in the 1980s but not when this repeatedly happens during the Iraq War or in Colombia? Why did Milošević in Serbia become a monster about whom we had to do something military, but not Mugabe in Zimbabwe or SLORC in Burma or Pol Pot in Cambodia or, until 9/11, the Taliban in Afghanistan? Why did nuclear power become a threat after Three Mile Island (which killed nobody) but coal remains warm and cuddly after well-publicized fatal mine accidents?

Idea entrepreneurs, a central concern of this book, are always trying to sell fears and threats. However, not all threats that have been promoted and could potentially have been seized upon have evoked anxiety and overreaction. For example, the American public and its leaders have remained remarkably calm about the potential damage that could be inflicted by the planet's intersection with large meteors or comets, and (perhaps more pertinently) they do not seem to be all that exercised by much-advertised dangers stemming from global warming (until recently perhaps) or from genetically modified food.

Perhaps the best, and certainly historically the most significant, example of an unwillingness to embrace a promoted threat concerns Hitler's Germany in the 1930s. Although there were many prominent people in the United States, including ultimately President Franklin Roosevelt, who were seeking to heighten awareness and concern over this gathering threat in Europe, the public and many elites remained substantially unmoved at least until late in the game. There was a palpable disgust with the warlike proclivities of the Europeans: it was Thomas Jefferson, after all, who characterized (or dismissed) the continent as an "arena of gladiators." Moreover, as I argue in *Retreat from Doomsday*, the supposition that the next major war would result in human annihilation was common, an assumption that led to the logical, but profoundly misguided, conclusion that Hitler could not possibly be willing to risk, much less start, one.

The Cold War as farce

The article includes a discussion of the policy of containment, arguing that it was logically flawed and that the collapse of Communism might have been reached earlier if its desire to expand had been tolerated rather than contained.

There is something inherently farcical about this and, even more so, about another quality of the Cold War: the arms race. Throughout, as discussed more fully in my *Atomic Obsession*, the contestants engaged in a security dilemma: each accumulated an impressive military arsenal to deter a threat of direct military aggression that didn't exist, and each took the other's buildup to be threatening, requiring them to accumulate more armaments in response. Surely, since it resulted primarily in frantic, if fundamentally insignificant, sound and fury, the theatrical form these antics most resemble is farce.

Because neither side had the slightest interest at any time in fighting the other militarily, there never really was much danger of a direct war between them—that is, neither actually had anything to deter. Nonetheless, each continued to pour massive resources into arms, and the absurdity of the situation is poignantly captured in an exasperated comment by President Dwight Eisenhower at a 1956 National Security Council meeting: "We are piling up armaments because we do not know what else to do to provide for our security."

Actually, Eisenhower does seem to have appreciated the farcical element, grasping the fundamental reality that the Soviets had no interest whatever in a direct military confrontation and therefore that an ever-enlarged military was scarcely required to deter them. He never summoned the political courage to say this openly however, choosing instead to flail at the "military-industrial complex" rather than at the faulty and under-examined premise, or idea, that gave that complex its political potency.

Domestic terrorism, domestic Communism, and the self-licking ice cream cone

During the Cold War, as discussed on p. 103, many became convinced that US Communists were devoted to a system dedicated not only to the revolutionary overthrow of the American government but also ultimately to a direct invasion of the country itself. Accordingly, fears about the dangers presented by "the enemy within" became greatly heightened and then fully internalized.

After 9/11 concern about the terrorist enemy within followed a similar trajectory. Agencies like the FBI, redirecting much of their effort from such unglamorous enterprises as dealing with organized crime and white-collar embezzlement (which have actually happened since 2001), have focused primarily on the terrorist threat. As with the quest to uncover Communists during the Cold War, almost all of this activity has led nowhere. In 2002, reports Bill Gertz, official US intelligence estimates held that there were as many as 5,000 al Qaeda terrorists and supporters in the country. And in testimony before the Senate Committee on Intelligence on February 11, 2003, FBI Director Robert Mueller proclaimed that "the greatest threat is from al Qaeda cells in the U.S. that we have not yet identified" and judged that the threat from these unidentified entities was increasing and that they had "the ability and the intent to inflict significant casualties in the U.S. with little warning." In the intervening years of intensive and well-funded questing, however, the FBI and other investigative agencies have been unable to uncover a single true al Qaeda sleeper cell within the country. Indeed, they have been scarcely able to unearth anyone who might even be deemed to have a "connection" to the diabolical group.

As with domestic Communist violence during the Cold War, just about all terrorist violence within the United States since 2001 has taken place on television, in novels, and at the movies. Nevertheless, official and public opinion in the United States will probably continue to labor under that internalized "false sense of insecurity" noted in the article.

The experience with domestic Communism also suggests that once a threat becomes really internalized, the concern can linger for decades even if there is no evidence to support such a continued preoccupation. It becomes self-perpetuating, a self-licking ice cream cone. Accordingly, we can expect there to be, for example, continued and costly efforts to reduce, or to seem to reduce, the country's "vulnerability" to terrorism even though the number of potential terrorist targets is essentially infinite, the probability any particular target will be hit by a terrorist is virtually zero, and inventive terrorists, should they ever actually show up, are free to redirect their attention from a target that is protected toward one of the many that aren't.

However, there is an important difference between concerns about domestic Communism and about domestic terrorism. The Communist monster, like Grendel (and his mother), could terminally and convincingly expire as a perceived threat. But, like crime, terrorism can be carried out by an individual or small group and can therefore never vanish from the human experience. Other colorful monsters may arise from time to time to charm the attention and to strut and fret their hour upon the stage. But the terrorism monster and the internalized fears it has inspired show distinct signs of being timeless.

The cost-effectiveness of counterterrorism

Enhanced expenditures within the United States on counterterrorism have totaled something over $1 trillion over the 10 years since 9/11, even without including in the cost tally such enterprises as the terror-induced wars in Afghanistan and Iraq. Expanding on the arguments arrayed in the last part of the "Simplicity and spook" article, Mark Stewart and I have made a sustained effort to subject these expenditures to standard cost-benefit and risk analytic procedures that have been accepted and applied for decades throughout the world. This is an obvious and routine process that, according to a 2010 study by the National Research Council of the National Academies of Science, simply hasn't been done by those in charge of doling out these massive sums over the decade: it could not find, it concluded, *any* "risk analysis capabilities and methods that are yet adequate" for supporting the decisions made, pointing out that "little effective attention" has been paid to "features of the risk problem that are fundamental." The results of our analysis, published in our book, *Terror, Security, and Money*, are pretty grim.

The key issue is not "are we safer?" but the one put by risk analyst Howard Kunreuther as noted in the "Simplicity and spook" article: "How much should we be willing to pay for a small reduction in probabilities that are already extremely low?" The book concludes that the much enhanced American homeland security expenditures have been wildly inefficient for dealing with the limited threat that terrorism presents: to be considered cost-effective, they would have had to save nearly 11,500 lives per year and to have averted terrorist acts inflicting $100 billion in damage at least twice every year. Or each year they would have needed to thwart 1,667 attacks like the one apparently intended by the Times Square would-be bomber in 2010—more than four a day. More specifically, analyses applying assumptions substantially biased toward the opposite conclusion suggest that the likelihood of a successful terrorist attack on a typical office-type building would have to be a thousand times higher than it is at present for protective security measures to be cost-effective.

We also argue that the existence of political and public pressures does not relieve those in charge from being responsible in the way they expend public funds. To be irrational with your own money may be to be foolhardy, to give in to guilty pleasure, or to wallow in caprice. But to be irrational with other people's money is to betray an essential trust, a dereliction of duty that cannot be justified by political pressure, bureaucratic constraints, or emotional drives. Moreover, the fact that the United Kingdom spends proportionately less than half as much on comparable expenditures suggests that the pressures do not necessary require such high spending levels.

The popular notion that all this is beside the point because terrorists are likely soon to come up with atomic weapons is addressed in some length in my *Atomic Obsession*. If they try, I conclude, there are a host of practical and organizational difficulties that make their likelihood of success vanishingly small.

Reflections references

Bill Gertz, 5,000 in U.S. Suspected of Ties to al Qaeda; Groups Nationwide Under Surveillance. *Washington Times*, July 11, 2002.

Howard Kunreuther, Risk Analysis and Risk Management in an Uncertain World. *Risk Analysis*, August 2002.

National Research Council of the National Academies. *Review of the Department of Homeland Security's Approach to Risk Analysis*. Washington, DC: National Academies Press, 2010.

Trevor Thrall and Jane Cramer (eds.), *Threat Inflation: The Theory, Politics, and Psychology of Fear Mongering in the United States*. London and New York: Routledge, 2009.

Stephen M. Walt, *The Origins of Alliances*. Ithaca, NY: Cornell University Press, 1987.

7 Faulty correlation, foolish consistency, fatal consequence

Democracy, peace, and theory in the Middle East

A foolish consistency is the hobgoblin of little minds, adored by little statesmen and philosophers and divines.

Ralph Waldo Emerson (1841)

Democracy, a messy gimmick for aggregating preferences, has proven to be not only superior to alternative methods but also a remarkably simple form of government that can rather easily be established, or imposed, whenever elites decide to do so and remain uninhibited by thugs with guns. Democracy, however, has been elevated into something of a mystique by philosophers and divines who maintain that this system of governance not only aggregates preferences but creates them. In addition, the rise of democracy has corresponded with the growing acceptance of another, essentially unrelated idea: war aversion. This faulty correlation has been thought to be causal. Putting theory into practice, American statesmen have sought to impose democracy on the Middle East partly operating under the foolish, if theoretically consistent, belief that this will cause peace and preferences favorable to US foreign policy to blossom in the area. The consequences have been fatal.

Democracy as a superior gimmick

Democracy is a device for aggregating and expressing policy preferences. It is characterized by government that is necessarily and routinely responsive—although this responsiveness is not always even, fair, or equal—and it comes into existence when the people effectively agree not to use violence to overthrow the government and the government effectively leaves them free to criticize, to pressure, to organize, and to try to overthrow it by any other means.[1] One is free to try to increase one's political importance by working in politics or by supplying money in appropriate places, or one can reduce it by succumbing to apathy and neglecting even to vote. In practice, then, democracy is a form of government in which the individual is left free to become politically unequal.[2]

Democracy is characterized by minority rule and majority acquiescence, and most of what democratic governments actually do on a day-by-day basis is the result not of elections, but of pressure and petition—lobbying, it's called—and of the reactions and policy initiatives of the government. The history of the oldest large democracy supplies much evidence for this: although it is often against the interests and the desires of the majority, bee-keepers gain price supports for honey, selected industries are insulated from competition, gun enthusiasts get protection from seizure, artists are given medals and subsidies.

The ultimate appeal of democracy is not that it is, or could become, a perfect or ideal form of government, but that, however imperfect, it has distinct advantages when compared to other forms. In an essay first published in 1939, E. M. Forster (1951, 69–70) adopted just such an appropriate comparative approach when he observed that democracy "is less hateful than other contemporary forms of government." Or, as it is usually put: democracy is the worst form of government except for all the rest.[3]

Democracy is, and will always be, distressingly messy, clumsy, and disorderly, and people are permitted loudly and irritatingly to voice opinions that are clearly erroneous and even dangerous. Moreover, decision making in democracies is often muddled, incoherent, and slow, and the results are sometimes exasperatingly foolish, short-sighted, irrational, and incoherent.[4] And some, including James Bryce, have lamented that democracies do not often promote the best people in the society to political leadership—assuming, presumably, that the society would be better off with the best in those positions rather than in science, business, or medicine (Hess 1987). But the key question is, "Compared to what?"

One might begin by looking at the quality of the people democracies have generally selected and compare them to leaders who have emerged in non-democratic societies. In general, democracy looks pretty good when one compares the leadership and decision-making qualities of the tsars of Russia or the kaisers of Germany or the kings of Saudi Arabia or the dictators of just about any place with the prime ministers of Britain or Canada or the presidents of the United States. Only democracies generally have been able to establish effective review and succession arrangements, thereby solving an elemental problem of governance. Moreover, democracy furnishes a safety valve for discontent: those with complaints may or may not ever see relief of their grievances, but, rather than wallowing in frustration, they are supplied with the opportunity to express themselves and potentially to change things.

In the end, William Riker's perspective (1982, 244–46) on all this seems sound: democracy is characterized not by "popular rule" but by various devices that provide for "an intermittent, sometimes random, even perverse, popular veto" that "has at least the potential of preventing tyranny and rendering officials responsive." He notes that this is "a minimal sort of democracy" but contends that it "is the only kind of democracy actually attainable."

The rise of this superior gimmick has essentially been the result of a 200-year competition of ideas, not the necessary or incidental consequence of grander changes in social, cultural, economic, or historic patterns. Democracy's promoters needed, first, to undermine the competition, to seize upon, and to bring out its defects. Since democracy's chief competitor initially was monarchy, a rather bizarre form of government that had unaccountably been around forever (but was to become extinguished in most of the world in just one century), this was not a terribly difficult task. They also needed to create demand for values which, if embraced, would rather automatically help their product to be accepted. For example, democracy will be aided (but its success will not necessarily be assured) if the notion becomes accepted that the government owes its existence and its perpetuation not to the dictates of God as expressed in the genetic process, but to the general consent and approval of the people at large. In addition, the product had to be market tested—put into practice somewhere to show it could actually work. Promoters of democracy were lucky that they first test-marketed their product in Britain and America (in the United States it was explicitly called "the American experiment") because, in the process, democracy came to be associated with countries which were held to be admirable—that is, which became fashion leaders or role models—for reasons that were often quite irrelevant to the institution itself. War also played a role. As European monarchy met its demise in World War I, fascism and Nazism, together with Japanese militarism, died, bloodied and discredited, in World War II.

In the last thirty years democracy has gained particularly wide acceptance (Huntington 1991; Mueller 1999, 214–27). The promoters improved neither the product nor the packaging. What changed was the receptivity of the customers: democracy caught on, at least among political elites, as an idea whose time had come. Indeed, just about the only set of countries where democracy has yet to penetrate deeply are the Islamic ones. As Samuel Huntington (1984, 216) has observed, Islam often associates democracy with the Western influences which many in the religion oppose. Thus the elites in many Islamic countries specifically do not find the Western democracies to be attractive fashion leaders, even as those in, say, Hungary, do. However, something similar was once said about Catholicism. Moreover, where leaders have allowed elections in the Middle East, as in Algeria and Iran in 1997, the voters displayed considerable ability to differentiate and express their interest even though the choice of candidates and the freedom of speech was limited. And some Muslim states, such as Mali, Turkey, Pakistan, and Qatar moved substantially toward democracy. That democracy could become fashionable even in the Middle East is suggested by a comment by the progressive emir of Qatar who sees the most progress in those states that adopted democratic rule.[5]

Democratic development, then, has principally been a matter of convincing leaders to do democracy.[6] In practice, it seems to be about as difficult to put on as a new suit of clothes, and it has spread not so much because it has been made cosmically inevitable by various economic or social developments, but because it has come into style: it's what just about everyone who is anyone is wearing this season. It is easy to establish and maintain because it is essentially based on giving people the freedom to complain—and, importantly, the freedom to organize with other complainers to attempt to topple or favorably influence the government. Complaining comes easily to most. Thus, as Americans should surely know by now, anyone can do democracy.

Democracy can also be established by force although, absent favorable market conditions, the forceful imposition of democracy has generally not worked very well. For example, the United States has repeatedly and often evangelically urged democracy upon its neighbors to the south, and it has often been prepared to use money (and sometimes military force) to coat the philosophic pill. Those efforts seem rarely to have made much lasting difference. Thus, in 1913 President Woodrow Wilson dramatically declared the United States to be the "champion" of democracy in the Americas and, to show he meant business, sent US troops to Nicaragua, Haiti, and the Dominican Republic to establish democracy. But all three countries subsequently lapsed into extended dictatorships (Whitehead 1986, 6). Latin America's remarkable move toward democracy after 1975 was accomplished almost entirely by the people there themselves when they were ready to buy, and became receptive to, the ideas.

However, when conditions are propitious, force may work. The times seem to have been right for democracy by force at the end of World War II in some places. At the war's end the victorious democracies set about foisting their form of government on the portion of Germany they occupied and on Italy, Austria, and Japan. By 1945, it must have seemed to the people of these countries that even democracy at its worst was better than the alternative that had just brought catastrophe upon them, and they took up, or lapsed into, democracy without a great deal of apparent effort. Similarly, when Panama's Manuel Noriega calmly stole an election that went against him in 1989, in the midst of Latin America's transition, he was deposed by an American military invasion. Liberated from this anachronistic tyrant, the country became a democracy. The United States also successfully imposed, or reimposed, democracy on Grenada in 1983. However, a somewhat similar process in Haiti in the 1990s met with far less success.

The democratic peace: faulty correlation

When ideas have filtered throughout the world in the last few hundred years, they have tended to do so in one direction. There has been, for better or worse, a long and fairly steady process of what is often called "Westernization": Taiwan has become more like Canada than Canada has become like Taiwan; Gabon has become more like Belgium than Belgium has become like Gabon (see also Nadelmann 1990, 484). Major ideas that have gone from the developed world to the less developed world include Christianity, the abolition of slavery, the acceptance of democratic institutions and Western economic and social forms, and the determined application of, and faith in, the scientific method. Not all of these have been fully or readily accepted, but the point is that the process has largely been unidirectional and that there has so far been little in the way of a reverse flow of ideas.

In the last couple of decades there has been a burgeoning and intriguing discussion about the connection between democracy and war aversion.[7] Most notable has been the empirical observation that democracies have never, or almost never, gone to war with each other. This relationship seems more correlative than causal, however. Like many important ideas over the last few centuries, the idea that war is undesirable and inefficacious and the idea that democracy is a good form of government have largely followed the same trajectory: they were embraced first in northern Europe and North America and then gradually, with a number of traumatic setbacks, became more accepted elsewhere. In this view, the rise of democracy not only is associated with the rise of war aversion, but also with the decline of slavery, religion, capital punishment, and cigarette smoking, and with the growing acceptance of capitalism, scientific methodology, women's rights, environmentalism, abortion, and rock music.[8]

While democracy and war aversion have taken much the same trajectory, however, they have been substantially out of sync with each other: the movement toward democracy began about 200 years ago, but the movement against war really began only about a century ago (Mueller 1989, 2004). Critics of the democracy/peace connection often cite examples of wars or near-wars between democracies. Most of these took place before World War I—that is, before war aversion had caught on.[9]

A necessary, logical connection between democracy and war aversion, accordingly, is far from clear. Thus, it is often asserted that democracies are peaceful because they apply their domestic penchant for peaceful compromise (something, obviously, that broke down in the United States in 1861) to the international arena or because the structure of democracy requires decision makers to obtain domestic approval.[10] Yet, authoritarian regimes must also necessarily develop skills at compromise in order to survive, and they all have domestic constituencies that must be serviced such as the church, the landed gentry, potential urban rioters, the *nomenklatura*, the aristocracy, party members, the military, prominent business interests, the police or secret police, lenders of money to the exchequer, potential rivals for the throne, and the sullen peasantry.[11]

Since World War I the democracies in the developed world have been in the lead in rejecting war as a methodology. Some proponents of the democracy–peace connection suggest that this is because the democratic norm of non-violent conflict resolution has been externalized to the international arena. However, developed democracies have not necessarily adopted a pacifist approach, particularly after a version of that approach failed so spectacularly to prevent World War II from being forced upon them. In addition, they were willing to subvert or to threaten— and sometimes apply military force—when threats appeared to loom during the Cold War contest. At times this approach was used even against regimes that had some democratic credentials such as in Iran in 1953, Guatemala in 1954, Chile in 1973, and perhaps Nicaragua in the 1980s (Rosato 2003, 590–91). And they have also sometimes used military force in their intermittent efforts to police the post-Cold War world (Mueller 2004, Chapters 7, 8).

It is true that developed democracies have warred little or not at all against each other; and, since there were few democracies outside the developed world until the last quarter of the twentieth century, it is this statistical regularity that most prominently informs the supposed connection between democracy and peace. However, the developed democracies hardly needed democracy to decide that war among them was a bad idea.[12] In addition, they also adopted a live-and-let-live approach toward a huge number of dictatorships and other non-democracies that did not seem threatening during the Cold War. In fact, they often aided and embraced such regimes if they seemed to be on the right side in the conflict with Communism.

The supposed penchant for peaceful compromise of democracies has not always served them well when confronted with civil unrest and secessionist demands. The process broke down into civil warfare in democratic Switzerland in 1847 and savagely so in the United States in 1861. Democracies have also fought a considerable number of wars to retain colonial possessions—six by France alone since World War II. And these can in many respects be labeled civil wars (Fearon and Laitin 2003, 76). To be sure, democracies have often managed to deal with colonial problems peacefully, mostly by letting the colonies go. But authoritarian governments have also done so: the Soviet Union, for example, withdrew from its empire in Eastern Europe and then dissolved itself, all almost entirely without violence.

Thus, while democracy and war aversion have often been promoted by the same advocates, the relationship does not seem to be a causal one. And when the two trends are substantially out of step today, democracies will fight one another. Thus, it is not at all clear that telling the elected hawks in the Jordanian parliament that Israel is a democracy will dampen their hostility in the slightest. And various warlike sentiments could be found in the elected parliaments in the former Yugoslavia in the early 1990s or in India and then-democratic Pakistan when these two countries engaged in armed conflict in 1999. If Argentina had been a democracy in 1982 when it seized the Falkland Islands (a very popular undertaking), it is unlikely that British opposition to the venture would have been much less severe. "The important consideration," observes Miriam Fendius Elman (1997, 484, 496) after surveying the literature on the subject, does not seem to be "whether a country is democratic or not, but whether its ruling coalition is committed to peaceful methods of conflict resolution." As she further points out, the countries of Latin America and most of Africa have engaged in very few international wars even without the benefit of being democratic. And, of course, the long peace enjoyed by developed countries since World War II includes not only the one that has prevailed between democracies, but also the even more important one between the authoritarian East and the democratic West. Even if there is some connection, whether causal or atmospheric, between democracy and peace, it cannot explain this latter phenomenon.

Democracy and the democratic peace become mystiques: the role of philosophers and divines

Democracy has been a matter of debate for several millennia as philosophers and divines have speculated about what it is, what it might become, and what it ought to be. Associated with these speculations has been a tendency to emboss the grubby gimmick with something of a mystique. Of particular interest for present purposes is the fanciful notion that democracy does not simply express and aggregate preferences, but actually somehow *creates* (or should create) them. In addition, the (rough) correlation between democracy and war aversion has also been elevated into a causal relationship.

Democratic philosophers and divines have often come to conclude that, rather than simply being a process of interest aggregation, democracy actually creates, inspires, or requires certain modes of thought or policy preferences. However, although democracy does by definition require that opposition and contention and special interest activity be peacefully preserved, and although it may be a (comparatively) desirable gimmick for aggregating policy preferences, it does not create the policy preferences themselves. This should be clear from experience.

Over the course of time, democracies variously have banned liquor and allowed it to flow freely; raised taxes to confiscatory levels and lowered them to next to nothing; refused women the right to vote and granted it to them; despoiled the environment and sought to protect it; subsidized certain economic groups and withdrawn subsidies; stifled labor unions and facilitated their creation; banned abortion and permitted and subsidized the operation; tolerated drug use and launched massive "wars" upon the practice; embraced slavery and determinedly sought to eradicate it; persecuted homosexuals and repealed or systematically failed to enforce the laws that did so; seized private property and turned over state assets to the private sector; discriminated against racial groups and given them preferential treatment; banned pornography and allowed it to be distributed freely; and tolerated the organization of peaceful political opposition and voted themselves out of existence by withdrawing the right to do so. Moreover, democracies have welcomed or committed naked aggression and fought to reverse it; devolved into vicious civil war and avoided it by artful compromise; embraced colonialism and rejected the practice entirely; tolerated and sometimes caused humanitarian disaster in other parts of the world and sought to alleviate it; adopted protectionist economic policies and been free traders; and gone to war with enthusiasm and self-righteousness and sought to outlaw the institution.[13]

Philosophers and divines not only encased democracy in a vaporously idealistic or ideological mystique, they have done the same for the democracy–peace correlation. After all, if correlation is taken to be the cause, it follows that peace will envelop the earth right after democracy does. Accordingly for those who value peace, the promotion of democracy, by force or otherwise, becomes a central mission.

This notion has been brewing for some time. Woodrow Wilson's famous desire to "make the world safe for democracy" was in large part an antiwar motivation. He and many others in Britain, France, and the United States had become convinced that, as Britain's Lloyd George put it, "Freedom is the only warranty of Peace" (Rappard 1940, 42–44). With the growth in the systematic examination of the supposed peace–democracy connection by the end of the century, such certain pronouncements became commonplace. Notes Bruce Russett (2005, 395), sentiments like those have "issued from the White House ever since the last year of the Reagan administration" (2005, 395).

Foolish consistency, fatal consequence: the role of little statesmen

It was left to George W. Bush to put mystique into practice. As he stressed to reporter Bob Woodward (2004, 88–89) during the run-up to his war with Iraq, "I say that freedom is not America's gift to the world. Freedom is God's gift to everybody in the world. I believe that. As a matter of fact, I was the person that wrote that line, or said it. I didn't write it, I just said it in a speech. And it became part of the jargon. And I believe that. And I believe we have a duty to free people. I would hope we wouldn't have to do it militarily, but we have a duty." And in an address shortly before the war, he confidently proclaimed, "The world has a clear interest in the spread of democratic values, because stable and free nations do not breed the ideologies of murder. They encourage the peaceful pursuit of a better life" (quoted in Frum and Perle 2003, 158).

In this, Bush was only trying to be consistent (foolishly so, perhaps), a quality that endears him to so many of his followers. If democracy is so wonderful, and if in addition it inevitably brings both peace and creates favorable policy preferences, then forcefully jamming it down the throats of the decreasing number of non-democratic countries in the world must be all to the good. Bush had already done something like that, with a fair amount of success, in Afghanistan; Bill Clinton had invaded Haiti and bombed Bosnia and Serbia with the same lofty goal at least partly in mind; George H. W. Bush had crisply slapped Panama into shape; and Ronald Reagan had straightened out Grenada. Further, the Australians had recently done it in East Timor and the British in Sierra Leone (Mueller 2004, Chapter 7). Critics have argued that democracy can't be spread at the point of a gun, but, as noted earlier, cases like these, as well as the experience with the defeated enemies after World War II, suggest that it sometimes can be, something that supporters of the administration were quick to point out (Kaplan and Kristol 2003, 98–99; Frum and Perle 2003, 163). Even Russett (2005, 398–400), a prominent democratic-peace analyst, eventually, if rather reluctantly, concedes the possibility (see also Peceny and Pickering 2006).

However, George W. Bush and some of his supporters—particularly those in the neoconservative camp—foolishly, if consistently, extrapolated to develop an even more extravagant mystique. Not only would the invasion crisply bring viable democracy to Iraq, but success there would have a domino effect: democracy would eventually spread from its Baghdad bastion to envelop the Middle East. This would not only bring blissful peace in its wake (because, as we know, democracies never fight each other), but the new democracies would also adopt all sorts of other policies as well including, in particular, love of, or at least much-diminished hostility toward, the United States and Israel (because, as we know, the democratic process itself has a way of making people think nice thoughts). As Woodward (2004, 428) has reported, Vice President Dick Cheney attests to Bush's "abiding faith that if people were given freedom and democracy, that would begin a transformation process in Iraq that in years ahead would change the Middle East."

Moreover, since force can establish democracy and since democracies automatically embrace peaceful intentions toward each other, military force would deftly be applied as necessary to speed up the domino-toppling process wherever necessary in the area. Such extravagant, even romantic visions filled neoconservative calls to arms. In their book *The War Over Iraq*, Lawrence Kaplan and William Kristol (2003, 104–5) applied due reverence to the sanctified correlation—"democracies rarely, if ever, wage war against on another"—and then extrapolate fancifully to conclude that "The more democratic the world becomes, the more likely it is to be congenial to America."

War architect Paul Wolfowitz also seems to have believed that the war would become an essential stage on the march toward freedom and democracy (Woodward 2004, 428). In an article proposing what he calls "democratic realism," Charles Krauthammer (2004, 23, 17) urged taking "the risky but imperative course of trying to reorder the Arab world," with a "targeted, focused" effort that would (however) be "limited" to "that Islamic crescent stretching from North Africa to Afghanistan." And Kaplan and Kristol (2003, 124–25) stressed that "The mission begins in Baghdad, but does not end there. . . . War in Iraq represents but the first installment. . . . Duly armed, the United States can act to secure its safety and to advance the cause of liberty—in Baghdad and beyond."

With that, lamented Russett (2005), democracy and democratic peace theory became "Bushwhacked." Democratic processes of pressure and policy promotion were deftly used by a dedicated group to wage costly war to establish both peace and congenial policy in the otherwise intractable Middle East. It could be argued, then, that the little statesmen of the Bush administration had the courage of the mystical convictions of the democracy and democratic peace philosophers and divines. However, although Bush's simple faith in democracy may perhaps have its endearing side, how deeply that passion is (or was) really shared by his neoconservative allies could be questioned. That is, did they really believe that the United States which, as Francis Fukuyama (2004, 60) noted, "cannot eliminate poverty or raise test scores in Washington, DC," could "bring democracy to a part of the world that has stubbornly resisted it and is virulently anti-American to boot"?

Although they hyped democracy, David Frum and Richard Perle (2003, 162–63) carefully cautioned that "in the Middle East, democratization does not mean calling immediate elections and then living with whatever happens next," but rather "opening political spaces," "creating representative institutions," "deregulating the economy," "shrinking and reforming the Middle Eastern public sector," and "perhaps above all" changing the educational system. Similarly, Krauthammer's "democratic realism" approach did not seem to stress democracy all that much.[14]

Most interesting is a call issued by neoconservatism's champion, Norman Podhoretz (2002, 28), in the run-up to the war. He strongly advocated expanding Bush's "axis of evil" beyond Iraq, Iran, and North Korea "at a minimum" to embrace "Syria and Lebanon and Libya, as well as 'friends' of America like the Saudi royal family and Egypt's Hosni Mubarak, along with the Palestinian Authority." However, Podhoretz proved to be less mystical (or simply less devious) than other neocons about democracy by pointedly adding: "the alternative to these regimes could easily turn out to be worse, even (or especially) if it comes into power through democratic elections." Accordingly, he emphasized, "it will be necessary for the United States to *impose* a new political culture on the defeated parties."[15] Although Podhoretz may be more realistic than others about democracy, his extravagant notion that the US would somehow have the capacity to impose a new political culture throughout the non-Israeli Middle East is, like Krauthammer's comparable vision, so fantastic as to border on the absurd.

Indeed, after looking beneath the boilerplate about democracy and the democratic peace, what seems to be principally motivating at least some of these people is a strong desire for the United States to use military methods to make the Middle East finally and once and for all safe for Israel (Drew 2003, 22; Fukuyama 2004; Roy 2003). Most Bush advisers were devoted supporters of Israel and seemed to display far less interest in advocating the application of military force to deal with unsavory dictatorial regimes in other parts of the world that did not threaten Israel.

As John Mearsheimer and Stephen Walt observed (2006) of what they call the "Israel Lobby," such policy advocacy is entirely appropriate and fully democratic. Democracy, as noted earlier, is centrally characterized by the contestings of isolated, self-serving, and often tiny special interest groups and their political and bureaucratic allies. What happened with Iraq policy was democracy in full flower. It does not follow, of course, that policies so generated are necessarily wise, and Mearsheimer and Walt considered that the results of much of the lobby's efforts—certainly in this case—were detrimental to American (and even Israeli) national interest. Yet, their contentions that the Lobby was "critical" or "a key factor" in the decision to go to war or that that decision would "have been far less likely" without the lobby's efforts need more careful analysis. In their view, the lobby has too much influence over US foreign policy—a conclusion, as it happens, that is shared by 68 percent of over 1,000 international relations scholars who responded to a 2006 survey.[16]

It should be noted, however, that, although Bush and Cheney and at least some of the neocons may actually have believed their prewar fantasies about the blessings that imposed democracy would in turn shower on the Middle East, the arguments they proffered for going to war stressed national security issues, not democracy ones. Specifically, this included the notion that Saddam's Iraq was a threat to the United States because of its development, or potential development, of weapons of mass destruction and because of its connections to terrorist groups out to get America (Roy 2003). The democracy argument rose in significance, noted Russett (2005, 396), only after those security arguments for going to war proved to be empty. As Fukuyama (2005) put it, a prewar request to spend "several hundred billion dollars and several thousand American lives in order to bring democracy to . . . Iraq" would "have been laughed out of court." Moreover, when given a list of foreign-policy goals, the American public has rather consistently ranked the promotion of democracy lower—often *much* lower—than such goals as combating international terrorism, protecting American jobs, preventing the spread of nuclear weapons, strengthening the United Nations, and protecting American businesses abroad (see Figure 7.1).

Support for the Iraq War eroded rather more slowly than one might have expected given the demise of the main reasons for going to war and the subsequent unexpectedly high American casualty levels (Mueller 2005, 45). This may reflect the fact that many people still connected the effort there to the campaign, or "war," against terror, an enterprise that continues to enjoy huge support. In addition, the toppling of Saddam Hussein remains a singular accomplishment, one the American people had been spoiling for since the Gulf War of 1991 (Larson and Savych 2005, 132–37). However, support for the war may be partly the result of acceptance by the American public, despite its pervasive cynicism about democracy in practice, of some of the democratic mystique so sonorously spun out by democratic philosophers and divines over the decades.

Saving democracy and peace

The cynicism (or realism) about democracy expressed by Podhoretz has proved to be sound, of course. As peace builders in Bosnia have repeatedly discovered, elections lead to the rise of people who can best engage and manipulate the political process to attract voters, and the winners are not necessarily the ones preferred by intervening foreign well-wishers.

Thus if the people detest Israel and the United States and let that passion influence their vote, they will elect politicians who voice—indeed, stoke—hatred for

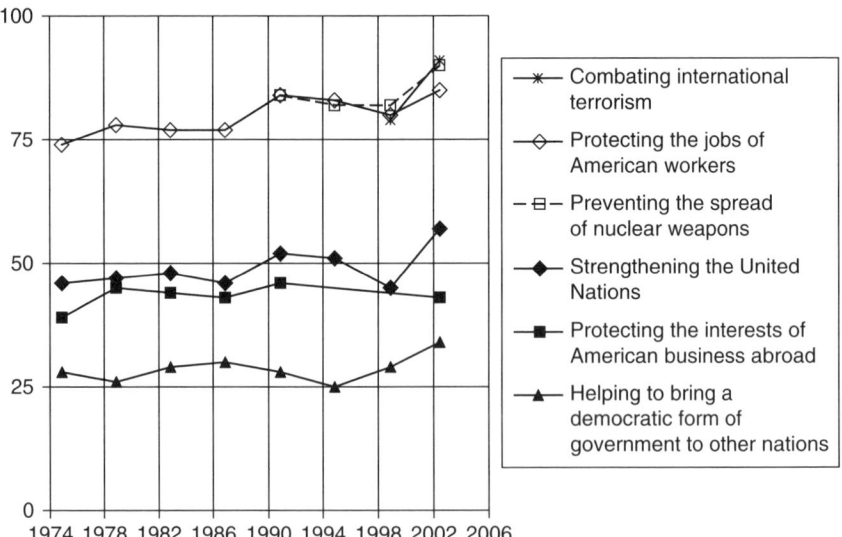

Figure 7.1 The public and US foreign-policy goals: percent saying "very important."

Source: Chicago Council on Foreign Relations quadrennial surveys.

Israel and the United States. Such hatreds have been very much enhanced by the American and British invasion of Iraq and by Israel's military actions against Palestinians during an internal rebellion between 2000 and 2005 and later against Lebanon in 2006. Nearly two-thirds of those elected to the Iraqi parliament in late 2005 explicitly advocated a stronger role for Islam in politics; Muslim Brotherhood candidates did very well in Egyptian elections at the same time and would have done even better had it not been for great electoral restrictions imposed by the government; and the militantly anti-Israel group Hamas triumphed in elections in Palestine in January 2006 (Gause 2006).

This is not to argue that efforts to force democracy on Iraq have necessarily failed. Using the minimal—but realistic—definitions of democracy proposed at the outset of this article, Iraq is acting very much like a standard democracy, albeit one with exceptionally high rates of crime and violence. Politicians are squabbling continuously, interest groups are seeking to loot the public treasury as best they can, people are rather freely expressing themselves even where this may entail the airing of ethnic and racial hatreds (those who use violence to do so are not democratic, however), and politicians are seeking to manipulate the system to advantage their supporters.[17] If the violence eventually comes under control, it is entirely possible that the country will remain democratic—though the demand for security may lead to a takeover by a strongman welcomed by the desperate population. However, even if democracy does survive in Iraq, it is to be expected that those in charge will remain loyal to the wishes of their constituencies. That may well mean, as Podhoretz suggests, intensified hostility to Israel and ungrateful animosity toward Iraq's naive, clumsy, and destructive democratic liberators.

On the brighter side, there is at least some hope that the disastrous experience in Iraq will terminally undercut both the democracy mystique and the democratic peace mystique that are so adored by philosophers, divines, and little statesmen. There are some signs that this may already be in process. Before elections in Egypt, US administration spokespeople made innumerable speeches seeking to prod that country into a more democratic direction, but this cheerleading largely stopped after the election with its discouraging, if democratic, results. It is all rather similar to the non-reaction of George H. W. Bush when the Algerian military in 1992 cancelled elections likely to bring Muslim fundamentalists to power there shortly after Bush had taken deep umbrage and instituted sanctions against Haiti where the military had done much the same thing.

There is, however, a considerable danger that the disastrous experience with democracy promotion in the Middle East will become a major setback to the rise of democracy there. The unwillingness of the United States to accept the results of elections in Egypt and especially in Palestine because they didn't come out "right" has led to understandable, and essentially correct, accusations of hypocrisy. And an additional danger is that the disastrous chaos visited upon Iraq by the American invasion will come to be associated with democracy, substantially discrediting the institution in the area.

In the end, maybe someone will explore the possibility that the supposed democracy–peace connection has been reversed in all this. The correlation between democracy and peace may not mean that democracy causes peace, but that peace causes, or facilitates, democracy—at least when other conditions are right. This already seems to hold for the relationship between peace and trade. Although expanding trade and interactions may enhance or reinforce the process, attitude toward war is likely to be the key explanatory variable in the relationship. Thus, it has frequently been observed that militarized disputes between countries reduce trade between them (Pollins 1989a, 1989b; Li and Sacko 2002). By contrast, if a couple of countries that have previously enjoyed a conflictual relationship lapse into a comfortable peace and become extremely unlikely to get into war, businesses in both places may well become inclined to explore the possibilities for mutually beneficial exchange.

Similarly, although international institutions and norms often stress peace, they, like expanded trade flows, are not so much the cause of peace as its result. Many of the institutions that have been fabricated in Europe, particularly ones like the coal and steel community that were so carefully forged between France and Germany in the years following World War II, have been specifically designed to reduce the danger of war between erstwhile enemies. It is difficult to see why the institutions should get the credit for the peace that has flourished between those two countries for the last half century and more.[18] They are among the consequences of the peace that has enveloped western Europe since 1945, not its cause. As Richard Betts (1992, 23–24) puts it for institutions of collective security, "peace is the premise of the system, not the product" (see also Schweller 2001, 183).

Something like that may hold for the democracy–peace connection: peace causes—or, more likely, facilitates—democracy (see also Pietrzyk 2002; Payne 2006). Countries often restrict or even abandon democracy when domestic instability or external military threat seems to loom. An Iraqi who had been imprisoned by the Saddam Hussein regime and who gleefully helped pull down a statue of the tyrant in 2003 became disillusioned by subsequent calamity and concluded in 2007, "We regret that Saddam Hussein is gone, no matter how much we hated him" (Raghavan 2007). And after the chaos of the 1990s, Russians continue to highly approve of their order-providing, if democracy-eroding president, Vladimir Putin. By the same token, when they are comfortably at peace, people may come to realize that they no longer require a strongman to provide order and can afford to embrace the comparative benefits of democracy even if those might come with somewhat heightened uncertainty and possibly with the potential for less reliable leadership.

If this is so, the prospects for continued democratization seem to be quite good. As it happens, there has been a remarkable decline in the incidence of war—both civil and international—over the last decade to the point where, outside of Iraq, scarcely any exist anywhere in the world (Mueller 2007). That is, although there has been a considerable increase in the number of democratic countries in the world, as noted earlier, trends in war aversion seem to have considerably outrun it. Thus if this pattern holds and if fashionable yearnings for democracy continue to grow, peace may help these yearnings to be realized. If so, however, this desirable development is not likely to owe much to little statesmen, philosophers, and divines, and to the damaging and sometimes fatal mystiques they cherish and nurture.

Notes

1 For further development of these ideas, see Mueller (1999, Chapter 6). This approach may be used to set up a sort of sliding scale of governmental forms. An *authoritarian* government may effectively and sometimes intentionally allow a degree of opposition—a limited amount of press disagreement, for example, or the freedom to complain privately, something sometimes known as the freedom of conversation. But it will not tolerate organized attempts to overthrow it, even if they are peaceful. A *totalitarian* government does not allow even those limited freedoms found under authoritarianism. On the other end of the scale is *anarchy*: a condition which holds when a government "allows" the use of violence to try to overthrow it—presumably mainly out of weakness or ineffectiveness.

2 See also Schmitter and Karl (1991, 83–84); Dahl (1956, Chapter 4).

3 The most famous expression of this sentiment comes from Winston Churchill (1950, 200) who, referring perhaps to Forster, observed in a House of Commons speech in November 1947 that "It has been said that Democracy is the worst form of government except all those other forms that have been tried from time to time." Twenty years before Forster, William Ralph Inge (1919, 5) had put it this way: "Democracy is a form of government which may be rationally defended, not as good, but as being less bad than any other."

4 Tocqueville (1990, 235), for example, argued in the 1830s that, particularly with respect to foreign policy, democracy "can only with great difficulty regulate the details of an important undertaking, persevere in a fixed design, and work out its execution in spite of serious obstacles. It cannot combine its measures with secrecy or await their consequences with patience."

5 As interviewed on *60 Minutes*, CBS, August 3, 2003. On Qatar, see also Jehl (1997). On Iran, see Bakhash (1998).

6 On elite transformations, see Higley and Gunther (1992).

7 See, for example, Doyle (1986), Russett (1990), Singer and Wildavsky (1993), Russett and Oneal (2001).

8 On this process, see Mueller (1995, 181–82; 1999, Chapter 8); Nadelmann (1990, 484).

9 For example, Layne (1994); Rosato (2003, 591–92); Elman (1997, Chapters 1–3); Pietrzyk (2002).

10 For a discussion, see Russett and Oneal (2001, 53–58).

11 See also Rosato (2003, 593–94, 596–97).

12 Nor is it likely, contrary to the suggestion by Rosato (2003, 599–600), that they needed "American preponderance" to do so.

13 See also Schweller (2002, 184); Rosato (2003, 594–96).

14 The theory's extravagant calls for massive warfare over a very substantial portion of the globe, only "limited" in comparison to Bush's expansive view, suggested it was rather lacking in realism as well.

15 Emphasis in the original. Richard Perle issued a similar litany of targets, adding for good measure, and possibly in jest, France and the State Department. He also suggested that "a short message" should be delivered to other hostile regimes in the area: "You're next" (Mearsheimer and Walt 2006).

16 Maliniak et al. (2007, 66). The complete survey results are at http://www.wm.edu/ TRIP (accessed July 9, 2009).

17 Alternatively, using the notions sketched out in note 1, Iraq could be considered mostly to be in a state of anarchy because of the inability of the government sufficiently to police political violence.

18 But they do: "The creation of a security community has made armed conflict between France and Germany . . . unthinkable" (Russett and Oneal 2001, 158). See also Ikenberry (2001, Chapter 6).

References

Bakhash, Shaul. 1998. Iran's Remarkable Election. *Journal of Democracy* 9(1) January: 80–94.

Betts, Richard K. 1992. Systems for Peace or Causes of War? Collective Security, Arms Control, and the New Europe. *International Security* 17(1) Summer: 5–43.

Churchill, Winston S. 1950. *Europe Unite: Speeches 1947 and 1948*, ed. Randolph S. Churchill. Boston: Houghton Mifflin.

Dahl, Robert A. 1956. *A Preface to Democratic Theory*. Chicago, IL: University of Chicago Press.

Doyle, Michael W. 1986. Liberalism and World Politics. *American Political Science Review* 80(4) December: 1151–69.

Drew, Elizabeth. 2003. The Neocons in Power. *New York Review of Books* June 12: 20–22.

Elman, Miriam Fendius, ed. 1997. *Paths to Peace: Is Democracy the Answer?* Cambridge, MA: MIT Press.

Emerson, Ralph Waldo. 1841. Self-Reliance. In *Essays: First Series*.

Fearon, James D., and David D. Laitin. 2003. Ethnicity, Insurgency, and Civil War. *American Political Science Review* 97(1) February: 75–90.

Forster, E. M. 1951. *Two Cheers for Democracy*. New York: Harcourt, Brace & World.

Frum, David, and Richard Perle. 2003. *An End to Evil: How to Win the War on Terror*. New York: Random House.

Fukuyama, Francis. 2004. The Neoconservative Moment. *National Interest* Summer: 57–68.

——. 2005. America's Parties and Their Foreign Policy Masquerade. *Financial Times* March 8: 21.

Gause, F. Gregory, III. 2006. Beware of What You Wish For. http://www.foreignaffairs.org, February 8.

Hess, Stephen. 1987. "Why Great Men Are Not Chosen Presidents": Lord Bryce Revisited. In *Elections American Style*, ed. A. James Reichley. Washington, DC: Brookings Institution, 75–94.

Higley, John, and Richard Gunther, eds. 1992. *Elites and Democratic Consolidation in Latin America and Southern Europe*. Cambridge: Cambridge University Press.

Huntington, Samuel P. 1984. Will More Countries Become Democratic? *Political Science Quarterly* 99(2) Summer: 193–218.

——. 1991. *The Third Wave: Democratization in the Late Twentieth Century*. Norman, OK: University of Oklahoma Press.

Ikenberry, G. John. 2001. *After Victory: Institutions, Strategic Restraint, and the Rebuilding of Order After Major Wars*. Princeton, NJ: Princeton University Press.

Inge, William Ralph. 1919. *Outspoken Essays*. London: Longmans, Green.

Jehl, Douglas. 1997. Persian Gulf's Young Turk: Sheik Hamad, Emir of Qatar. *New York Times* July 10: A1.

Kaplan, Lawrence F., and William Kristol. 2003. *The War Over Iraq: Saddam's Tyranny and America's Mission*. San Francisco, CA: Encounter Books.

Krauthammer, Charles. 2004. In Defense of Democratic Realism. *National Interest* Fall: 15–25.

——. 2006. Past the Apogee: America Under Pressure. http://www.fpri.org, December.

Larson, Eric. V., and Godgan Savych. 2005. *American Public Support for U.S. Military Operations from Mogadishu to Baghdad*. Santa Monica, CA: RAND Corporation.

Layne, Christopher. 1994. Kant or Cant? The Myth of the Democratic Peace. *International Security* 19(2) Fall: 5–49.

Li, Quan, and David Sacko. 2002. The (Ir)Relevance of Militarized Interstate Disputes for International Trade. *International Studies Quarterly* 46(1) March: 11–34.

Maliniak, Daniel, Amy Oakes, Susan Peterson, and Michael J. Tierney. 2007. Inside the Ivory Tower. *Foreign Policy* March/April: 62–68.

Mearsheimer, John, and Stephen Walt. 2006. The Israel Lobby. *London Review of Books* March 23.

Mueller, John. 1989. *Retreat from Doomsday: The Obsolescence of Major War*. New York: Basic Books.

——. 1995. *Quiet Cataclysm: Reflections on the Recent Transformation of World Politics*. New York: HarperCollins.

——. 1999. *Capitalism, Democracy, and Ralph's Pretty Good Grocery*. Princeton, NJ: Princeton University Press.

——. 2004. *The Remnants of War*. Ithaca, NY: Cornell University Press.

——. 2005. The Iraq Syndrome. *Foreign Affairs* 84(6) November/December: 44–54.

——. 2007. The Demise of War and of Speculations about the Causes Thereof. Paper Presented at the Annual Convention of the International Studies Association. Chicago, IL, March 1.

Nadelmann, Ethan A. 1990. Global Prohibition Regimes: The Evolution of Norms in International Society. *International Organization* 44(4) Autumn: 479–526.

Payne, James L. 2006. Election Fraud: Democracy is an Effect, not a Cause, of Nonviolence. *American Conservative* March 13: 11–12.

Peceny, Mark, and Jeffrey Pickering. 2006. Can Liberal Intervention Build Liberal Democracy? In *Conflict Prevention and Peacebuilding in Post-War Societies: Sustaining the Peace*, ed. T. David Mason and James D. Meernik. London and New York: Routledge, 130–48.

Pietrzyk, Mark E. 2002. *International Order and Individual Liberty: Effects of War and Peace on the Development of Governments*. Lanham, MD: University Press of America.

Podhoretz, Norman. 2002. In Praise of the Bush Doctrine. *Commentary* 114(2) September: 19–28.

Pollins, Brian. 1989a. Conflict, Cooperation, and Commerce: The Effect of International Political Interactions on Bilateral Trade Flows. *American Journal of Political Science* 33(3): 737–61.

——. 1989b. Does Trade Still Follow the Flag? *American Political Science Review* 83(2) June.

Raghavan, Sudarsan. 2007. 4 Years After Hussein's Fall, Regret in Iraq: Harley Fan Who Helped Topple Statue Wants Old Order Back. *Washington Post* April 9: A8.

Rappard, William E. 1940. *The Quest for Peace since the World War*. Cambridge, MA: Harvard University Press.

Riker, William H. 1982. *Liberalism Against Populism*. San Francisco, CA: Freeman.

Rosato, Sebastian. 2003. The Flawed Logic of Democratic Peace Theory. *American Political Science Review* 97(4) November: 585–602.

Roy, Olivier. 2003. Europe Won't Be Fooled Again. *New York Times* May 13: A31.

Russett, Bruce. 1990. *Controlling the Sword: The Democratic Governance of National Security*. Cambridge, MA: Harvard University Press.

——. 2005. Bushwhacking the Democratic Peace. *International Studies Perspectives* 6(4) November: 395–408.

Russett, Bruce M., and John R. Oneal. 2001. *Triangulating Peace: Democracy, Interdependence, and International Organizations*. New York: Norton.

Schmitter, Philippe, and Terry Lynn Karl. 1991. What Democracy Is . . . And Is Not. *Journal of Democracy* 2(3) Summer: 75–88.

Schweller, Randall L. 2001. The Problem of International Order Revisited: A Review Essay. *International Security* 26(1) Summer: 161–86.

——. 2002. Correspondence. *International Security* 27(1) Summer: 181–85.

Singer, Max, and Aaron Wildavsky. 1993. *The Real World Order: Zones of Peace, Zones of Conflict*. Chatham, NJ: Chatham House.

Tocqueville, Alexis de. 1990. *Democracy in America*. Trans. Henry Reeve. New York: Vintage.

Whitehead, Laurence. 1986. International Aspects of Democratization. In *Transitions from Authoritarian Rule: Comparative Perspectives*, ed. Guillermo O'Donnell, Philippe C. Schmitter, and Laurence Whitehead. Baltimore, MD: Johns Hopkins University Press, 3–46.

Woodward, Bob. 2004. *Plan of Attack*. New York: Simon & Schuster.

REFLECTIONS

Democracy, capitalism, and peace: interrelations and causal connections

Over the last few centuries there have been quite remarkable changes in many major ideas about the way societies and the world should be arranged. For example, there have been notable declines in formal slavery, capital and corporal punishment, torture, vendetta, blood feuds, monarchy, and smoking, and there has been the rising acceptance of humane prisons, pornography, abortion, racial and class political equality, women's rights, the string quartet, labor unions, environmentalism, gay rights, and the determined application of the scientific method.

Many of the ideas that have grown in acceptance relate to one another, and sometimes they have been promoted by the same idea entrepreneurs. However, as suggested in the article, although the ideas have taken parallel, and often overlapping or correlated, trajectories, it is not clear whether they are consequentially or logically or necessarily dependent on each other. It is quite possible, for example, to oppose slavery but not war; to promote the political freedoms necessary for democracy without accepting the economic liberties necessary for free-market capitalism; to embrace class or ethnic equality, but not gender equality. And people who strongly oppose abortion on moral grounds may still accept capital punishment and may be appalled by those who have the opposite predispositions. It may in general be best, then, to see each idea movement as an independent phenomenon rather than as contingent on something else or on another idea stream, rather in the way that skirt lengths are determined far more by fashion whims than by the availability of cloth and thread. There will be a correlation between the acceptance of the ideas, but it may be essentially spurious.

The article discusses this in evaluating any causal connections between democracy and war aversion. Similar considerations may apply to the notion that there is a "capitalist peace": countries may have come to embrace international peace in about the same order as they embraced capitalism, but that should not be taken to imply that capitalism necessarily "leads to" peace.

Indeed, although the idea strands of war aversion and the acceptance of free-market capitalism have undergone parallel and substantially overlapping historical trajectories, support for capitalism does not on its own necessarily imply war aversion or support for peace. In fact, people must not only embrace capitalism as an economic system, but must logically accept at least three other, or underlying, ideas as well. They must take economic prosperity and development as a dominant goal—that is, they must value economic well-being above passions that are often economically absurd, and the single-minded pursuit of wealth must be accepted as behavior that is desirable, beneficial, and even honorable. Second, they must see peace as a better motor than war for development, progress, and innovation. And, third, they must come to believe that trade, rather than conquest, is the best way to achieve their chief goal.

All three propositions have now gained wide currency, and, although international war has hardly evaporated from the planet, it has become quite rare, as documented in the "War has almost ceased to exist" article. This remarkable development may at least partly be due to the increasing joint acceptance of the capitalist/peace propositions. Over time, most countries in most areas of the world have opted for peace and, not unrelatedly, for the banal pleasures of capitalist economic development, connections discussed more fully in my 2010 article, "Capitalism, peace, and the historical movement of ideas." That article extends the discussion in the "Faulty correlation" article (some of it also found in the "War has almost ceased to exist" article), and argues that, insofar as there is a causal relationship between the ideas of peace, democracy, and capitalism, it may be best to see peace as an independent variable—a condition that facilitates (more than causes) democracy and capitalism—not, as in the common approach, as a dependent one.

However, the relationship by which peace facilitates market capitalism and economic growth is likely to be considerably stronger than the one by which it facilitates democracy. This presumably holds especially with respect to international trade. International tensions and the prospect of international war have a strong dampening effect on trade because each threatened nation has an incentive to cut itself off from the rest of the world economically in order to ensure that it can survive if international exchange is severed by military conflict.

This line of thought also related to studies such as those by Michael Mousseau concluding that any democratic peace is conditioned by economic development. Peace does probably facilitate democratic development, but it likely facilitates economic development far more—hence there is a closer relationship between peace and capitalism than between peace and democracy. But the causal relationship is not that democracy and/or capitalism cause peace. Rather, if other issues are in proper alignment, it is peace that causes—facilitates, makes more possible—democracy and capitalism.

Democracy without prerequisites

As Robert Dahl has pointed out, democracy has been "strongly associated" with a wide variety of social and economic characteristics: "a relatively high level of income and wealth per capita, long-run growth in per capita income and wealth, a high level of urbanization, a rapidly declining or relatively small agricultural population, great occupational diversity, extensive literacy, a comparatively large number of persons who have attended institutions of higher education, an economic order in which production is mainly carried on by relatively autonomous firms whose decisions are strongly oriented toward national and international markets, and relatively high levels of conventional measures of well-being."

That such characteristics are more nearly correlates than causes, Dahl observes, is suggested by the case of India, where political leaders were able to establish a viable democracy even though "the population was overwhelmingly agricultural, illiterate . . . and highly traditional and rule-bound in behavior and beliefs." Or "even more tellingly" there is the case of the United States which took to democracy when it was still "overwhelmingly rural and agricultural."

So it goes with the other supposed relationships—political culture, for example. Democracy may have been established earlier in Protestant countries than in Catholic ones, but once Catholic countries took a notion to become democratic, their religious tradition did not seem to cramp their style very much. Some analysts have held that a sizeable middle class is necessary for democracy: as one has put it, "No bourgeois, no democracy." The cases of India and quite a few other places call that generalization into question, and the recent experience in eastern Europe seems to shatter it.

Over the last two centuries the world has experienced great changes that accompanied democracy's rise: the industrial revolution, enormous economic growth, the rise of a middle class, a vast improvement in transportation and communication, surging literacy rates, and massive increases in international trade. But if these developments somehow "caused" the growth of democracy, they also stimulated its direct opposites: Nazism, fascism, Bolshevism.

Experiences over the last two decades in the post-Communist countries and elsewhere suggest that democracy is not terribly difficult to institute, that it can come about very quickly, and that it need not necessarily come accompanied by, or preceded by, the social, economic, and cultural clutter that some have often found necessary. This in turn suggests that the pessimism of some of democracy's analytic well-wishers (see note 9 in Chapter 6) may be substantially overdrawn and that the agile excuses of authoritarian foot-draggers are invalid.

As Dahl points out, the role of beliefs is "pivotal" for the rise of democracy: it is difficult to see, he notes, how democracy could exist "if there is a weak commitment to democratic principles among the political activists." By the same token, it seems to me that, as suggested in the article, a country can quite easily become democratic—*fully* democratic—without any special historical preparation and whatever the state of its social or economic development if elites or political activists generally come to believe that democracy is the way things ought to be done and if they aren't physically intimidated or held in check by authoritarian thugs. For example, it is likely that about the *only* thing keeping isolated, backward, impoverished, prerequisite-free Burma from being democratic is a group of thugs with guns. About the only prerequisite for democracy is that people—probably only the ones who happen to be in charge at the moment, actually—become convinced to allow it to come into effect.

Experience also suggests that, contrary to the gloomy and sometimes strident claims of many analysts, democracy can function remarkably well even when its constituents participate only as moved to do so and even when they exhibit little in the way of self-discipline, restraint, commitment, knowledge, or sacrifice for the general interest. For democracy to operate, people do not generally need to be good or noble, nor do they need to be deeply imbued with some sort of democratic spirit or culture. They need merely to muse about how they think things ought to be, relying on their best guesses about what would be in their own best interests or what they think might be in the general society's best interests, and, if they happen to be sufficiently moved by these musings, to express them in non-violent ways. Maybe someone will listen.

Reflections references

Robert A. Dahl, *Polyarchy*. New Haven, CT: Yale University Press, 1971.
Robert A. Dahl, *Democracy and Its Critics*. New Haven, CT: Yale University Press, 1989.
Michael Mousseau, The Social Market Roots of Democratic Peace. *International Security*, Spring 2009.

Part III

Public opinion, foreign policy, and war

Introduction

Because I consider ideas to be so important, I am strongly interested in the goings-on of people attempting to sell ideas—idea entrepreneurs. When an idea takes flight, its trajectory can very often be traced back to the deliberate efforts of agile and effective promoters. In my view, the successful promotion of the idea of war aversion can be so traced, and I try to demonstrate how this took place in *Retreat from Doomsday, Quiet Cataclysm*, and *The Remnants of War*. In *Capitalism, Democracy, and Ralph's Pretty Good Grocery*, I attempt to do the same thing for the idea entrepreneurs who eventually were so important in the increasing acceptance of democracy and capitalism over the last 250 years.

However, as with any marketing process, idea entrepreneurs fail far more often than they succeed. H. L. Mencken argued that "The whole aim of practical politics is to keep the populace alarmed (and hence clamorous to be led to safety) by menacing it with an endless series of hobgoblins, all of them imaginary." That may be a goal, but success of the effort is by no means guaranteed.

I explore some of the problems idea entrepreneurs face in "American foreign policy and public opinion in a new era: Eleven propositions" which investigates the relevance of, and the ups and downs of, foreign policy concerns to the American public since 1945. Particularly in the area of foreign policy, would-be manipulators of public opinion including the president have their work cut out for them because most people most of the time pay little attention to foreign policy. Opinion thus establishes limitations and constraints for foreign-policy makers like the president, but the inattention can sometimes also supply them with opportunities.

For example, a burgeoning literature, stemming from an article by James Fearon, has been concerned with "audience costs" – the notion that foreign policy decision-makers need to worry about unfavourable domestic reaction and consequent electoral punishment if they back down from an unwise commitment or from an incautious threat issued during a crisis. The public opinion data suggest that, although this is a sensible concern, in a large number of situations any audience cost stemming from backing off is likely to be fleeting as the public quickly settles back into its more comfortable pose of inattention to foreign policy matters and moves onto issues of greater concern to it.

"The Iraq War and the management of American public opinion" evaluates American public opinion for the Iraq War and compares the opinion patterns generated by that war to ones found earlier for the Korean and Vietnam Wars as explored in my 1973 book, *War, Presidents and Public Opinion*, and for the Gulf War of 1991 as explored in my 1994 book, *Policy and Opinion in the Gulf War*. As the title suggests, the article focuses particularly on the difficulties opinion managers face when trying to sell intervention and war.

References

Fearon, James D. Domestic Political Audiences and the Escalation of International Disputes, *American Political Science Review*. September 1994.

H. L. Mencken, *A Mencken Chrestomathy*. New York: Knopf, 1949.

8 American foreign policy and public opinion in a new era

Eleven propositions

American foreign policy is being reshaped in the wake of the cold war (Mueller 1996). And, as in the past, public opinion will play an important role in this process—indeed, it has already shown itself to be a notable impelling factor in some of the key policy decisions of the 1990s (see also Holsti 1996, chap. 6).

I would like to advance a set of propositions about American public opinion, stressing ones that seem to have implications for the practice of foreign policy in the new era. Although I focus on opinion in the United States, many of the propositions may hold as well for other countries, particularly for other developed democracies.[1]

In general, it seems, Americans are inclined to pay little attention to foreign policy issues unless there appears to be a direct threat to the United States, though they have not become more isolationist in the wake of the cold war. They are also very sensitive to the degree to which a policy is likely to cost American lives. So long as American casualties are kept low, the president has quite a bit of leeway to deal with ventures that are not highly valued, such as humanitarian interventions. Because of public inattention, however, the long-term political consequences from such ventures—whether successful or not—are likely to be low. By the time of the next election, people will have forgotten all about them.

Proposition 1

The public generally pays very little attention to international affairs.

A useful way to assess the emphasis Americans place on foreign affairs is to consider the results generated by the frequently asked poll question, "What do you think is the most important problem facing this country today?" The question poses something of a contest: the hapless respondents are essentially asked to select the most notable irritant from the huge array of calamities paraded daily in the news. Although they are allowed to give more than one response, the question does not encourage this.

The results of this question overstate concerns about political and international issues. A filter question asking the respondents whether they have given any attention to the country's problems would likely reduce the numbers of cited problems greatly—probably by half (Sterngold, Warland, and Herrmann 1994).

Moreover, the responses would be quite a bit different if the question were broader, like the one asked by Samuel Stouffer in a classic study (1955, chap. 3): "What kinds of things do you worry about most?" The "big, overwhelming response," Stouffer found, "was in terms of personal and family problems." Indeed, 80 percent "answered *solely* in these terms." The poll then posed a follow-up question, "Are there other problems you worry or are concerned about, especially political or world problems?" Fully 52 percent responded they had nothing to add.[2]

The pattern of Americans' concerns can be seen by scanning Figure 8.1, which displays results derived from responses to the question about the country's most important problem as it was posed from 1935 until the beginning of 2001. The figure shows what percentage of respondents in each poll selected an international or foreign policy issue. It appears that the American public's natural tendency with regard to international issues is to pay them little heed: people principally focus on domestic matters when asked to designate the country's most important problem. Their attention can be diverted by major threats or by explicit, specific, and dramatic dangers to American lives, but once these concerns fade, people return their attention to domestic issues with considerable alacrity—rather like "the snapping back of a strained elastic," as Gabriel Almond once put it (1960, 76).

In the 1930s, domestic problems dominated even as the approach of a major war was signaled by such dangerous events as the Munich crisis of 1938. Only when war actually began in Europe in September 1939, and then when war against Japan approached in the Pacific—from late 1939 through November 1941—did foreign affairs come to dominate the public's professed concerns.

War presumably became the chief preoccupation after the Japanese attack at Pearl Harbor in December 1941. There are no exact data, but when the most important problem question was twice asked during the war, it was prefaced by

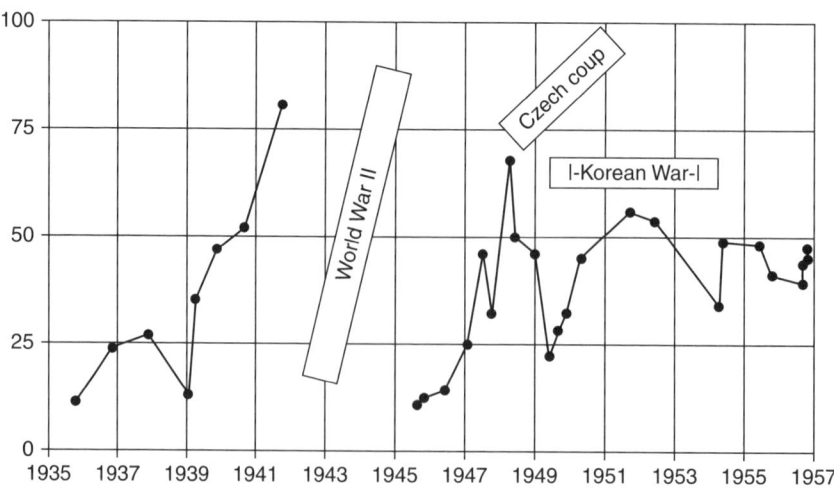

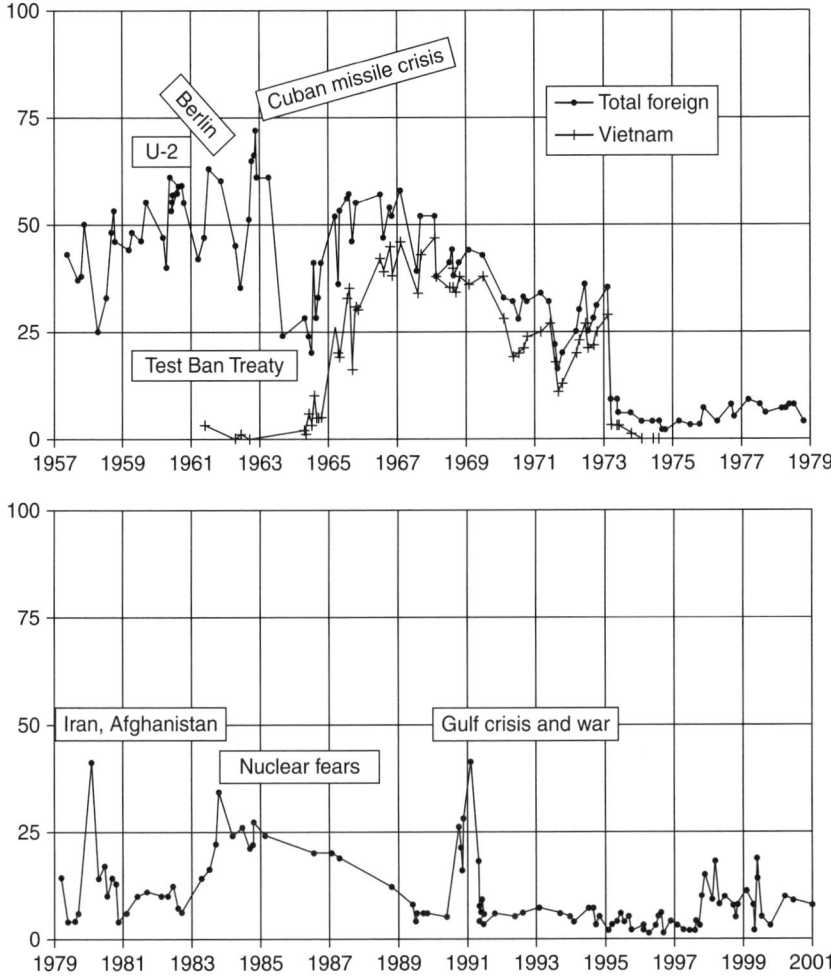

Figure 8.1 Percentage choosing a foreign policy issue as the most important problem, 1935–2001.

Source: Materials on deposit at the Roper Center for Public Opinion, Storrs, Conn., and Niemi, Mueller, and Smith 1989.

the words, "Aside from winning the war . . ." (see Smith 1985; Niemi, Mueller, and Smith 1989, 39–46). Obviously and quite reasonably, the pollsters expected respondents overwhelmingly to mention the war if they posed the question in its original form.

Attention to international concerns dropped to almost nothing at the end of the war in 1945. It rose again only two years later, as the cold war was launched, and it reached highs during the Korean War and at the time of various cold war crises through the end of 1962.

Then, in mid-1963, what might be called the classic cold war came to an end with the Soviet–American détente surrounding the signing of the Partial Test Ban Treaty (Mueller 1989, 156–62). Again, as had happened at the end of the hot war in Europe and Asia in 1945, Americans' attention to foreign affairs dropped substantially.[3]

By 1966, Vietnam had come to dominate the public's attention, and the conflict there far outstripped all other foreign concerns. Attention to international issues declined by the 1970s as U.S. casualty rates in Vietnam were reduced and as troops began to be withdrawn. The Vietnam War essentially came to an end as far as the American public was concerned with the January 1973 agreement to halt direct American participation in the fighting and, in particular, with the consequent release of American prisoners of war. Even though the United States was still committed to the area, and even though the war continued for more than two years, attention to Vietnam remained low and did not revive even when America's long-time allies, the South Vietnamese, fell to Communist forces in the spring of 1975.

Since then, few events have been able to focus the public's attention on foreign affairs. Indeed, at no time from 1969 through 2000 did foreign policy issues outweigh domestic ones in the public's concerns.

Only three international issues notably intruded upon the American public's perceptions during that period. One was a rise in attention after the Soviet invasion of Afghanistan in December 1979, a concern apparently embellished by the Iran hostage crisis, which had begun in November 1979. Even this rise is more fleeting and less impressive than might be expected, however: there was a brief spike of heightened interest in January 1980, but then a speedy and very substantial decline during the rest of that year. Another instance was the remarkably heightened anxiety over thermonuclear war that materialized in the early and mid-1980s and then withered with the rise of the disarmingly agreeable Mikhail Gorbachev in the USSR (see also Oreskes 1990). Although the episode has been substantially forgotten, as late as 1986 and 1987 over a fifth of the American public designated the danger of war as the country's greatest problem.[4] The final attention-arresting international concern of the period was the Persian Gulf crisis and war of 1990–1991. Predictably, interest dropped precipitously as soon as the war was over.

This pattern of overall inattention was abruptly shattered in September 2001 by the devastating terrorist destruction at the World Trade Center and Pentagon. For the first time in over three decades, international concerns came to outnumber domestic ones (not shown in Figure 8.1).

In the past sixty years, then, the few events that have notably caused the public to divert its attention from domestic matters have been these:

- World War II
- Certain cold war crises before 1963
- The Korean War
- The Vietnam War

- Fleetingly, the Soviet invasion of Afghanistan in late 1979 (presumably embellished by the Iran hostage crisis of 1979–1981)
- The apparently heightened prospect in the mid-1980s of nuclear war
- The Persian Gulf crisis and war
- Terrorist bombings in New York and Washington, D.C., in 2001

The central conclusion from this survey of public opinion trends is that Americans show little interest in foreign and international matters unless they espy what appears to be a clear and present threat. It could be argued that the future of ordinary Americans today is likely to be significantly affected by international developments like globalization and the political direction that Russia and China take. But issues like that are unlikely to register on a survey, crowded out as they are by such parochial domestic concerns as education, crime, drugs, and the condition of the economy. A 1998 poll, for example, asked people to list not one, but two or three problems facing the country, and no international issue even made it into double percentage figures (Rielly 1999, 7–11). In fact, in some polls in the 1990s a few percent held the country's most important problem to be that it was spending too much time worrying about foreign concerns or was spending too much money on foreign aid—responses that were dutifully included in the "foreign policy" category for the purposes of Figure 8.1 (see also Rielly 1999, 11).

However, as Figure 8.2 suggests, people do voice concern about some international issues, as least when they are specifically asked about them. Nuclear weapons remain a potentially potent concern—even as the weapons themselves dwindle in number and relevance from cold war days. The same can be said for

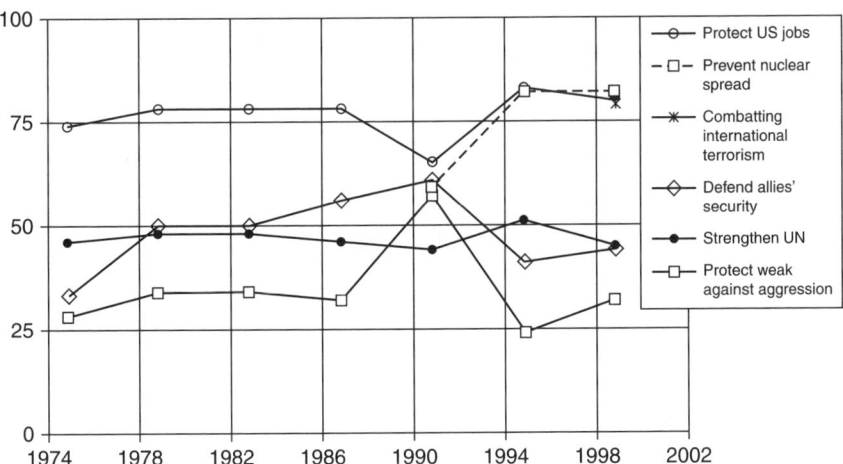

Figure 8.2 Percentage saying foreign policy goals "very important".

Source: Materials on deposit at the Roper Center for Public Opinion, Storrs, Conn., and Niemi, Mueller, and Smith 1989.

terrorism. Until the bombings of 2001, international terrorists had killed far fewer Americans than lightning or accidents caused by deer.[5] Yet, international terrorism registered as a top foreign policy concern in 1998. The bombings, obviously, will only heighten that concern. (See also p. 152.)

Proposition 2

The public's agenda and attitude on foreign affairs are set much more by the objective content of the issue and by the position of major policymakers (including the political opposition) than by the media.

Given the public's limited attention span, the media are often given great credit for setting the political agenda (Iyengar and Kinder 1987; Iyengar 1993). However, it is difficult to argue that the media had much independent impact in whipping up interest in most of the eight international concerns that have notably diverted the public's attention away from domestic matters over the last several decades.[6] Rather, the chief determinant has been the often overwhelming weight and drama of the events themselves and opinion leadership exercised by the major policymakers, especially the president—who is, after all, in part elected explicitly to direct the country's foreign policy.

Thus, Franklin D. Roosevelt was important in leading the nation toward World War II, though he hardly had to do much to focus the public's concerns after Pearl Harbor (Cantril 1944, 1967) anymore than President George W. Bush had to after the terrorist destruction of 2001. President Harry S. Truman consciously led the country into the cold war, a momentum that was continued by Dwight D. Eisenhower and John F. Kennedy (Lovell 1985, 122–23). As part of this process, Truman led the country into the Korean War, as did Lyndon Johnson into the Vietnam War and George Bush into opposing Iraq's invasion of Kuwait in 1990. In all these cases, the president found that he enjoyed a wide degree of backing among the political elite. Any notable independent impact by the media in these cases would be difficult to discern.

Much the same can be said for Jimmy Carter and his enveloping Iran hostage crisis. The president was acting within a wide consensus, though it seems possible in this case that he could have used his leadership position to dampen somewhat the concern which was, it could be argued, over something of less than massive importance (see Mueller 1984b, 1987). Following the lead of Carter—whose popularity ratings soared when the hostages were seized (Stanley and Niemi 1992, 280)—the media certainly hyped this issue, apparently in response to the actions of the president and to the demands of their customers.

The final attention-arresting international issue was the fear of war during the 1980s. Although the media unquestionably played a role by transmitting information about the issue to the public, they do not seem to have had an independent impact in this case either. After the end of the classic cold war in 1963, fears of nuclear war subsided substantially (Paarlberg 1973; Mueller 1977, 326–28). Renewed anxiety came almost out of the air: it was an old idea whose time had come again. Insofar as the issue was consciously promoted, credit must be given to the opposition parties in Europe (see Joffe 1987) and to their counterparts in the United States who were looking for an issue that they could use to undermine support for governments in office at the time—though such political exploitation of the issue seems to have come *after* nuclear concerns became popular, not before. The noisy cold war debate over missiles in Europe was also a central element in all this, it seems, as was Ronald Reagan's occasionally loose and casual verbiage about nuclear war (see Mueller 1989, 202–5).

Overall, the media seem not so much to act as agenda-setters as purveyors of information they hope will tantalize and will, accordingly, boost sales and ratings. Like any other entrepreneurial organization, they are susceptible to the market, and they follow up on those proffered items that stimulate their customers' interest. In that very important sense, the media do not set the agenda; ultimately the public does.

For example, notable public concern over a famine in Ethiopia in the mid-1980s is often taken to have been media-generated because it was only after the suffering received prominent play in the media that the issue entered the public's agenda. But Christopher Bosso's study (1989) of the phenomenon suggests a different interpretation. At first the media were reluctant to cover the story because they saw African famine as a dog-bites-man story. However, going against this journalistic consensus, NBC television decided to do a three-day sequence on the famine in October 1984, something that inspired a huge public response. NBC then gave the story extensive follow-up coverage while its television and print competitors scrambled to get on the bandwagon, deluging their customers with information that, to the surprise of those in the media, was suddenly in demand. There is a sense in which it could be said that NBC put the issue on the public's agenda. But the network is constantly doing three-day stories, and this one just happened to catch on. It seems more accurate to say that NBC put the issue on the shelf—alongside a great many others—and that it was the public that put it on the agenda.[7]

Proposition 3

The "CNN effect" is vastly exaggerated.

It is often argued that television pictures set the public's agenda and policy mood: the so-called CNN effect. Usually pictures of horrors are said to cause the public to want to do something to relieve the situation, but sometimes the pictures are said to cause the public to be repelled and to want to avoid intervention. Or we get arguments on the one hand that violent pictures on television caused people to want to get out of Vietnam, and on the other that violent pictures on television have inspired people to go out and commit violence themselves.

At any rate, the CNN effect theory essentially assumes people are so unimagi-native that they react only when they see something visualized. Yet Americans somehow managed to become outraged at and mobilized over the Pearl Harbor attack weeks—or even months—before they saw pictures of the event (see Mueller 1995a, 97–101). The Vietnam War was not noticeably more unpopular than the Korean War for the period in which the wars were comparable in American casualties, despite the fact that Vietnam is often seen to be a "television war" while Korea was fought during the medium's infancy (Mueller 1973, 167; Mandelbaum 1981; Hallin 1986).[8]

That the conventional wisdom about the CNN effect lingers on is impressive in light of the example of Bosnia during the first half of the 1990s. For years the public was deluged by vivid pictures of the problems there. Although these may have influenced the opinion of some editorial writers and columnists, they inspired remarkably little public demand to send American troops over to fix the problem (Sobel 1998; Larson 2000).

On those rare occasions when pictures have had—or seem to have had—an effect, as in Ethiopia in the mid-1980s, pundits espy a CNN effect. When pictures *fail* to have any notable impact, these theorists fail to notice—or they come up with other tortuous accountings. One explanation for the unwillingness of the American public to send troops to Bosnia is that the constant suffering shown on television did not "sensitize" the public but rather "inured" it to the violence (Orwin 1996, 49). Thus, whether the public in its collective wisdom concludes that troops should be sent or should not be sent, television always remains the convenient leader of public opinion (on this issue, see also Strobel 1997).

Proposition 4

The public applies a fairly reasonable cost-benefit analysis when evaluating foreign affairs, but it values the lives of Americans very highly and tends to undervalue the lives of foreigners.

In general, the American public seems to apply a fairly reasonable, common-sensical standard of benefit and cost when evaluating foreign affairs (see also Key 1966; Page and Shapiro 1992; Nincic 1992; Jentleson 1992; Holsti 1996, chap. 2). An assessment of probable and potential American casualties is particularly important in its evaluation (see also Wittkopf 1990, 229; Larson 1996; Klarevas 1999; Mueller 2000a).

After Pearl Harbor, the public had no difficulty accepting the necessity, and the costs, of confronting the threats presented by Germany and Japan. Then, during the cold war, it came to accept international communism as a similar source of threat and was willing to enter the wars in Korea and Vietnam as part of a perceived necessity to confront Communist challenges there—though as these wars progressed, the public engaged in a continuing reevaluation, and they had increasing misgivings about the wisdom of participating in the armed conflicts. This decline of support appears primarily to have been a function of accumulating American casualties, not of television coverage or antiwar protest: the decline of enthusiasm followed the same pattern in both wars, even though public protest and television coverage were uncommon in the Korean case (see Mueller 1973, chaps. 3–6).[9]

Policy in the Gulf War seems to have been subjected to a similar calculation. A fair number of Americans bought President Bush's notion that it was worth some

American lives—perhaps a thousand or two, far fewer than were suffered in Korea or Vietnam—to use war to turn back Saddam Hussein's invasion of Kuwait. But it is clear from poll data that, led by Democrats who had opposed the war in the first place, support for the effort would have eroded quickly if very many casualties had been suffered (see Table 8.1). A similar pattern (at much lower casualty levels) is evident when the public was asked about peacekeeping in Bosnia (see Table 8.2).

Table 8.1 American casualties and the Persian Gulf War

Question: Assuming Iraq leaves Kuwait, would you consider the war with Iraq a success if 500 American troops died, or not? (If yes) Would you consider it a success if 1,000 American troops died, or not? (If yes) Would you consider the war with Iraq a success if 5,000 American troops died, or not? (If yes) And would you consider the war with Iraq a success if 10,000 American troops died, or not? (If yes) And would you consider the war with Iraq a success if 20,000 American troops died, or not? (Accept "considers no American troops died as a success" as a volunteered response.)

Consider war with Iraq a success if Iraq leaves Kuwait and

No	American troops die	80%
500	American troops die	50
1,000	American troops die	37
5,000	American troops die	27
10,000	American troops die	20
20,000	American troops die	16
Don't know		13
Refused		7

Source: Los Angeles Times poll, January 17–18, 1991.

Table 8.2 American casualties and Bosnia

Question: Suppose you knew that if the United States sent U.S. troops to Bosnia as part of an international peacekeeping force, no/25/100/400 American soldiers would be killed. With this in mind, would you favor or oppose sending U.S. troops to Bosnia?

Projected casualties	Favor sending troops	Oppose sending troops	Don't know
No soldiers killed	68%	29	4
25 soldiers killed	31%	64	4
100 soldiers killed	30%	65	6
400 soldiers killed	21%	72	7

Source: Gallup/CNN/*USA Today* poll, October 19–22, 1995.

Although concern about American lives often seems nuanced when the public assesses foreign affairs, there are times when public abhorrence of American casualties becomes so obsessive that policy may suffer.

For example, it could be maintained that the Vietnam War was essentially supported until the prisoners of war held by Hanoi were returned. Although it may not make a great deal of sense to continue a war costing thousands of lives to gain the return of a few hundred prisoners, it would be difficult to exaggerate the political potency of this issue. In a May 1971 poll, 68 percent agreed that U.S. troops should be withdrawn from Vietnam by the end of the year. However, when asked if they would still favor withdrawal "even if it threatened [not *cost*] the lives or safety of United States POWs held by North Vietnam," support for withdrawal dropped to 11 percent (Mueller 1973, 97–98).

The emotional attachment to prisoners of war was also central to the lengthy and acrimonious peace talks in Korea, and outrage at the fate of American POWs on Bataan probably intensified hatred for the Japanese during World War II almost as much as the attack on Pearl Harbor did. Concern about American prisoners and of those missing in action continued to haunt discussions about Vietnam for decades.

A dramatic case in point was the remarkable preoccupation by politicians and press with Americans held hostage by Iran during the crisis of 1979–1981, to the virtual exclusion of issues and events likely to be of far greater importance historically. Later in the 1980s, the fate of a few hostages in Lebanon seems to have held the Reagan administration hostage, an obsession that helped to generate the Iran-contra scandal. In another episode, until the Americans taken by Iraq after its invasion of Kuwait were released in December 1990, freeing them was a major concern among Americans—far more important in the public mind than liberating Kuwait (see Table 8.3).

Although Americans are extremely sensitive to American casualties, they seem to be remarkably *in*sensitive to casualties suffered by foreigners, including essentially uninvolved—that is, innocent—civilians. It may not be surprising to discover that there was little sympathy with the Japanese civilian population during World War II—many, after all, saw Japanese civilization as one huge war machine targeted against the United States.[10] But the Gulf War was radically different in this respect: for example, 60 percent of the American public held the Iraqi people to be innocent of any blame for their leader's policies (Mueller 1994, 316). However, this lack of animosity toward the Iraqi people did not translate into a great deal of sympathy among the American public for civilian casualties caused by air attacks. Extensive pictures and publicity about the civilian casualties resulting from an attack on a Baghdad bomb shelter on February 13, 1991 had no impact on support for bombing (Mueller 1994, 317). Moreover, images of the "highway of death" and reports that 100,000 Iraqis had died in the war[11] scarcely dampened enthusiasm at the various "victory" and "welcome home" parades and celebrations. Nor was much sympathy or even interest shown for the Iraqi civilian deaths that resulted from the severe sanctions imposed on Iraq by the United States during the 1990s (see Mueller and Mueller 1999, 2000; Mueller 2000a).

Table 8.3 Reasons for fighting Iraq

Question: Now that the U.S. (United States) forces have been sent to Saudi Arabia and other areas of the Middle East, do you think they should engage in combat if Iraq . . .

Date of poll	Engage in combat	Do not engage in combat	Don't know
A. invades Saudi Arabia?			
1990 Aug 9–10	67%	23	10
1990 Oct 18–19*	68%	19	13
B. refuses to leave Kuwait and restore its former government?			
1990 Aug 9–10	42%	40	18
1990 Oct 18–19*	45%	37	18
1990 Nov 15–16*	46%	40	14
C. continues to hold U.S. civilians hostage?			
1990 Aug 9–10**	61%	30	9
1990 Oct 18–19*	57%	32	11
1990 Nov 15–16*	55%	34	11
D. kills American civilians in Kuwait and Iraq?			
1990 Aug 9–10	79%	14	7
E. begins to control or cut off oil?			
1990 Aug 9–10	58%	31	11
F. attacks U.S. forces?			
1990 Aug 9–10	94%	4	2
1990 Oct 18–19 *	93%	3	4
1990 Nov 15–16 *	91%	6	3

Source: Gallup polls.

* Response items rotated from interview to interview to deal with the possibility that the order in which the items are asked affects the response.
** Holds American civilians hostage.

Proposition 5

The public has not become newly isolationist: it is about as accepting of involvement in foreign affairs as ever, but it does not have—and never has had—much stomach for losing American lives in ventures and arenas that are of little concern to it.

After the cold war, some people have become worried that the American public has turned—or may turn—isolationist since it has been able notably to contain its enthusiasm for sending American troops to police such trouble spots as Bosnia and Haiti. But it seems more likely that there has been little essential change in Americans' standards. Figure 8.3 displays the results for a set of questions

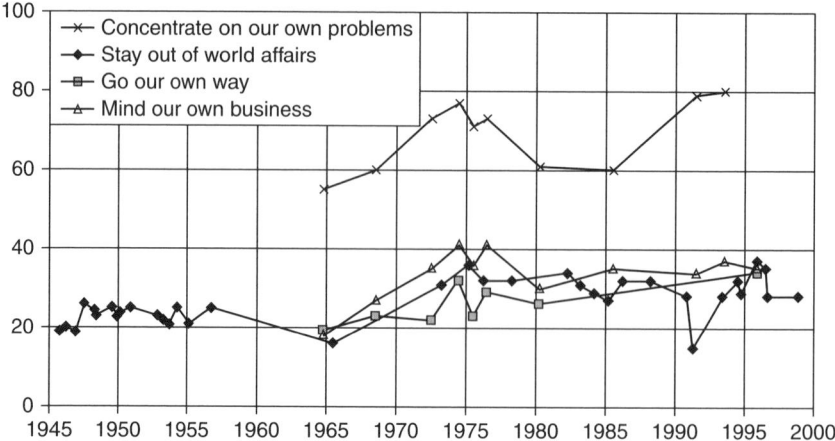

We shouldn't think so much in international terms but concentrate more on our own national problems and building up our strength and prosperity here at home.

Do you think it will be best for the future of this country if we take an active part in world affairs, or if we stayed out of world affairs?

Since the United States is the most powerful nation in the world, we should go our own way in international matters, not worrying too much about whether other countries agree with us or not.

The United States should mind its own business internationally and let other countries get along as best they can on their own.

Figure 8.3 Isolationism questions.

Source: Materials on deposit at the Roper Center for Public Opinion, Storrs, Conn., and Niemi, Mueller, and Smith 1989.

designed to tap isolationism. As usual in public opinion surveys, the response percentages vary with the wording of the question. However, if we focus on consistently worded questions, we find that the ending of the cold war did not have much impact. There was some rise in isolationism after Vietnam in the mid-1970s, and something of a decline since then (an abrupt drop registered at the end of the Gulf War in 1991 was quickly corrected). For the most part, overall changes have been modest.

With respect to foreign interventions, the public seems to apply, as usual, a fairly reasonable cost-benefit calculus. A substantial loss of American lives may have been tolerable if the enemy was a threat like international communism or the country that bombed Pearl Harbor, but risking lives to police small, distant, unthreatening, and apparently perennially troubled countries has proved difficult for the public to accept.

For example, the international mission to Somalia in 1992–1993 helped to bring a degree of order to a deadly situation that was causing a famine reportedly killing at its peak thousands of people per day. Perhaps never before has so much been done for so many at such little cost. There seems to have been considerable support for the mission when Bush put it into effect in late 1992 (cautiously waiting, however, until after the presidential election). But it seems clear that the policy of nation building, shaped by the new Clinton administration in 1993 and much criticized by Republicans as unwise "mission creep," was dampening support for the venture even before eighteen Americans were killed in a firefight on the night of October 3–4, 1993 (Larson 1996; Strobel 1997, 166–83; Burk 1999, 66–67; Klarevas 1999). After that, support, already substantially reduced, it seems, to its hardcore supporters, dropped even further, and criticism became rampant.[12]

In essence, when Americans asked themselves how many American lives peace in Somalia was worth, the answer came out rather close to zero, as Table 8.4 forcefully suggests (see also Dole 1995, 41). The general reluctance to become involved in the actual fighting in Bosnia (despite years of the supposed CNN effect) suggests that Americans reached a similar conclusion for that trouble spot—as have, it seems, others in their own terms, including Britons, Germans, and Canadians.[13] It seems clear that policing efforts will be tolerated only as long as the costs in lives for the policing forces remain extremely low.

It is true that during the cold war Americans were willing, at least at the outset, to send troops to die in Korea and Vietnam, but that was because they subscribed to the containment notion which held communism to be a genuine threat to the United States. Polls from the time make it clear that the public had little interest in losing American lives simply to help out the South Koreans or South Vietnamese (see Table 8.5 and Mueller 1973, 44, 48–49, 58, 100–1). Similarly, as Figure 8.2 suggests, "protecting weaker nations against foreign aggression" (much less, fighting to do so) has usually achieved comparatively low ratings among foreign policy goals both during and after the cold war (though it did rise notably during the Gulf crisis of 1990). Thus an unwillingness to send Americans to die for purposes that are essentially humanitarian is hardly new.[14]

Table 8.4 American casualties and Somalia

Question: Nothing the U.S. could accomplish in Somalia is worth the death of even one more U.S. soldier.

60%	Agree
35	Disagree
5	Not sure

Source: Time/CNN/Yankelovich poll, October 7, 1993.

Table 8.5 Reasons for continuing the Vietnam War

Question: Here is a list of arguments that have been given for our military effort in Vietnam. I'm going to ask you to read over this card carefully. Then I'm going to ask you to tell me which *two or three* of these you yourself feel are the *very* strongest arguments.	
49%	If we do not continue, the Communists will take over Vietnam and then move on to other parts of the world
48%	We must support our fighting men
33%	If we quit now, it would weaken the will of other countries to defend their freedom
33%	If we give up now, the whole expenditure of American lives and money will have been in vain
24%	The United States should never accept defeat
23%	If we do not continue, we will lose prestige and the confidence of our friends and allies abroad
19%	We are committed to South Vietnam
14%	If we pull out and the Communists take over, they will kill many of the Vietnamese who have opposed them
8%	If we persevere, we are sure to gain our objectives

Source: Institute for International Social Research, February 1968.

Proposition 6

Foreign policy has become less important in judging the performance of the president and of presidential contenders.

During the cold war, foreign policy was often a prominent theme in presidential campaigns. The Berlin Blockade accompanied the 1948 election; Korea was important in 1952;[15] the Suez crisis and Soviet intervention in Hungary were in the background in 1956; Kennedy and Nixon battled it out over who could stand up best to Khrushchev and Castro in 1960; and Vietnam was a notable concern in the elections of 1964, 1968, and 1972.

Thereafter, as is also suggested by the data in Figure 8.1, foreign policy declined in significance. It was of very little relevance in the 1976 election campaign between Carter and Ford (Mueller 1977, 328). It played more of a role in 1980, with the Iran hostage crisis, and in 1984 and 1988, with anxiety about nuclear war, arms control, and defense spending; overall, however, these elections were substantially dominated by domestic issues like inflation, unemployment, crime, government spending, and drug policy (Aldrich, Sullivan, and Borgida 1989).

In the wake of the cold war, any tendency by the American public to ignore foreign policy has surely been heightened. With his Gulf War success and with his opponent's complete lack of experience in foreign policy, George Bush tried very hard to make foreign affairs an important issue in the 1992 campaign. But he failed, as the public quickly refocused its attention on domestic matters (see

Mueller 1994, 90, 103–7). Foreign policy was also substantially missing from the election campaigns of 1996 and 2000. Whether concern over international terrorism after the attacks of 2001 will change this in future elections remains to be seen.

Proposition 7

There is little or no long-term political gain from successful international ventures.

When American troops are sent abroad into dangerous situations, there is usually a "rally round the flag" effect: the commander in chief's approval ratings rise abruptly (Mueller 1973, 208–13). But it is important to note that this phenomenon tends to be fleeting. The public does not seem to be very interested in rewarding—or even remembering—foreign policy success.

If Bush found little lasting electoral advantage in a large dramatic victory like the Gulf War (or, earlier, for his successful intervention in Panama), lesser accomplishments seem to have been at least as unrewarding. Nobody gave Eisenhower much credit for a successful venture into Lebanon in 1958, to Johnson for success in the Dominican Republic in 1965, to Carter for husbanding an important Middle East treaty in 1979, to Reagan for a successful invasion of Grenada in 1983, or to Bill Clinton for resolving the Bosnia problem in 1995. Even Truman, who presided over the massive triumph in World War II, saw his approval plummet to impressive lows within months because of domestic concerns.[16]

At the time of the Kosovo bombings of 1999, press accounts argued that the presidential ambitions and political future of Clinton's vice president, Al Gore, hung in the balance and that the outcome would "make or unmake Clinton's much-discussed legacy" (Kettle 1999; Zelnick 1999; Page 1999; Balz and Neal 1999). From the standpoint of public opinion, the Kosovo venture seems to have been a success. But when he launched his campaign for the presidency a few months later, Gore scarcely thought it important or memorable enough to bring up, and Clinton's "much-discussed legacy" seems to have centered on rather different matters.[17]

Proposition 8

There is little or no long-term political loss from international failures when the perceived stakes are low unless the failure becomes massively expensive; this means that U.S. leaders can abruptly pull out of failed peacekeeping missions without having to worry much about political costs.

While Americans place a high, even sometimes exaggerated, value on the lives of other Americans, their reaction when Americans are killed varies considerably. In some cases the death of Americans leads to demands for revenge, in others for cutting losses and withdrawing. Which emotion prevails seems to depend on an evaluation of the stakes involved.

When Americans were killed at Pearl Harbor, the outraged call for revenge against the Japanese was overwhelming. But Japan was also seen as a palpable threat to the United States itself—indeed, many were anticipating an attack on the U.S. mainland. Much of this could also be seen in the public response to the terrorist attacks on New York and Washington in 2001. Similarly, although American decision makers apparently thought differently at the time, it seems clear from poll results like those in Table 8.3 that if Iraq had attacked American troops in the Saudi desert, where they were placed after Iraq's invasion of Kuwait, the Pearl Harbor syndrome would have been activated: Saddam Hussein would likely have been seen as an aggressor whose appetite knew no bounds and who must be confronted immediately (see also Mueller 1994, 123). Table 8.3 also suggests that if Saddam had killed some of his American hostages, his deed would have formed a major reason to go to war (far more than his cutting off oil supplies to the United States).

When the value of the stakes does not seem to be worth additional American lives, however, the public has shown a willingness to abandon an overextended or untenable position. Thus the public came to accept—even substantially to support—the decision to withdraw U.S. policing troops from Lebanon in 1983 after a terrorist bomb killed 241 U.S. marines in the chaotic civil war there. Public opinion data on the episode are sparse, but they tend to suggest that the Lebanon venture was never very popular with the public (Larson 1996, 48; Burk 1999, 65). In the two or three days after the marines were killed, the polls detected a sharp rise in the percentage calling for the sending in of more troops to avenge or deal with the tragedy; but this reaction dissipated within a few days. Meanwhile, the percentage advocating removal of the troops remained high and then grew considerably during the next weeks (see Table 8.6). Similarly, the deaths of eighteen U.S. soldiers in Somalia in 1993 helped lead to outraged demands for withdrawal, not for calls to avenge the humiliation. Unlike the problems with Japan in 1941 or Iraq in 1990, the situations in Lebanon and Somalia did not present much of a wider threat to American interests, and the public was quite willing to support measures to cut its losses and leave.

These episodes demonstrate that when peacekeeping leads to unacceptable deaths, peacekeepers can be readily removed with little concern about saving face. As Table 8.7 suggests, after the fact, Americans said that although they considered Reagan's expedition to Lebanon to have been a failure, many, with reasonable nuance, felt it still to have been "a good idea at the time." The lessons of Korea and Vietnam suggest that there can be electoral consequences if casualties are allowed to rise very substantially. But if a venture is seen to be of little importance, a president can, precisely because of that, cut and run without fear of inordinate electoral costs. As the experiences with Lebanon and Somalia suggest, by the time the next election rolls around, people will have substantially forgotten the whole thing. Thus, the situation does not have to become a quagmire.[18] Presidential adviser Dick Morris has argued that "if foreign policy is misplayed, it can hurt an incumbent's image faster than can domestic errors" (1999, 164). The tarnishing of the image may be swift, but it need not be debilitating in the long term.

Table 8.6 U.S. policy in Lebanon

Question: Would you say . . .

	the U.S. should send more troops to Lebanon	leave the number of troops about the same	or remove the troops that are there now	Don't know
Sept 22–26, 1993	7%	48	40	5
Oct 23, 1993	241 Marines are killed in bomb attack			
Oct 23, 1993	21%	21	48	10
Oct 24, 1993	Reagan gives press conference			
Oct 25, 1993	31%	26	39	5
Oct 26, 1993	16%	33	45	6
Oct 27, 1993	Reagan gives speech on Lebanon, Grenada			
Oct 28, 1993	17%	41	37	5
Nov 3–7, 1993	13%	41	39	7
Dec 8–13, 1993	9%	38	48	5
Jan 3, 1994	5%	30	59	6
Jan 4, 1994	8%	29	57	6
Jan 12–17, 1994	7%	31	58	4
Feb 1994	U.S. troops are redeployed to ships offshore			
Mar 30, 1994	Reagan formally withdraws from peacekeeping			

Source: ABC, ABC/*Washington Post* polls.

Table 8.7 Success and failure in Lebanon

Question: Do you think the removal of the U.S. Marines from Lebanon means that Ronald Reagan's policies were a success or failure?

19%	Success
15	Neither (volunteered)
54	Failure
15	Not sure

Question: Which of the following statements come closest to your opinion about sending U.S. Marines to Lebanon?

33%	It was a big mistake to send them at all
45	It was a good idea at the time but it didn't work
15	We should have sent more of them to begin with
7	Not sure

Sources: NBC News poll, March 8–11, 1984, and CBS/*New York Times* poll, February 21–25, 1984.

Proposition 9

If they are not being killed, American troops can remain in peacekeeping ventures virtually indefinitely.

Although there is an overwhelming political demand that casualties in ventures deemed of little importance be extremely low, there seems to be little problem about keeping occupying forces in place as long as they are not being killed—for the most part, nobody will even remember that they are there. Thus, it is not important to have an "exit strategy," a "closed-end commitment," or "a time-certain for withdrawal," except perhaps to sell an interventionist policy in the first place.

After the Somalia fiasco, for example, the Americans stayed on for several months; since none were killed, Americans at home paid little attention and voiced little concern. Similarly, although there was little public or political support for sending U.S. troops to Haiti in 1994, there was almost no protest about keeping them there since no one was killed—in fact, when the last of them were withdrawn in March 1996 the story was given eleven inches in a lower corner of page 14 of the *New York Times* (Mitchell 1996). Although Clinton suggested that policing troops sent to Bosnia in 1995 might be withdrawn after one year, there was hardly any protest when their stay was extended. And Americans tolerated—indeed, hardly noticed—the stationing of hundreds of thousands of U.S. troops in Europe, Japan, and South Korea for decades on end. If they are not being killed, it scarcely matters whether the troops are in Macedonia or in Kansas.

On the other hand, if American troops start being killed in low-valued ventures, there will be public and political demands to get them out, whatever the initial plans for withdrawal had been. Thus, despite calls for knowing in advance what the endgame will be (see Powell 1992/93; Sciolino 1993), the only exit strategy required is a tactical arrangement to yank the troops abruptly and painlessly from the scene should things go awry.

Therefore, presidents would be wise to sell low-valued ventures not with cosmic internationalist hype, but rather as international social work that can be shrugged off if necessary. For all his high-flown rhetoric about the importance of Bosnia, Clinton was never able to increase the number of Americans who saw wisdom or value in sending U.S. policing troops there, even though it was expected that there would be few casualties (Sobel 1998; Larson 2000; see also Mueller 2000b, 2000c). Similarly, his echoing in 1994 of Bush's earlier amazing hyperbole about the antidemocratic coup in Haiti—that it posed "an unusual and extraordinary threat to the national security, foreign policy, and economy of the United States"—seems to have had no resonance with the American public, which may very well see such hyperbole as nonsense and an insult to their intelligence.

Fortunately, the public often seems more sensible than its leaders. When he sent the marines to help police Lebanon, Ronald Reagan declared that "in an age of nuclear challenge and economic interdependence, such conflicts are a threat to all the people of the world, not just to the Middle East itself" (1983, 1096). Despite having gotten such an overblown sales pitch from the president, however, the public had no difficulty accepting Reagan's later decision to have the marines "redeployed to the sea" after 241 of them had been killed by a terrorist bomb.

Proposition 10

A danger in peacekeeping missions is that Americans might be taken hostage, something that can suddenly and disproportionately magnify the perceived stakes.

Because of the overriding importance Americans place on American lives, as discussed in proposition 4, policy remains vulnerable to hostage taking. I have argued that peacekeeping ventures need not become quagmires because a president can still abruptly withdraw troops from an overextended position with little long-lasting political cost. However, this principle can be dramatically reversed if even a small number of Americans are taken hostage.

The process is illustrated best by some evidence from the Somalia episode. After the debacle of October 1993, a Somalia group captured one American soldier. The public's determination to remain until the prisoner was recovered (and then to withdraw) is clear from Table 8.8.

Policymakers seem well aware of this problem. Much of the reticence about bombing in Bosnia stemmed from fear that West European peacekeepers might be caught in the crossfire or taken hostage. Accordingly, extensive bombing was begun in 1995 only after troops had been quietly removed from vulnerable areas. The same thing happened with bombing campaigns against Iraq in 1998 and against Serbia in 1999.

Table 8.8 U.S. policy in Somalia

Question: Which of these three policies do you most favor for U.S. policy in Somalia?

11%	withdraw all U.S. troops immediately
67	withdraw all U.S. troops but only after all U.S. servicemen are returned
19	or stay in Somalia until political stability is restored?
3	Not sure

Source: NBC News poll, October 6, 1993.

Proposition 11

The degree to which notable international events linger in the public mind after they are over varies rather curiously and does not appear to depend on their inherent historical importance.

As is clear from the preceding analysis, few international events and issues have managed to arrest the public's attention substantially. The degree to which notable and noted events have had a long-range impact varies in a sometimes rather puzzling manner. Some linger on more or less continuously in the public consciousness, some vanish quickly and never revive, some linger for a while and then suddenly vanish, and some vanish for a while but then become revived in memory.

Events that linger

The best example of an international event that continued uninterruptedly to live in memory long after it was over is undoutedly World War II. The war was a massive affair, affecting all strata of society, and it continued, and continues, to affect popular perceptions. On the domestic side, something somewhat comparable could probably be said for the Great Depression—an unpleasant event that had a long, lingering impact.

Events that vanish

The Gulf War seems prototypical of international events that vanish. On the eve of the war, half of the American people claimed that they thought about the crisis at least once an hour (Mueller 1994, 214). But when it was over, it quickly, and apparently permanently, vanished from sight and recall—as its author, George Bush, ruefully found out in his unsuccessful reelection campaign a year later. In this, public opinion may appropriately be reflecting historical reality: it is difficult to escape the conclusion that from the standpoint of world history the war was really quite a minor event (Mueller 1994, chap. 9). However, the cold war cannot so easily be dismissed as a historical sideshow. Yet it seems already to be picking up a patina of quaintness as it recedes from memory.[19]

Events that linger, then vanish

The Korean War may well have been the most important event since World War II. It was the most costly war in the period (Small and Singer 1982), and it essentially crystallized the cold war (see Gaddis 1974; Jervis 1980; May 1984; Mueller 1989, chap. 6). Moreover, it seems to have importantly affected public perceptions throughout the 1950s (see Mueller 1979, 314–15). The War of 1812 also lingered for quite a while and influenced several elections. Yet both wars eventually sagged from public consciousness, and both, interestingly enough, have inspired books with titles labeling them "forgotten" conflicts (Blair 1987; Hickey 1989).

Events that vanish, then revive

The Vietnam War was the great nonissue of the 1976 election campaign—just a year after the war concluded—and it continued to be neglected by the public for several years (see Lovell 1992, 389–91). Americans, it seemed, did not want to think about a costly and unpleasant failure like Vietnam—in part, perhaps, because they did not want to have to consider doing something about the consequent Khmer Rouge genocide in Cambodia, a catastrophe that garnered a total of less than twenty-nine minutes of coverage on all three networks at the time (Adams and Joblove 1982). Yet, by the 1980s, Vietnam had become a fabled and memorable event, even a haunting one, in the American consciousness, and it seems likely to remain one for a long time. Something similar happened with the Civil War—probably the most important event in American history. For twenty years there was a considerable desire to forget the conflict, but then the building of myths—and of memorials and monuments—began (see Linderman 1987).

Overall, then, neither the scope of the event nor its objective historical importance seems precisely to determine the pattern it takes in public recall.

Notes

1 Unless otherwise indicated, all data come from materials on deposit at the Roper Center for Public Opinion, Storrs, Conn., and from Niemi, Mueller, and Smith (1989). This paper is dedicated to the memory of John Lovell and was written in part while the author was a guest fellow at the Norwegian Nobel Institute in Oslo. The Institute's support is gratefully acknowledged.

2 Results like these frequently elicit disapproving tongue-clicking. It is not clear, however, why one should expect people to spend a lot of time worrying about national or international problems, particularly when democratic capitalism not only leaves them free to choose other ways to get their kicks but in its seemingly infinite quest for variety is constantly developing seductive distractions. Some people are intensely interested in government and world affairs, but it verges on the arrogant to suggest that others are somehow inadequate or derelict unless they share the same curious passion (see Mueller 1999, chap. 6).

3 For an analysis of American expectations of war during the classic cold war period, see Mueller (1979).

4 For data, see Mueller (1994, 211–12). It could be argued that, objectively speaking, thermonuclear war is the most important problem facing the country, considering the potential devastation. Clearly, however, the poll respondents are not unreasonably building an estimate of probability into their responses. For example, it appears that no one has ever suggested that the explosion of the sun might be the country's most important problem.

5 In almost all years, fewer than ten Americans die at the hands of international terrorists (U.S. Department of State 1998, 85). By contrast, an average of ninety Americans are killed each year by lightning (National Safety Council 1997, 120), and about 100 die in accidents caused by deer (Revkin 1998). The destructiveness of the 2001 bombings in which thousands perished is thus unprecedentedly extreme.

6 Nor, it might be added, has the speed with which the public receives news significantly increased in recent decades. Once the telegraph was established in the nineteenth century, information that had previously taken days, weeks, months, or even years to travel could be relayed almost instantly, reaching ordinary citizens within a very few hours as newspapers came out with special editions. With the arrival of radio and, much later, television, the information delay was further reduced—at least for those who happen to have their radio or television sets turned on at the time. But this is a comparatively minor improvement.

7 In some important respects, the Gulf War experience also calls into question, or at least delimits, the notion that the media has a great independent impact in agenda-setting in international affairs. Throughout, journalists and editors reported what was going on, and they correctly doped out what their public wanted (especially supportive, uncritical news during the war itself). So instructed, they supplied that need, but they did not invent it nor did they invent the issues that, for a while, so engrossed the public. Then, following their customers, the media dutifully shifted their attention to domestic

concerns at the end of the war, despite the strenuous efforts of the previously influential president to keep the war euphoria and glow alive. The message and the customer dominated, even intimidated, the medium. For a fuller discussion, see Mueller (1994, 129–36).

8 During World War II an experiment was made to determine whether "realistic" war pictures would hurt morale. It found that those who were exposed to such pictures were not any more or less likely to support the war than an unexposed control group. Those exposed, however, did become more favorable to showing people realistic war pictures (National Opinion Research Center 1944). Other studies found that efforts of the military to use propaganda films to indoctrinate new draftees were ineffective (Kinder and Sears 1985, 706).

9 This conclusion is principally derived from trend data on the percentage holding the wars to have been a mistake. Opinion data concerning policy options do not permit a precise trend assessment about whether the public came to support withdrawal or escalation during the course of the wars because the polling agencies constantly changed the wording of the relevant questions in important ways (for an extensive display and analysis of such data, see Mueller 1973, chap. 4). For an analysis that seems to be insensitive to this issue, see Schwarz (1994); for a correction, see Larson (1996).

10 Asked what should be done with the Japanese after the war, 10 to 15 percent volunteered the solution of extermination. And after the war was over, 23 percent said they regretted that many more atomic bombs had not "quickly" been used on Japan before it "had a chance to surrender" (Mueller 1973, 172–73).

11 This figure is almost certainly much too high, probably by a factor of more than 10; see Mueller (1995b).

12 The popularly accepted notion that the debacle was importantly caused by the UN (Dole 1995, 37) is not only wrong but grotesque; see Gordon and Friedman (1993). Despite the criticism of the UN that this episode inspired, especially from Republicans, there has been no notable decline in public support for the UN (Murray, Klarevas, and Hartley 1997; see also Figure 8.2).

13 After Spanish troops had suffered some seventeen deaths in the Bosnian war, their government indicated that this was enough, and they withdrew from further confrontation, something that greatly encouraged the Croat gangs the Spanish had been dealing with (Hedges 1997). Similarly, Belgium abruptly withdrew from Rwanda—and, to save face, urged others to do so as well—when ten of its policing troops were massacred and mutilated early in the genocide (Gourevitch 1998, 114, 149–50). For the remarkable conclusion, based on a single poll question, that Americans might be willing, on average, to sacrifice 6,861 U.S. military deaths in order to stabilize a democratic government in Congo, see Feaver and Gelpi (1999). For a similar take, see Kull and Destler (1999, 106–8), critiqued by Larson (1999, 625).

14 Actually, this is not such an unusual position for humanitarian ventures. If Red Cross or other workers are killed while carrying out humanitarian missions, their organizations frequently threaten to withdraw, no matter how much good they may be doing. Essentially what they are saying, then, is that the saving of lives is not worth the deaths of even a few of their service personnel.

15 The Republican presidential campaign apparently was able to raise the salience of the Korean War as an issue, however; see Harris (1954, 25).

16 The truly big electoral loser of World War II was Britain's Winston Churchill, voted out of office even as he was attending a peace conference at the end of the war. Nor did Woodrow Wilson or his party derive long-term benefit from victory in World War I. There may be some partial exceptions to this pattern, however. Eisenhower benefited from the Korean War, but that was not because he had instituted it. Rather, his achievement was in apparently bringing it to an end within six months of his inauguration in 1953, something that may well have been the most significant achievement turned in by any postwar president: it was still remembered as a great accomplishment seven years

later when Eisenhower was leaving office, and it was pointedly brought up again by Republicans in the 1968 election, a full fifteen years after the event (Mueller 1973, 234). A good case for an exception seems to be the War of 1812, which apparently benefited the Republicans who had instituted it (see Mueller 1994, 108–11), and something similar may have happened after the Civil War. The successful Falklands War of 1982 may have helped British prime minister Margaret Thatcher in the elections of 1983, but the effect is confounded by the fact that the economy was improving impressively at the same time; see Norpoth (1987a, 1987b).

17 Conceivably, a successful venture will help if it comes close enough to the next election—Bush might have benefited, perhaps, if he had been able to stage the Gulf War so that it wrapped up within a few days or weeks of the election. There may have been such an effect in the March 2000 presidential election in Russia, where the popular invasion of Chechnya seems to have boosted Vladimir Putin's election prospects even higher than they might otherwise have been.

18 Most remarkably in this regard, the utter collapse of the American position in Vietnam in 1975 was actually used by the man who presided over it, Gerald Ford, as a point in his favor in his reelection campaign of 1976. When he came into office, he observed, "We were still deeply involved in the problems of Vietnam" but now "we are at peace. Not a single young American is fighting or dying on any foreign soil" (Kraus 1979, 538–39; see also Mueller 1984a).

19 In 1945, the Western victors of the war faced two major international problems: what to do about the defeated countries, Germany and Japan, and what to do about the emerging conflict with the USSR. Since it involved a lot of interesting conflict, the latter problem has inspired a much greater literature. But it seems quite possible that in time the cold war will be remembered as something of a historical curiosity. By contrast, the successful solution of the Japan–Germany problem—making those countries over into moderate and prosperous allies and peaceful competitors whose view of the world is much like that of the Western victors—may well come to be seen as a much more momentous development historically.

References

Adams, William C., and Michael Joblove. 1982. The Unnewsworthy Holocaust: TV News and Terror in Cambodia. In *Television Coverage of International Affairs*, ed. William C. Adams. Norwood, NJ: Ablex Publishing.

Aldrich, John H., John L. Sullivan, and Eugene Borgida. 1989. Foreign Affairs and Issue Voting: Do Presidential Candidates "Waltz Before a Blind Audience?" *American Political Science Review* 83(1) March: 123–41.

Almond, Gabriel A. 1960. *The American People and Foreign Policy*. New York: Praeger.

Balz, Dan, and Terry M. Neal. 1999. Gore Benefits, but Will War Issue Stay Hot? *Washington Post* 6 June.

Blair, Clay. 1987. *The Forgotten War: America in Korea, 1950–1953*. New York: Times Books.

Bosso, Christopher. 1989. Setting the Agenda: Mass Media and the Discovery of Famine in Ethiopia. In *Manipulating Public Opinion: Essays on Public Opinion as a Dependent Variable*, ed. Michael Margolis and Gary A. Mauser. Pacific Grove, CA: Brooks/Cole.

Burk, James. 1999. Public Support for Peacekeeping in Lebanon and Somalia: Assessing the Casualties Hypothesis. *Political Science Quarterly* 114(1) Spring: 53–78.

Cantril, Hadley. 1967. *The Human Dimension: Experiences in Policy Research*. New Brunswick, NJ: Rutgers University Press.

Cantril, Hadley and Associates. 1944. *Gauging Public Opinion*. Princeton, NJ: Princeton University Press.

Dole, Bob. 1995. Shaping America's Global Future. *Foreign Policy* Spring: 29–43.

Feaver, Peter D., and Christopher Gelpi. 1999. Casualty Aversion; How Many Deaths Are Acceptable? A Surprising Answer. *Washington Post* 7 November.

Gaddis, John Lewis. 1974. Was the Truman Doctrine a Real Turning Point? *Foreign Affairs* 52(2) January: 386–401.

Gourevitch, Philip. 1998. *We Wish to Inform You That Tomorrow We Will Be Killed With Our Families: Stories from Rwanda*. New York: Farrar Straus and Giroux.

Hallin, Daniel C. 1986. *The "Uncensored War": The Media and Vietnam*. New York: Oxford University Press.

Harris, Louis. 1954. *Is There a Republican Majority? Political Trends, 1952–1956*. New York: Harper's.

Hedges, Chris. 1997. On Bosnia's Ethnic Fault Lines, It's Still Tense, but World Is Silent. *New York Times* 28 February.

Hickey, Donald R. 1989. *The War of 1812: A Forgotten Conflict*. Urbana and Chicago: University of Illinois Press.

Holsti, Ole R. 1996. *Public Opinion and American Foreign Policy*. Ann Arbor: University of Michigan Press.

Iyengar, Shato. 1993. Agenda Setting and Beyond: Television News and the Strength of Political Issues. In *Agenda Formation*, ed. William H. Riker. Ann Arbor: University of Michigan Press.

Iyengar, Shanto, and Donald R. Kinder. 1987. *News That Matters: Television and American Opinion*. Chicago, IL: University of Chicago Press.

Jentleson, Bruce W. 1992. The Pretty Prudent Public: Post Post-Vietnam American Opinion on the Use of Military Force. *International Studies Quarterly* 36(1) March: 49–74.

Jervis, Robert. 1980. The Impact of the Korean War on the Cold War. *Journal of Conflict Resolution* 24(4) December: 563–92.

Joffe, Josef. 1987. Peace and Populism: Why the European Anti-Nuclear Movement Failed. *International Security* 11(4) Spring: 3–40.

Kettle, Martin. 1999. Kosovo Holds the Key to Gore's Prospects. *Guardian Weekly* 6 June.

Key, V.O., Jr. 1966. *The Responsible Electorate: Rationality in Presidential Voting, 1936–1960*. New York: Vintage.

Kinder, Donald R., and David O. Sears. 1985. Public Opinion and Political Action. In Vol. 2, *Handbook of Social Psychology*, ed. Gardner Lindzey and Elliot Aronson. New York: Random House.

Klarevas, Louis J. 1999. *American Public Opinion on Peace Operations: The Cases of Somalia, Rwanda, and Haiti*. Dissertation American University.

Kraus, Sidney. 1979. *The Great Debates: Carter vs. Ford, 1976*. Bloomington: Indiana University Press.

Kull, Steven, and I. M. Destler. 1999. *Misreading the Public: The Myth of a New Isolationism*. Washington, DC: Brookings.

Larson, Eric V. 1996. *Casualties and Consensus: The Historical Role of Casualties in Domestic Support for U.S. Military Operations*. Santa Monica, CA: RAND Corporation.

——. 1999. Review of Kull and Destler, *Misreading the Public. Public Opinion Quarterly* 63(4) Winter: 624–27.

——. 2000. Putting Theory to Work: Diagnosing Public Opinion on the U.S. Intervention in Bosnia. In *Being Useful: Policy Relevance and International Relations*, ed. Miroslav Nincic and Joseph Lepgold. Ann Arbor: University of Michigan Press.

Lovell, John P. 1985. *The Challenge of American Foreign Policy: Purpose and Adaptation*. New York: Macmillan.

——. 1992. The Limits of "Lessons Learned": From Vietnam to the Gulf War. *Peace & Change* 17(4) October: 379–401.

Mandelbaum, Michael. 1981. Vietnam: The Television War. *Daedalus* Fall: 157–69.

May, Ernest R. 1984. The Cold War. In *The Making of America's Soviet Policy*, ed. Joseph S. Nye, Jr. New Haven, CT: Yale University Press.

Mitchell, Alison. 1996. Clinton Honors Troops That Served in Haiti. *New York Times* 19 March: A14.

Morris, Dick. 1999. *The New Prince: Machiavelli Updated for the Twenty-First Century*. Los Angeles: Renaissance Books.

Mueller, John. 1973. *War, Presidents and Public Opinion*. New York: Wiley.

——. 1977. Changes in American Public Attitudes toward International Involvement. In *The Limits of Military Intervention*, ed. Ellen Stern. Beverly Hills, CA: Sage.

——. 1979. Public Expectations of War During the Cold War. *American Journal of Political Science* 23(2) May: 301–29.

——. 1984a. Reflections on the Vietnam Protest Movement and on the Curious Calm at the War's End. In *Vietnam as History*, ed. Peter Braestrup. Lanham, MD: University Press of America.

——. 1984b. Lessons Learned Five Years After the Hostage Nightmare. *Wall Street Journal* 6 November.

——. 1987. Presidents and Terrorists Should Not Mix. *Wall Street Journal* 31 March.

——. 1989. *Retreat from Doomsday: The Obsolescence of Major War*. New York: Basic Books.

——. 1994. *Policy and Opinion in the Gulf War*. Chicago, IL: University of Chicago Press.

——. 1995a. *Quiet Cataclysm: Reflections on the Recent Transformation of World Politics*. New York: HarperCollins.

——. 1995b. The Perfect Enemy: Assessing the Gulf War. *Security Studies* 5(1) Autumn: 77–117.

——. 1996. Policy Principles for Unthreatened Wealth-Seekers. *Foreign Policy* Spring: 22–33.

——. 1999. *Capitalism, Democracy, and Ralph's Pretty Good Grocery*. Princeton, NJ: Princeton University Press.

——. 2000a. Public Opinion as a Constraint on U.S. Foreign Policy: Assessing the Perceived Value of American and Foreign Lives. Paper presented at the Annual Convention of the International Studies Association. Los Angeles.

——. 2000b. The Banality of "Ethnic War." *International Security* 25(1) Summer: 42–70.

——. 2000c. The Banality of "Ethnic War": Yugoslavia and Rwanda. Paper presented at the Annual Meeting of the American Political Science Association, Washington, DC.

Mueller, John, and Karl Mueller. 1999. Sanctions of Mass Destruction. *Foreign Affairs* 78(3) May/June: 43–53.

——. 2000. The Methodology of Mass Destruction: Assessing Threats in the New World Order. In *Preventing the Use of Weapons of Mass Destruction*, ed. Eric Herring. London: Frank Cass, 163–87.

Murray, Shoon Kathleen, Louis Klarevas, and Thomas Hartley. 1997. Are Policymakers Misreading Public Views Toward the United Nations? Paper presented at the Annual Convention of the International Studies Association, Toronto, Canada, 18–22 March.

National Opinion Research Center. 1944. *The Effect of Realistic War Pictures: Report EW 20, March 13*. Chicago: National Opinion Research Center.

National Safety Council (Chicago). 1997. *Accident Facts*.

Niemi, Richard G., John Mueller, and Tom W. Smith. 1989. *Trends in Public Opinion: A Compendium of Survey Data*. Westport, CT: Greenwood.

Nincic, Miroslav. 1992. *Democracy and Foreign Policy: The Fallacy of Political Realism*. New York: Columbia University Press.

Norpoth, Helmut. 1987a. The Falklands War and Government Popularity in Britain: Rally without Consequence or Surge without Decline? *Electoral Studies* 6(1): 3–16.

——. 1987b. Guns and Butter and Government Popularity in Britain. *American Political Science Review* 81(3) September: 949–59.

Oreskes, Michael. 1990. American Fear of Soviets Declines, Survey Finds. *New York Times* 30 May.

Orwin, Clifford. 1996. Distant Comparison: CNN and Borrioboola-Gha. *National Interest* Spring: 42–49.

Paarlberg, Rob. 1973. Forgetting About the Unthinkable. *Foreign Policy* Spring: 132–40.

Page, Benjamin I., and Robert Y. Shapiro. 1992. *The Rational Public: Fifty Years of Trends in American Policy Preferences*. Chicago, IL: University of Chicago Press.

Page, Susan. 1999. Kosovo Can Help or Haunt Gore. *USA Today* 14 April.

Powell, Colin L. 1992/93. U.S. Forces: Challenges Ahead. *Foreign Affairs* 72(5) Winter: 32–45.

Reagan, Ronald. 1983. *Public Papers of the Presidents of the United States*. Washington, DC: United States Government Publishing Office.

Revkin, Andrew C. 1998. Coming to the Suburbs: A Hit Squad for Deer. *New York Times* 30 November.

Rielly, John E., ed. 1999. *American Public Opinion and U.S. Foreign Policy, 1999*. Chicago, IL: Chicago Council on Foreign Relations.

Schwarz, Benjamin C. 1994. *Casualties, Public Opinion, U.S. Military Intervention: Implications for U.S. Regional Deterrence Strategies*. Santa Monica, CA: RAND Corporation.

Sciolino, Elaine. 1993. Christopher Explains Conditions For Use of U.S. Force in Bosnia. *New York Times* 28 April.

Small, Melvin, and J. David Singer. 1982. *Resort to Arms: International Civil Wars, 1816–1980*. Beverly Hills, CA: Sage.

Smith, Tom W. 1985. The Polls: America's Most Important Problems. *Public Opinion Quarterly* 49(2) Summer: 264–74.

Sobel, Richard. 1998. The Polls—Trends: United States Intervention in Bosnia. *Public Opinion Quarterly* 62(2) Summer: 250–78.

Stanley, Harold W., and Richard G. Niemi. 1992. *Vital Statistics on American Politics*, 3rd edn. Washington, DC: Congressional Quarterly Press.

Sterngold, Arthur, Rex H. Warland, and Robert O. Herrmann. 1994. Do Surveys Overstate Public Concerns? *Public Opinion Quarterly* 58(2) Summer: 255–63.

Stouffer, Samuel A. 1955. *Communism, Conformity, and Civil Liberties*. Garden City, NY: Doubleday.

Strobel, Warren P. 1997. *Late-Breaking Foreign Policy: The News Media's Influence on Peace Operations*. Washington, DC: United States Institute of Peace Press.

United States Department of State. 1998. *Patterns of Global Terrorism, 1997*, April.

Wittkopf, Eugene R. 1990. *Faces of Internationalism: Public Opinion and American Foreign Policy*. Durham, NC: Duke University Press.
Zelnick, Bob. 1999. Kosovo Crisis Carries Grave Risks for Gore. *USA Today* 8 April.

REFLECTIONS

Reason and caprice

Although politicians and other idea entrepreneurs, including the media, actively try to sell and promote issues that they think should be of concern to the public, it is difficult, as noted at various points in this book, to predict which of the concerns placed on the public menu will actually be taken up, or even noticed, by the public. On the one hand, policy leaders need to pay attention to those fears and perceived threats that have been accepted, and particularly to those that have been internalized, by the public—like the supposed threat presented by domestic Communists and terrorists as discussed earlier. On the other hand, issues presented with great urgency may generate no response at all.

Ultimately, then, the process is substantially bottom-up: would-be opinion leaders may propose, but the public disposes. Proposition 11 in the article takes a somewhat bemused, long-term perspective on this phenomenon. Not only is there a fair amount of apparent caprice in the manner in which the public chooses what to grasp, but the degree to which notable international events linger in the public mind after they are over "varies rather curiously," and would be difficult to predict.

The most important problem since 2001

This article was in press at the time of the 9/11 terrorist attacks, and it was published a few months later. The following article in this collection was written later and it examines public opinion in the years after 2001, particularly with respect to the Iraq War. But a few comments updating the specific assessments in this earlier one may be in order.

In a poll conducted in the few days before September 11, 2001, the number of people who picked terrorism as the most important problem facing the country registered at a flat zero. That jumped to 46 percent in October while another 10 percent registered fear of war and others voiced general concerns about national security. If one considers terrorism to be a foreign policy issue rather than a domestic one (an arguable designation, of course, under the circumstances), concern about international issues in the aftermath of 9/11 registered at a higher level for the American public than at any time since the Cuban Missile Crisis of 1962.

However, although international terrorism did not weigh in heavily before 9/11 according to the most important problem question, it did so when people were specifically asked about the relative importance of various foreign policy goals: in 1998, in the wake of the bombings of two American embassies in Africa, over 75 percent picked it as a "very important" goal, a percentage, of course, that soared even higher after 9/11 (see Figure 7.1 on p. 152).

The focus on foreign policy generally remained high for several years after 2001. Specific mentions of terrorism as the country's greatest problem declined to around 20 percent by early 2003, but they were substantially replaced by other foreign policy concerns including those over the war in Afghanistan that began shortly after 9/11 and then by ones relating to the war in Iraq that began in March 2003.

By the end of the decade, however, as the Iraq War declined in intensity and the financial crisis broke out, concerns as voiced on this question snapped back (applying Gabriel Almond's metaphor once again) primarily to domestic issues. Moreover, proposition 6 in the article was soon restored: foreign policy did play a considerable role in the 2004 election, but much less of one in 2008.

Comparing dates of infamy

In urging a declaration of war against Japan after it had bombed American territory at Pearl Harbor, President Franklin Roosevelt pronounced the day of the attack, December 7, 1941, to be "a date which will live in infamy." On September 11, 2001, with a similar combination of guile, careful planning, secrecy, ruthlessness, and luck, a band of suicidal terrorists attacked American territory and managed to kill even more Americans than had perished at Pearl Harbor. And that date, too, seems likely to be remembered with the same special designation.

The events appear to be most similar in the impact they had on public opinion. Historian Gordon Prange observes that after the Pearl Harbor attack, "The American people reeled with a mind-staggering mixture of surprise, awe, mystification, grief, humiliation, and, above all, cataclysmic fury." One could use the same language to characterize the public's response to the September 11 events. In both cases planners of the attack (idea entrepreneurs in their way) severely misjudged the public and official response their acts would inspire.

As Prange notes, the Japanese presumed "that in the face of this type of attack the American people might think the Japanese such a unique and fearless race that it would be useless to fight them." This proved, of course, to be one of the greatest miscalculations in military history, but a thoughtful caveat by Scott Sagan ought to be kept in mind: "Anyone who has lived through the war in Vietnam cannot easily dismiss the possibility that the United States public and elite opinion might have decided that the costs of continuing a war in Asia were greater than any possible gains to be made." Be that as it may, the attack on Pearl Harbor was phenomenally successful in its shock effect, but the results of the shock were exactly the opposite of the one the would-be opinion manipulators hoped for.

Although he altered his rationale later, Osama bin Laden was impressed in particular by the American reaction to rather small losses in Lebanon in 1983 and in Somalia in 1993 (discussed in proposition 8 of the article). This, he concluded, demonstrated "impotence," "weakness," and "false courage," and he appears to have believed that the country would respond to a direct attack by withdrawing from the Middle East. What he clearly failed to understand was that the US withdrew from Lebanon and Somalia not simply because of the losses, but because it also did not value the stakes very much in those humanitarian ventures. As discussed in proposition 5, for Americans (and Canadians, Swedes, Belgians, the Red Cross, and so on) peacekeeping is simply not worth many of their own lives. By contrast, the American public concluded from 9/11 that the country's very survival was at stake in the conflict with bin Laden's form of terrorism, and a willingness to confront the danger (and to exact revenge) was, as after Pearl Harbor, monumental. In particular, support for chasing down the terrorists in Afghanistan, even though there was a prospect for considerable American losses there, was exceedingly high—considerably higher, as can be seen in the updated figure on p. 200, than at the beginnings of the wars in Vietnam, Korea, or Iraq.

In some respects, then, it may be useful to consider opinion on the "war" against terrorism and the Afghan venture (at least in its early years) to be similar to opinion on World War II or on the cold war. In all three instances, a willingness to support a long-term venture was internalized and maintained, although it could sour on certain specific projects within that campaign like the wars in Korea, Vietnam, or Iraq.

An immediate beneficiary after both 12/7 and 9/11 was the president of the United States, as the events, not surprisingly, had a pronounced rally-round-the-flag effect in boosting his approval rating. Before Pearl Harbor Roosevelt's approval was quite high, 73 percent, but when next tapped, about a month after Pearl Harbor, it had risen to 84 percent. The impact of September 11 on President George W. Bush's ratings was similar—except that he had further to go. Only about 53 percent expressed approval of the job he was doing before the attacks, but this abruptly soared into the 80s, even into the 90s in some polls, after they took place—the greatest up-tick ever recorded in the data series.

More interestingly, the decline for each president's approval ratings from those stratospheric highs was very gradual—probably because each was leading the country in a continuing enterprise focused on a palpable, direct threat to American lives. Two years after December 7, when the polls last sought to tap Roosevelt's approval rating, it still stood at 66 percent. And a year and a half after September 11 (but before he began the Iraq War) Bush's rating had declined only into the 60s, a particularly impressive achievement in light of his tepid pre-September 11 approval ratings.

Reflections references

Gordon W. Prange with Donald M. Goldstein, and Katherine V. Dillon, *At Dawn We Slept: The Untold Story of Pearl Harbor*. New York: McGraw-Hill, 1981.
Scott Sagan, Origins of the Pacific War, *Journal of Interdisciplinary History*, Spring 1988.

In promoting and prosecuting its war against Iraq, the administration of George W. Bush sought to accomplish two tasks in the management of American public opinion. In the run-up to the war, it tried to rally the public to support its planned venture, and, during the war itself, it tried to maintain public backing for the war even as costs increased.

It failed in both of these endeavors. During the run-up, it was unable to increase enthusiasm for going to war, and during the war, despite continuing efforts to reverse the process, support eroded rather inexorably as American casualties accrued. Moreover, in the process the administration's whole policy approach—often labeled "the Bush Doctrine"—became severely undermined and is likely to be supplanted by an "Iraq Syndrome" that will be hostile to such ventures in the future.

Public opinion and the promotion of war

In its drive toward war with Iraq in 2002, the Bush administration was working from a position of some strength with the public. Hostility toward Saddam Hussein was generated at the time of the 1990–1 Gulf crisis and war following Iraq's August 1990 seizure of neighboring Kuwait, an episode that had been presided over by Bush's father, George H. W. Bush. Throughout, Saddam played the role of demon with consummate skill, and the public responded accordingly. More-over, the antipathy did not diminish after the event was over. The war succeeded in liberating Kuwait, destroying the Iraqi army, and humiliating Saddam at remarkably low cost in American casualties. Yet, in its aftermath Americans increasingly expressed dissatisfaction because the venture had failed to remove Saddam from office.[1]

In addition, they continued to support a decade of severe economic sanctions on Saddam's regime, and they remained oblivious to reports that the sanctions were a necessary cause of hundreds of thousands of deaths in that country. For example, in 1996 it was put to Madeleine Albright, then America's ambassador to the United Nations, on her country's most popular television news program, *60 Minutes*, that the sanctions had taken the lives of half a million Iraqi children, and she was bluntly asked if the price was worth it. Without denying the numbers, Albright acknowledged that "this is a very hard choice," then firmly concluded, "we think the price is worth it."[2] This remarkable conclusion stirred no comment anywhere in the country's media, though it became famous in the Arab world.[3] Generally, politicians seem to have concluded, quite possibly correctly, that any voiced opposition to the sanctions would be politically detrimental since it would imply support for the demonic Saddam Hussein.[4]

In fact, throughout the decade after the Gulf War, polls document a fair degree of support for the use of military force to depose Saddam.[5] As Figure 9.1 documents, in early 2001 55 percent were still responding favorably to the idea of "invading Iraq with US ground troops in an attempt to remove Saddam Hussein from power."

However, despite this potential opening, politicians and others apparently still considered an invasion to be a nonstarter, and few, if any, advocated such a course at the time: there were public declarations and congressional appropriations to support opposition groups, but no one was really calling for a war to depose him. For example, defense department advisor Richard Perle, who would prove to be one of the most ardent proponents of war in 2003, published an article in 2000 that, while strongly advocating a policy hostile toward Saddam, recommended only protecting and assisting resistance movements within Iraq, not anything resembling an invasion by American troops.[6]

As the figure also discloses, this percentage leaped to nearly 75 percent in the wake of the September 11, 2001 terrorist attacks in the United States, a reaction that may have helped encourage the discussions that began at that time within the Bush administration about launching such a war. By January 2002 Bush publicly positioned Iraq prominently on his "axis of evil" hit list and announced that, unlike all of Iraq's neighbors except Israel, the United States had come to imagine that Saddam presented a "grave and growing danger."

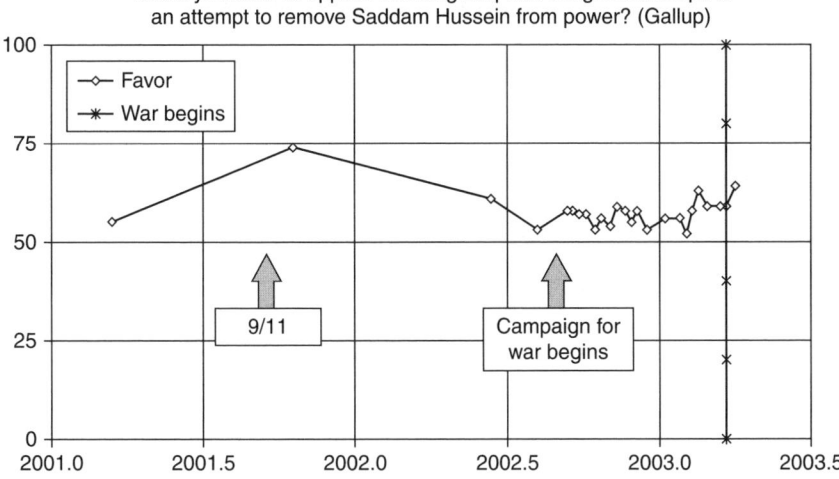

Figure 9.1 Support for removing Saddam Hussein, 2001–3.

However, despite such dramatic fulminations and despite the fact that polls found around half of the population professing to believe Saddam had been personally involved in the 9/11 attacks,[7] support for war against Iraq dwindled during the next several months to about where it had stood before 9/11.

A concentrated campaign to boost support for going to war began in August and September 2002 with speeches by Bush and Vice President Dick Cheney. As can be seen in Figure 9.1, the administration may conceivably have been able to halt further erosion of support, but, despite strenuous efforts, it was unable notably to increase support for going to war: from September 2002 to the launching of war in March 2003, attitudes did not change notably. There was something of a bump upwards to 63 percent at the time of Secretary of State Colin Powell's much-publicized speech at the United Nations on February 5, 2003, but this lift proved to be temporary. There is also an upward push in the last poll of the series, but that one was conducted as the war was beginning in mid-March and represents part of a "rally 'round the flag' " effect as troops were being sent into action. With those exceptions, approval for sending the troops never ranged more than 4 percentage points higher or lower than the 55 percent figure tallied when George W. Bush was taking office, nine months before 9/11.[8]

An interesting comparison can be made with the run-up to the 1991 war presided over by Bush's father. He, too, spent a great deal of time and effort seeking to boost support for sending the American military into action to force Iraq's forces from Kuwait. For the most part, however, during the entire course of the debate over war, there was little change in the degree to which popular opinion supported the idea of initiating a war in the Gulf. People did not become consistently more hawkish or dovish, more war eager or war averse, or more or less supportive of Bush or his policies. And their perceptions of the reasons behind involvement and the reasons for going to war apparently did not change very much either.[9]

Overall, then, neither Bush was able to swing public opinion toward war—though, conceivably, they were able to arrest a deterioration of support for war. This experience suggests there are rather distinct limits to the effectiveness of the bully pulpit.[10]

The president's ability to go to war

Nonetheless, obviously, each president did manage to get his war. But this was because, as president, each was able to order troops into action, not because of his ability to move the public to his point of view. Moreover, they were able to keep the issue brewing as an important one and they could unilaterally commit the country to a path that dramatically increased a sense of fatalism about war and perhaps convinced many that there was no honorable alternative to war. The lessons of the wars suggest, then, that a great deal lies in the president's ability to deploy troops and thus to commit the country's honor and destiny. With such moves he can make an issue important and convey a compelling sense of obligation as well as of entrapment and inevitability.

More generally, it does not appear that the president necessarily needs public support in advance to pull off a military venture.[11] The public generally seems to be willing to go along (not that it has much choice), but it reserves the right to object if the cost of the war comes to outweigh its perceived value. Sometimes the public has apparently been quite supportive of going to war, as in World War II (after Pearl Harbor), in Korea (1950), in Vietnam (1965), in Panama (1989), in Somalia (1992–3), and in Afghanistan (2001). At other times, the public has been at best divided as in Lebanon (1958), Grenada (1983), Lebanon (1983), the Gulf War (1991), Haiti (1994), Bosnia (1995), Kosovo (1999), and the Iraq War (2003). In some cases, the ventures have been accomplished at acceptable cost as in World War II, Panama, Lebanon 1958, Grenada, the Gulf War, Haiti, Bosnia, and Kosovo. In others, support dropped as costs grew, as in Korea, Vietnam, and Iraq (and maybe, now, in Afghanistan). And in others, the public's dismay at rising costs was met by abrupt early withdrawal as in Lebanon in 1983 and in Somalia.

But the hope in all this for the president would be that if the venture appears to be worth the cost, the public will accept, even laud, it despite any prewar misgivings. This happened quite clearly in the case of the controversial Gulf War of 1991. Before the war polls found the public split about 50/50 on a question asking whether they preferred continued sanctions or military action. After the war, however, the percentage recalling that they had supported war over sanctions registered at 76 percent.[12]

The extraordinary partisan divide

In one respect there was a great—and rather unexpected—difference in public opinion between the run-ups to the 1991 and 2003 wars against Iraq. In each, Democrats were less likely to support the prospective wars than were Republicans, but what is surprising is that the partisan gap was *far* wider in the 2003 case than in the 1991 one even though the behavior of leading Democrats in Congress would suggest that the relationship should be the reverse. In the earlier war, Democratic leaders stood in strong opposition to going to war, and it was reasonable to expect that many ordinary Democrats would follow their lead. In the later war, by distinct contrast, the leaders mostly remained silent or were even generally supportive of the effort.[13] Yet ordinary Democrats, even though there were few cues being issued by congressional Democrats, departed far more fully from ordinary Republicans on this war.[14]

A truly satisfying explanation for this remarkable finding has yet to be established. There may be some explanation in the very substantial contempt many Democrats harbored for George W. Bush stemming from the controversial 2000 election.[15] However, the gap between Democrats and Republicans on approval of the president greatly diminished for a while after the 9/11 terrorist events, and widened only later.[16] What may have been peculiar to the second war was that George W. Bush was exceptional in that he was much more able to retain the support of the Republicans than was his father. Since it takes *two* to make a gap, some of the differences between the two wars may stem from this.

Public opinion and the prosecution of war

Once the war against Iraq began in March 2003, there was a rally round the flag effect as opinion swung to support the country's military efforts, something that was rather predictable—and predicted. The partisan gap also closed somewhat for a while.[17]

At the outset, the war looked like it might resemble the Gulf War of 1991 as the Iraqi military performed in about the same manner as it had previously: basically, it disintegrated under the onslaught and seems to have lacked any semblance of a coherent strategy of resistance.[18] Indeed, total battle deaths for the invading American and British forces during this period were well under 150—even lower than had been borne in the Gulf War of 1991. And, as Figure 9.2 demonstrates, public support for the venture during this period remained high and even increased—something that had also happened during the brief war of 1991.[19]

The two wars quickly ceased to resemble each other militarily, however. Once Iraq was summarily expelled from Kuwait in 1991, the Kuwaiti regime came back from exile and took over, and American troops could go home to parade victoriously in American cities. No such pleasant fate awaited their successors in 2003: after President Bush prominently and triumphally declared "major combat

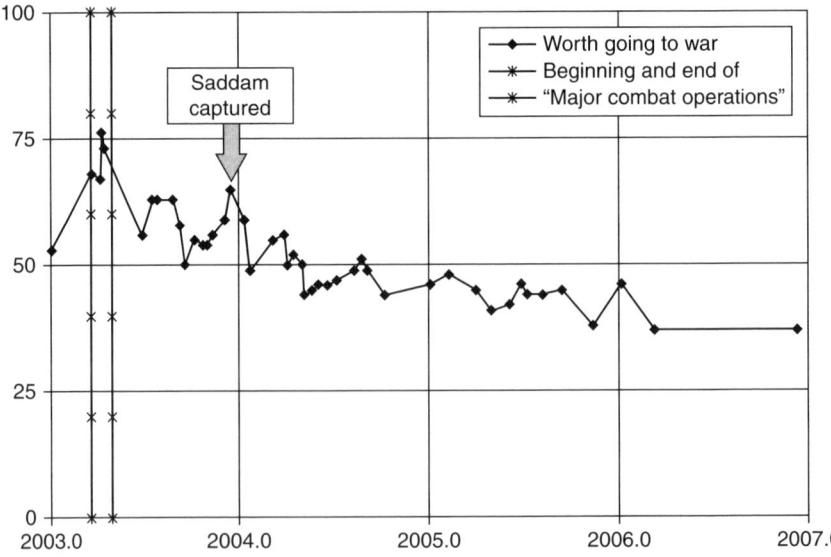

Figure 9.2 Value of going to war in Iraq, 2003–6.

operations" to be over on May 1 of that year, the conquerors found they had to hang around and fight in an attempt to build a viable national government out of the rubble that remained after Saddam, economic sanctions, and the war had taken their toll. It had been hoped that the Iraqis would greet the conquerors by dancing happily in the streets and somehow coordinate themselves into a coherent, and appreciative, government. But, although many were glad to see Saddam's tyranny ended, the invaders often found the population resentful and humiliated, rather than gleeful or grateful. Moreover, bringing order to the situation was vastly complicated by the fact that the government-toppling invasion had effectively (and instantly) created a failed state which permitted widespread criminality and looting. In addition some people—including apparently some foreign terrorists drawn opportunistically to the area—were dedicated to sabotaging the victors' peace and to killing the policing forces.[20] Eventually, communal violence and gang warfare were added to the destructive mix.

The decline of support

American troops have been sent into harm's way many times since 1945, but in only three of those ventures—in Korea, Vietnam, and now Iraq—have they been drawn into sustained ground combat and suffered more than 300 deaths in action (though Afghanistan may soon join this list).

Data from questions asking people if the war was a "mistake" allow for a fairly direct comparison of public support for the wars as in Figures 9.3 and 9.4. All

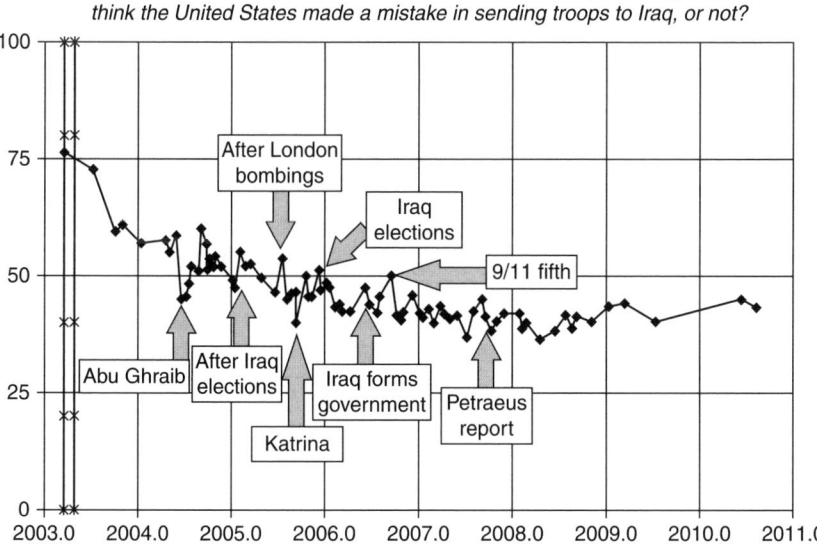

Figure 9.3 Opinion on whether Iraq was a mistake (*percent of those with an opinion*).

Note: This figure has been updated from the one in the original article.

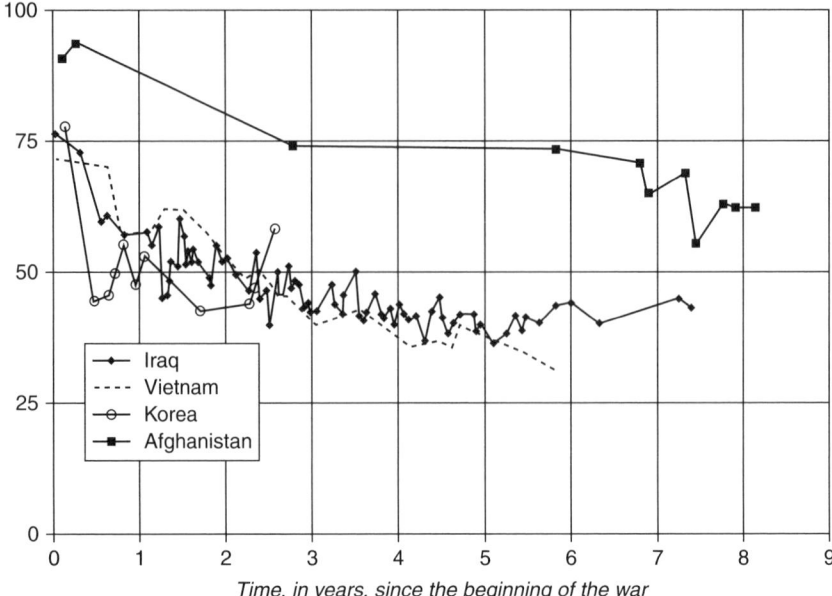

Figure 9.4 Support for wars in Korea, Vietnam, Iraq, and Afghanistan.

Note: This figure has been updated from the one in the original article and data for Afghanistan have been added.

three military ventures were quite substantially supported by the public as the troops were sent in and, in all cases, support decreased as casualties—whether of draftees, volunteers, or reservists—were suffered. The decline was steeper in the early stages of the war as reluctant approvers were rather quickly alienated, and the erosion slowed as support progressively became reduced to the harder-core—the pattern is essentially logarithmic.[21] The process is almost uncannily illustrated in Figure 9.5. (See also the data on p. 173.) In addition, Figure 9.6 shows the dramatic dropoff in acceptance of casualties in the Iraq War after the end of "major combat operations" and the slower erosion thereafter as additional casualties continued to be suffered.

There is one important difference between the wars, however: the data suggest the public places a far lower value on the stakes in Iraq than it did in the earlier wars. As Figure 9.4 demonstrates, after two years of war, support for war on this measure had slumped to around 50 percent. However at that point around 20,000 Americans had been killed in Vietnam and Korea, but only about 1,500 in Iraq. Korea and Vietnam were seen, initially at least, to be important and necessary components in dealing with international Communism. In Vietnam, for example, there was widespread agreement with the 1965 views of future war critic David Halberstam that Vietnam was a "strategic country in a key area . . . perhaps one of only five or six nations in the world that is truly vital to US interests."[22] Although

Suppose President George W. Bush decides to order US troops into a ground attack against Iraqi forces. Would you favor or oppose that decision? (If support) The number of possible casualties in a ground war with Iraq had been estimated at between 100 American soldiers, if the Iraqi military offers little resistance, to as many as 5,000 American soldiers if the Iraqi Republican Guard fight an effective urban defense. With this in mind, would you still support sending ground troops to fight in Iraq if it meant that up to 100 American soldiers would be killed in battle, or not? (If yes) Would you still support sending ground troops if up to 500 American soldiers were killed in battle or not? (If yes) Up to 1,000? (If yes) Up to 5,000? (If yes) Would you say you would support sending ground troops to fight in Iraq no matter what it cost in American casualties, or not? (*Los Angeles Times*)

    December 15–17, 2002: before the war
- 35% Oppose war
- 7% Don't know if favor or oppose
- 58% Favor war
- 49% Still favor if any killed
- 46% Still favor if 100 killed
- 43% Still favor if 500 killed
- 37% Still favor if 1,000 killed
- 32% Still favor if 5,000 killed
- 24% Still favor if more than 5,000 but not unlimited
- 17% Still favor no matter the cost in American casualties
- 6% Don't know about casualties

Do you favor or oppose the US war in Iraq? (*Washingon Post*)
    December 15–17, 2006: nearly 3,000 US fatalities
- 31% Favor war
- 67   Oppose war
- 8   Unsure

Figure 9.5 Casualty tolerance in Iraq.

Americans eventually soured on the war, it took far more American deaths to accomplish this than in Iraq. That is, casualty for casualty, support dropped off far more quickly in the Iraq war than in either of the earlier two wars.[23]

Contributing to this difference in casualty tolerance may be the fact that the main threats Iraq was deemed to present to the United States when troops were sent in—fears of its "weapons of mass destruction" and of its connections to international terrorism—quickly became, to say the least, severely undermined. With those justifications gone, Iraq became something of a humanitarian venture, and, as Francis Fukuyama has put it, a prewar request to spend "several hundred billion dollars and several thousand American lives in order to bring democracy to . . . Iraq" would "have been laughed out of court."[24] However, it should be noted that, applying consistent Cold War standards, the stakes in Korea and Vietnam also declined during the course of the wars there. In the latter war, for example, early fears that Indonesia might fall to Communism unless a stand was taken in Vietnam,

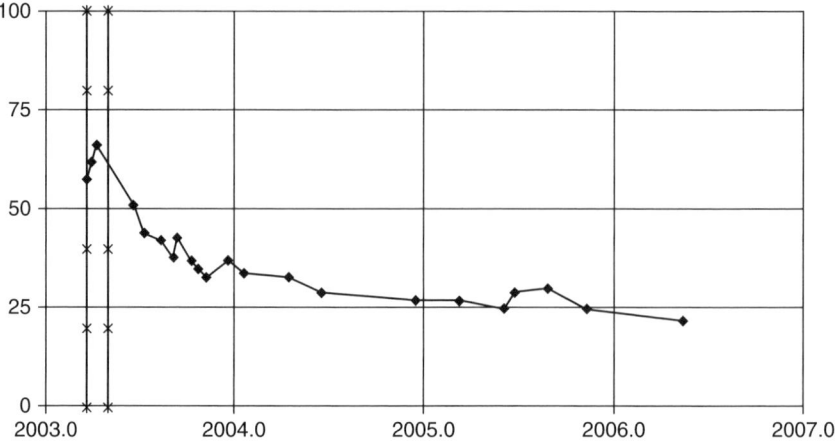

Figure 9.6 Opinion on acceptance of US casualties, 2003–6 (*percent acceptable*).

evaporated with an anti-Communist coup there after US troops had been committed to Vietnam.[25]

Actually, given the demise of the main reasons for going to war and the subsequent unexpectedly high American casualty levels, it is impressive that support for the war in Iraq remained as high as it did. This may reflect the fact that many people still connect the effort there to the campaign—or "war"—against terror, an enterprise that continues to enjoy huge support, as did World War II or (despite Vietnam) the Cold War. In addition, the toppling of Saddam remains a singular accomplishment, one, as noted earlier, that the American people had been spoiling for at least since 1990. And, despite continual assertions to the contrary from all sides, a fair number of Americans continued to see a connection between Saddam and the events of 9/11: in September 2006, two-and-a-half years into the Iraq War, 38 percent still remained convinced that Saddam Hussein was personally involved in the attacks.[26] However, as Figure 9.7 suggests, the appeal of that result declined as costs grew.

When one shifts from questions about whether the war was a "mistake" or "worth it" to ones about whether the US should get out, much the same pattern holds across Korea, Vietnam, and Iraq: relatively steep declines in support for continuing the war in the early stages, slower erosion later. However, judging how many people want to get out or stay the course at any point in time is essentially impossible because so much depends on the question wording. For example, there is far more support for "gradual withdrawal" or "begin to withdraw" than for "withdraw" or "immediate withdrawal." Thus in June 2005, the *Washington Post* found 58 percent for staying and 41 percent for withdrawing (much the same as in

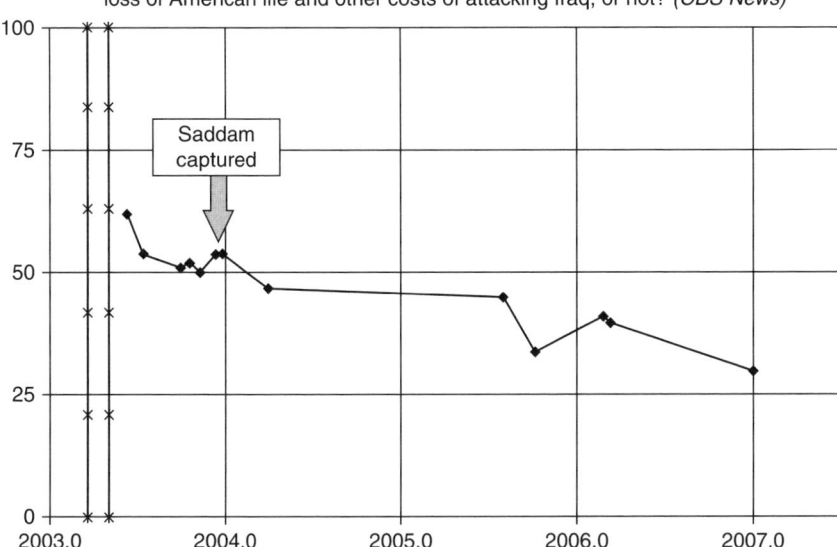

Figure 9.7 Value of removing Saddam Hussein, 2003–7 *(percent worth it)*.

October 2003) when the options were posed this way: "Do you think the United States should keep its military forces in Iraq until civil order is restored there, even if that means continued US military casualties, or, do you think the United States should withdraw its military forces from Iraq in order to avoid further US military casualties, even if that means civil order is not restored there?" But in the same month, the Harris poll tallied only 33 percent for staying and 63 percent for withdrawing (much changed from October 2003) when it asked, "Do you favor keeping a large number of US troops in Iraq until there is a stable government there or bringing most of our troops home in the next year?" All questions, however, have logged substantial increases in withdrawal sentiment over the course of the war.[27]

Insofar as the erosion of support, however measured, is related to casualties, the phenomenon is likely caused by the simple fact of cumulating combat deaths. Pictures of dead bodies, body bags, or flag-draped coffins are not necessary. Somehow, the notion that support declines with casualties became expressed as "support drops when they start seeing the body bags," and this metaphor apparently led, in turn, to the naive notion that for people to become disaffected they actually need to *see* the body bags. In consequence, perhaps, the military in the Iraq War enterprisingly tried to keep people from viewing pictures of body bags and flag-draped coffins presumably in the futile, bizarre hope that this will somehow arrest the decline of support.[28]

The decline in support seems to take place whether there is an active anti-war protest movement or not. There has been little so far for the Iraq War (except within the ranks of the Democratic Party), but there was also little during the Korean War and support for that venture still eroded in very much the same way as in Vietnam where anti-war protest was common. In fact, since the Vietnam protest movement became so associated with anti-American values and activities, it may ultimately have been somewhat counterproductive in its goal of reducing support for the war.[29]

Support can also erode when war opponents simply voice discontent but are unable to come up with specific alternatives. Dwight Eisenhower never seemed to have much of a plan for getting out of the Korean War—though he did say that, if elected, he would visit the place—but discontent with the war still worked well for him in the 1952 election. Richard Nixon's proposals in the 1968 election for fixing the Vietnam mess were distinctly unspecific, though there were some suggestions from time to time that he had a "secret plan."

Politically, the wars seem to have hurt the war-instituting political party not because the opposition comes up with a coherent clashing vision (George McGovern tried that unsuccessfully against Nixon in 1972), but because discontent over the war vaguely, but damagingly, translates into discontent over the capacities of the people in charge and causes people to yearn for a change. Britain's Tony Blair, presiding over a robust economy and a decidedly unpopular war, saw his margin cut very substantially in elections in 2005. In like manner, George W. Bush, with high marks on terrorism, but low ones on the war, would have done considerably better if the war hadn't been there in his reelection campaign of 2004. Examining polls from 1952 to the present, Gary Jacobson reports that the partisan division in the 2004 election was the most intense in the period: almost all the Republicans voted for Bush and almost all the Democrats for John Kerry.[30] Without the war, Bush would have still held the Republicans and would doubtless have done better with Democrats as well as with Independents whose opinion on the war more nearly traces Democratic patterns than Republican ones.[31] Then, in the congressional elections of 2006, Bush's party took a shellacking that seems to have come about substantially because of discontent over the war in Iraq.

Failures of efforts to reverse the decline

The ability of a president to reverse the erosion of support for an increasingly unpopular war seems limited. George W. Bush, like Vietnam's Lyndon Johnson before him, sought many times to turn things around by making speeches explaining what the war is about, urging patience, and repeatedly asserting that progress is being made. He also proved to be particularly adept at hitching the war, often by implication, to the traumatic 9/11 experience. This effort was seen in particular in a set of speeches at the end of 2005 in which Bush repeatedly applied the word, "victory." In one speech, surrounded by signs that said, "Plan for Victory," he used the word fifteen times, twice with the modifier, "complete," as: "Against this adversary there is only one effective response: We will never back down, we will never give in, and we will never accept anything less than complete victory."[32] As with his very considerable efforts to sell his Social

Security plan earlier that year (or like Woodrow Wilson's campaign to sell the League of Nations sixty-five years earlier), this experience suggests once again that the efficacy of the bully pulpit has often been much overrated.[33]

But if the impact of Washington rhetoric is limited at least in situations like this, favorable happenings in the war can boost support from time to time. Figures 9.2 and 9.3 supply evidence for the war in Iraq. There were notable upward shifts in support when Saddam was captured at the end of 2003[34] and when elections were held. The problem for the president and his policy is that these rises proved to be temporary, and support soon relapsed to where it had been before and then continued its generally downward course. The happy events proved more nearly to be bumps on the road than permanent shifts. The same can be seen for negative experiences: a drop in support at the time of the Abu Graib disclosures was eventually mostly reversed. Episodes in 2005 further illustrate the process. Support for the war dropped at the time of Hurricane Katrina as Americans were led to wonder about the nation's priorities, but this was more than reversed by the successful Iraq elections of November 15. Within days, however, war support dropped again to a level slightly lower than was registered before either event took place. In all, the phenomenon suggests that a significant, lasting reversal of the erosion of support is unlikely. Those who now consider the costs of the war already to be too high will probably not permanently reverse their opinion very much even with good news.

Partisan differences regarding Bush and the Iraq War, already seen in the run-up to the war, continued to be incredibly deep as the war progressed. Jacobson has documented that the partisan divide on Iraq is considerably greater than on any military action over the last half century and that the partisan split on presidential approval ratings, despite a major narrowing after 9/11 and at the time of the height of the war in Afghanistan, is greater than for any president over the period—wider than for Reagan, for Clinton, for Nixon.[35] To give a rather extreme example, by the time of the 2004 election, over 80 percent of well-informed Republicans supported the Iraq War while only about 3 percent of well-informed Democrats did so.[36] This means that Bush could scarcely look for increased Republican support because he already had practically all of it, while the Democrats were unlikely to budge much. There might be some hope for him among Independents, but, as noted, their war support patterns more nearly tracked those of the almost completely disaffected Democrats than those of the amazingly loyal Republicans.

In all this, what chiefly matters for public opinion is American losses, not those of the people defended. By some estimates, the number of Iraqis who have died in the upheaval following the invasion has reached well into six figures. As noted earlier, sanctions on Iraq were probably a necessary cause of the deaths of an equally great number of Iraqis, mostly of children, yet little concern is voiced about this. The only cumulative body count that seems to matter, and is routinely reported, is the American one.

This phenomenon is nothing new. The official estimate at the end of the 1991 Gulf War (though later determined almost certainly to be much too high) was that 100,000 Iraqis had been killed in that war.[37] This unpleasant fact scarcely dampened enthusiasm at the victory and "welcome home" parades for returning troops, however. And, although there was considerable support for the wars in Korea and Vietnam, polls make it clear that this was because people saw them as vital to confront the Communist threat: the defense of the South Koreans or the South Vietnamese per se was never perceived to be as remotely important a war goal.[38]

Some scholars have argued that support for war is determined by the prospects for success rather than by casualties—that Americans are "defeat phobic" rather than "casualty phobic." They proclaim it a "myth" that "Americans are casualty shy" and attempt to demonstrate that "a majority of the American people will accept combat deaths—so long as the mission has the potential to be successful." To support their case, they prominently employ results from a poll they conducted indicating that, contra Fukuyama, Americans would on average be entirely willing to accept 6,861 battle deaths to "stabilize a democratic government in Congo" and 29,853 battle deaths "to prevent Iraq from obtaining weapons of mass destruction."[39] Essentially, the argument seems to hold that Americans don't really care how many casualties they suffer so long as their side comes out the winner. In a later book they acknowledge in a footnote that these numbers were "overly susceptible to misinterpretation," and they then rejigger their analysis of the same poll question and essentially conclude that the original figure was some 6,800 percent too high.[40] The damage, however, has already been done: the op-ed had been widely cited and applied (and misinterpreted), particularly in military publications.[41]

In general, it is difficult to separate the effect of casualties from the prospects of success because casualty rates are generally part of what one uses to determine whether the war is going well or not. Where there is a disconnect, however, casualties seem to dominate the consideration. Thus the Tet offensive in Vietnam greatly heightened the public sense that the war was going badly even though American deaths did not surge; yet support for the war (contrary to common assumption) did not drop precipitously in response to the heightened frustration, but rather simply continued to erode tracing casualty patterns (the Tet offensive occurred at the two-and-a-half-year mark in Figure 9.4). Similarly, in the spring of 2005 there was a considerable increase in the sentiment that the war in Iraq was going badly or that the United States was becoming bogged down, yet support for the war declined only modestly over the period, as can be seen in Figures 9.2 and 9.3.

There never were periods of continuous good news in the wars in Korea or Vietnam, but should that happen in Iraq—including, in particular, a decline in American casualty rates—it would be more likely to cause the erosion in support to slow or even cease rather than to trigger a large upsurge in support. For support to rise notably, many of those disaffected by the war would need to reverse their position, and that seems rather unlikely: where polls seek to tap intensity of feeling, something over 80 percent of those opposed to the war say they "strongly" feel that way.[42] If you purchase a car for twice what it is worth, you are likely still to consider the deal to have been a mistake even if you come to like the car.

Moreover, it is difficult to see what a spate of continuous good news would look like. Put directly if perhaps a bit confusingly, it may well be that Iraq simply can't not be a mess. The invading forces were too small to establish order and some of the early administrative policies proved misguided (which, however, didn't prevent those chiefly responsible from later being awarded the Medal of Freedom). In effect the invaders almost instantly created a failed state, and clambering out of that condition is going to be difficult in the best of circumstances. If the worst violence diminishes, and therefore Iraq ceases to be quite so much of a *bloody* mess, there is still likely to be plenty of official and unofficial corruption, sporadic vigilantism, police misconduct, militia feuding, political back-stabbing, economic travail, regional separatism, government incompetence, rampant criminality, religious conflict, and posturing by political entrepreneurs who attract votes and support by spouting anti-American and anti-Israeli rhetoric. Under those circumstances Iraq may attract less attention, but the American venture there is unlikely to be seen as a great victory by those who now oppose it.

The politics of debacle

In Iraq, as in Vietnam, Britain and the United States face an armed opposition that is dedicated, resourceful, capable of replenishing its ranks after losses, and seemingly determined to fight forever if necessary. In Vietnam, the hope was that after suffering enough punishment the enemy would reach its "breaking point" and then either fade away or seek accommodation. Great punishment was inflicted, but the enemy never broke; instead it was the United States that faded away after signing a face-saving agreement.[43] Whether the insurgency in Iraq has the same determination and fortitude is yet to be seen, but the signs thus far are not very encouraging.

In the meantime, the policy of Vietnamization has been updated and applied to Iraq—Iraqization, some are calling it, if possible an even uglier word. Thus, strenuous efforts are being made, as in Vietnam, to fabricate a reasonably viable local government, police, and military that can take over the fight, allowing the American and British forces judiciously to withdraw. In Vietnam, of course, that government and military collapsed to the Communists a couple of years after the face-saving agreement. But the enemy they were up against possessed a massive military force backed by, indeed centered in, North Vietnam. The insurgency in Iraq, albeit deadly and dedicated, represents a much smaller and less well organized force and would likely have far more difficulty taking over the country. Moreover, many of the insurgents are probably fighting simply to get the United States out of the country and can be expected to cease doing so when the Americans leave—as happened to some of the insurgents when the Soviets left Afghanistan and when the Israelis left southern Lebanon. To that degree, the insurgency might become more manageable without the American presence there though there could still be a determined effort by at least some of the rebels to go after the remaining, American-fabricated government consisting, in their eyes, of Quislings and collaborators.

It was widely feared that there would be a bloodbath in Vietnam if that country fell to Communism. And indeed upon taking control, the Communists executed tens of thousands, sent hundreds of thousands to "reeducation camps" for long periods, and mismanaged the economy so badly that hundreds of thousands desperately fled the country, often in unseaworthy boats. And what happened in neighboring Cambodia when the Communists took over makes even the word "bloodbath" seem an understatement.[44]

There are understandable and somewhat comparable concerns that Iraq could devolve into full-scale civil war after the Americans leave, particularly as conditions considerably worsened in 2006. Much to be feared would be what happened in Afghanistan among those combatants who remained in the fray after the Soviets left in 1989—a cruel, scrabbling conflict between warlord groups, many of them essentially criminal. Images of the lengthy and incredibly chaotic civil war in Lebanon also come to mind.

It is often also argued—including by President Bush—that a precipitous exit from Iraq would be exhilarating to international terrorists who would see it as an even greater victory than the one over the Soviets in Afghanistan. Osama bin Laden's theory that the Americans can be defeated, or at least productively inconvenienced, by inflicting comparatively small, but continuously draining, casualties on them will achieve apparent confirmation. Thus, a venture designed and sold in part as a blow against international terrorists will end up emboldening and energizing them.

The dilemma is that almost any exit from Iraq will have this effect. People like bin Laden believe that America invaded Iraq as part of its plan to control the oil in the Middle East and to dominate the world, a perspective, polls suggest, that enjoys huge popularity in Muslim countries as well as in such non-Muslim ones as France and Germany.[45] But the United States does not intend to do that (at least not in the direct sense bin Laden and others doubtless consider to be its goal), nor does it seek to destroy Islam as many others around the world also bitterly assert. Thus just about any kind of American withdrawal will be seen by such people as a victory for the harassing terrorist insurgents, who, they will believe, are due primary credit for forcing the United States to leave without accomplishing what they take to be its key objectives.

In some important respects, therefore, Iraq is shaping up to be a major debacle, rather like Vietnam. However, on the brighter side for the administration, unless failure in Iraq leads directly to terrorism in the United States, history suggests that the American people are quite capable of taking debacle in their stride—they have not proven to be terribly "defeat phobic." They supported the decision to withdraw policing US troops from Lebanon in 1984 after a terrorist bomb killed 241 of them in the civil war there, and the man who presided over the debacle, Ronald Reagan, readily won reelection a few months later. Something similar happened to Bill Clinton when he withdrew policing troops from Somalia in 1994: by the time the next election rolled around, people had largely forgotten the whole episode.

Most remarkable, and relevant, in this regard, the utter collapse of the American position in Vietnam in 1975 as the Communists won was actually used by the man who presided over it, Gerald Ford, as a point in his favor in his reelection campaign the next year. When he came into office, he proudly pointed out, "we were still deeply involved in the problems of Vietnam;" but now "we are at peace. Not a single young American is fighting or dying on any foreign soil."[46] His challenger, Jimmy Carter, apparently did not think it good politics to point out the essential absurdity of Ford's declaration. Moreover, even if disaster follows in Iraq after American withdrawal—as it did in Lebanon, Somalia, and Vietnam— the people dying will be Iraqis, not Americans. And the deaths of foreigners, as noted earlier, are not what move the public.[47]

Public opinion and the aftermath of war: the Iraq Syndrome

After Vietnam, there was a strong desire—usually called the Vietnam Syndrome— not to do that again, and something similar happened after Korea. And, in fact, there never were other Koreas or Vietnams for the United States during the Cold War. Due to fears of "another Vietnam," the administration was kept by Congress even from rather modest anti-Communist ventures in Africa and, to a lesser extent in Latin America (though there was bipartisan support for aiding the anti-Soviet insurgency in Afghanistan, a venture, however, that of course did not involve sending American troops). Meanwhile, Communist genocide in Cambodia after the Vietnam War was studiously ignored in part from fears that paying attention might dangerously lead to the conclusion that American troops should be sent over to rectify the disaster: over most of its course the three network news telecasts devoted a total of twenty-nine minutes to the cataclysm in which millions died.[48]

No matter how the war there comes out, a rather comparable "Iraq Syndrome" seems likely. It probably doesn't matter much how the Bush administration is able to spin the Iraq experience. If a presumed "victory"—or non-defeat—is deemed to have been too costly, any desire for a repeat performance will be, to say the least, attenuated. Thus, a poll in relatively war-approving Alabama in 2005 asked whether America should be prepared to send troops back to establish order if full-scale civil war erupted in Iraq after a US withdrawal. Only a third of the respondents favored doing so.[49]

Among the casualties of the Iraq Syndrome for American policy could be the Bush Doctrine, empire, unilateralism, pre-emption (actually, preventive war), last-remaining-superpowerdom, and indispensable-nationhood. Indeed, as the world's last remaining superpower found itself incapable even of supplying Baghdad with reliable electricity, these once-fashionable (and sometimes self-infatuated) concepts are already picking up a patina of quaintness.

Specifically, there will probably be notable increases in skepticism over the notion that the United States should take unilateral military action to correct situations or regimes it considers reprehensible but which present no very direct and very immediate threat to it. As part of this, there will also be very substantial suspicions about any administration claims that such entities do present a threat. In particular, as the Democrats (and quite a few Republicans) strongly opposed other potential Vietnams after the American debacle there, they are hugely likely (as they emerge after the 2006 election out of their self-imposed cage) severely to question any other Iraqs proposed by the administration unless there is severe, unambiguous provocation.

Also declining in force will be the notions that the United States can and should apply its military supremacy to straighten out lesser peoples even if a result of this policy becomes the establishment of something of a new American "empire," that the United States should and can forcibly bring democracy to nations not now so blessed, that it has the duty to bring order to the Middle East, that it should embrace a mission to rid the world of evil, that international cooperation is of only very limited value, and that Europeans and other well-meaning foreigners are naive and decadent wimps. The country may also become more inclined to seek international cooperation, sometimes possibly even showing perceptible signs of humility.

At the end of the Vietnam experience, there was a substantial negative impact on the armed forces of the United States—some people even call it disintegration. Although this seems unlikely to be repeated in the wake of the war in Iraq, there may well be new pressures to reduce the military and to question whether having by far the largest defense budget in the world mostly brings benefits and, in fact, is all that necessary. In addition there will be a tendency (already partly acted upon) to withdraw American troops from overseas and perhaps to putting the frustrating and endless Israel-Palestine turmoil on a back burner.

The chief beneficiaries of the Iraq War are likely to be the rogue/axis-of-evil (or devil du jour) states of Iran and North Korea. In part because of the American military and financial overextension in Iraq (and Afghanistan), the likelihood of any coherent application of military action or even of focused military threat against these two unpleasant entities substantially diminished, as it has against what at one time seemed to be the next targets: Syria especially, as well as Libya, Saudi Arabia, Egypt, and Lebanon.[50] Accordingly, all such entities have the greatest incentive to make the American experience in Iraq as miserable as possible.

Evidence of the Iraq Syndrome is already emerging. When North Korea abruptly declared in February 2005 that it now actually possessed nuclear weapons, the announcement was officially characterized as "unfortunate" and as "rhetoric we've heard before."[51] Iran has been notably defiant, and its new elected president has actually had the temerity to suggest—surely, the unkindest cut—that he does not consider the United States to be the least bit indispensable.

Notes

1 John Mueller, *Policy and Opinion in the Gulf War* (Chicago, IL: University of Chicago Press, 1994), pp. 88–9.
2 "Punishing Saddam; Sanctions Against Iraq Not Hurting Leaders of the Country, But the Children are Suffering and Dying," *60 Minutes*, CBS Television, May 12, 1996.
3 Andrew Cockburn and Patrick Cockburn, *Out of the Ashes: The Resurrection of Saddam Hussein* (New York: HarperCollins, 1999), p. 263. On this issue more broadly, see John Mueller and Karl Mueller, "The Methodology of Mass Destruction: Assessing Threats in the New World Order," in *Preventing the Use of Weapons of Mass Destruction*, ed. Eric Herring (London: Frank Cass, 2000), pp. 163–87; also in *Journal of Strategic Studies* 23:1 (March 2000).

4 This is particularly impressive because Americans did not blame the people of Iraq— the chief victims of the sanctions—for that country's actions: even at the height of the Gulf War, fully 60 percent said they held the Iraqi people to be *innocent* of *any blame* for their leader's policies. Mueller, *Policy and Opinion*, p. 316.

5 Eric V. Larson and Bodgan Savych, *American Public Support for US Military Operations from Mogadishu to Baghdad* (Santa Monica, CA: RAND Corporation, 2005), pp. 132–8.

6 Richard N. Perle, "Iraq: Saddam Unbound," in *Present Dangers: Crisis and Opportunity in American Foreign and Defense Policy*, ed. Robert Kagan and William Kristol (San Francisco, CA: Encounter Books, 2000), pp. 108–9.

7 Gary C. Jacobson, *A Divider, Not a Uniter: George W. Bush and the American People* (New York: Pearson Longman, 2007), p. 139.

8 For similar data using a wide variety of questions, see Jacobson, *A Divider*, pp. 97, 109. See also Ole R. Holsti, *Public Opinion and American Foreign Policy*, revised edition (Ann Arbor, MI: University of Michigan Press, 2004), p. 278. By contrast, see Chaim Kaufmann, "Threat Inflation and the Failure of the Marketplace of Ideas: The Selling of the Iraq War," *International Security* 29:1 (Summer 2004), pp. 30–2.

9 Mueller, *Policy and Opinion*, ch. 2.

10 See also George C. Edwards III, *On Deaf Ears: The Limits of the Bully Pulpit* (New Haven, CT: Yale University Press, 2003).

11 See also John Mueller, "Public Support for Military Ventures Abroad," in *The Real Lessons of the Vietnam War: Reflections Twenty-Five Years After the Fall of Saigon*, ed. John Norton Moore and Robert F. Turner (Durham, NC: Carolina Academic Press, 2002), pp. 187–9.

12 Mueller, *Policy and Opinion*, pp. 87, 229.

13 The Democrats presumably were more or less expecting a repeat of 1991: Bush would get his war, it would generally be a success, and most American troops would be withdrawn in a few months. Best, then, to be on board for the war and hope, as in 1992, that the brief, successful war would become a distant memory by the time of the next election a year and a half later.

14 Jacobson, *A Divider*, pp. 133, 136.

15 Ibid, pp. 60–7.

16 Ibid, pp. 5, 7.

17 Ibid, p. 5.

18 A reporter's observation from the later war could hold as well for the earlier one: "The battlefields I walked over revealed signs of panicky flight: Iraqi gas masks and uniforms abandoned; armored vehicles left in revetments where they could not see advancing US armor, much less shoot at it; blanket rolls left out in the open. I searched for bodies and bloodstains but saw neither on battlefields where Iraqi vehicles hit by Marines were still smoking. Defenders must have run before Marine fire reached them. Iraqi officers deserted their men . . . and this abandonment almost certainly triggered full flight by all ranks." George C. Wilson, "Why Didn't Saddam Defend His Country?," *National Journal*, April 19, 2003, p. 1222. For similar observations in the earlier war, see John Mueller, "The Perfect Enemy: Assessing the Gulf War," *Security Studies* 5:1 (Autumn 1995), pp. 77–117.

19 Mueller, *Policy and Opinion*, pp. 70–1, 77–8.

20 Something that was predictable, and predicted: John Mueller, "Suicide Watch," *Reason*, January 2003, p. 45.

21 John Mueller, *War, Presidents and Public Opinion* (New York: Wiley, 1973), pp. 59–62.

22 David Halberstam, *The Making of a Quagmire* (New York: Random House, 1965), p. 319.

23 The bump upward in support for the Korean War in early 1953 (at the two-and-a-half-year mark in Figure 9.6) was apparently based on wishful thinking as Dwight Eisenhower was

elected president and took office. Other related data document a decline again over the course of 1953 to the end of the war: Mueller, *War, Presidents and Public Opinion*, pp. 44–52.

24 Francis Fukuyama, "America's Parties and Their Foreign Policy Masquerade," *Financial Times*, March 8, 2005, p. 21.

25 John Mueller, *Retreat from Doomsday: The Obsolescence of Major War* (New York: Basic Books, 1989), pp. 177–8. Robert J. McMahon, *The Limits of Empire: The United States in Southeast Asia Since World War II* (New York: Columbia University Press, 1999), pp. 119–24.

26 ABC polls under "Iraq" at pollingreport.com.

27 Data at pollingreport.com.

28 Actually, whatever its effect on war support, the best remembered pictorial display during Vietnam was not of coffins or body bags at all. Rather, it was the array in the June 27, 1969 issue of *Life Magazine* of unstaged shots of the 242 young men who had been killed in one week in the war, each smiling or staring awkwardly into the camera not long before their lives were extinguished.

29 Mueller, *War, Presidents and Public Opinion*, pp. 164–5.

30 Jacobson, *A Divider*, pp. 189–90.

31 Ibid, pp. 132, 136.

32 On this development, see Scott Shane, "Bush's Speech on Iraq Echoes Analyst's Voice," *New York Times*, December 4, 2005, p. 1. Bush's speech is at www.cnn.com/2005/POLITICS/11/30/bush.transcript1/index.html.

33 On Bush's ineffective Social Security sales job, see Jacobson, *A Divider*, pp. 206–18.

34 This is seen only in Figure 9.2. The question in Figure 9.3 was not asked at appropriate times to capture the uptick.

35 Jacobson, *A Divider*, p. 7. The gap appears to have been great as well during the Great Depression over the extremely controversial president of the time, Franklin Roosevelt. Three polls conducted in early 1941 found that between 90 and 97 percent of Democrats said they would vote for him as against only 33 to 45 percent of Republicans, generating a gap that approaches, but that still does not reach that obtained by G. W. Bush: Hadley Cantril and Mildred Strunk, *Public Opinion 1935–1946* (Princeton, NJ: Princeton University Press, 1951), p. 758.

36 Jacobson, *A Divider*, pp. 177–8. The group consists of the 8 percent of the sample that got four out of four political identification questions right.

37 The estimate appears to have been too high by a factor of at least 10: Mueller, "Perfect Enemy," pp. 87–95.

38 Mueller, *War, Presidents and Public Opinion*, pp. 44, 48–9, 58, 100–1.

39 Peter D. Feaver and Christopher Gelpi, "Casualty Aversion; How Many Deaths Are Acceptable? A Surprising Answer," *Washington Post*, November 7, 1999, p. B3.

40 Peter D. Feaver and Christopher Gelpi, *Choosing Your Battles: American Civil–Military Relations and the Use of Force* (Princeton, NJ: Princeton University Press, 2004), p. 109n.

41 In *Choosing Your Battles*, Feaver and Gelpi repeatedly declare that "the public is defeat phobic, not casualty phobic." However, their analysis actually concludes not that "the public" is defeat phobic, but only some 20 percent of it (p. 145). In their view, this minority group is particularly sensitive to seeming advances or setbacks in the war. My caution is simply to add that any such shifts tend to prove temporary when additional American casualties are suffered. The Feaver approach seems to have been at the back of Bush's failed effort to jigger support for his war in Iraq in late 2005: see Shane, "Bush's Speech."

42 *Washington Post* polls in pollingreport.com.

43 John Mueller, "The Search for the 'Breaking Point' in Vietnam: The Statistics of a Deadly Quarrel," *International Studies Quarterly* 24:4 (December 1980), pp. 497–519.

44 Mueller, *Retreat from Doomsday*, pp. 188–91.

45 Pew Global Attitudes Project, "A Year After Iraq War: Mistrust of America in Europe Ever Higher, Muslim Anger Persists," March 16, 2004.
46 Kraus, Sidney, *The Great Debates: Carter vs. Ford, 1976* (Bloomington, IN: Indiana University Press, 1979), pp. 538–9.
47 In one important respect, withdrawal from Vietnam was much more difficult politically than it would be from Iraq. North Vietnam held some 500 Americans—including John McCain—prisoner in Hanoi, and leaving Vietnam without getting those prisoners back seems to have been a political non-starter. Although 68 percent agreed in a May 1971 poll that US troops should be withdrawn from Vietnam by the end of the year, this number plummeted to 11 when they were asked if they would still favor withdrawal "even if it threatened [not *cost*] the lives or safety of United States POWs held by North Vietnam" (Mueller, *War, Presidents and Public Opinion*, pp. 97–8). There is no comparable problem in Iraq.
48 William C. Adams and Michael Joblove, "The Unnewsworthy Holocaust: TV News and Terror in Cambodia," in *Television Coverage of International Affairs*, ed. William C. Adams (Norwood, NJ: Ablex Publishing, 1982), pp. 217–25.
49 Sean Reilly, "Poll Shows Alabamians Still Support President," *Mobile Register*, May 22, 2005.
50 On these putative targets, see John Mueller, "What if We Leave?," *American Conservative*, February 26, 2007.
51 Sonni Efron and Bruce Wallace, "North Korea Escalates Its Nuclear Threat," *Los Angeles Times*, February 11, 2005, p. A1.

REFLECTIONS

The president's ability to go to war

The observation in this article about going to war could bear some additional emphasis: essentially the president, as commander in chief, can pretty much do it anytime the urge materializes. Any constraint from public opinion would be after the fact. Whatever the venture, the president can usually count on a surge of support as the troops are sent in and, even where that is missing, as it was when Bill Clinton sent policing troops into Bosnia in 1995, there will be a substantial tolerance for the action. There will be negative political payback if the public comes to sour on the venture as costs come to be seen to have outweighed benefits. However, as noted in proposition 7 in the previous article (Chapter 8), even if the venture proves to have been worthwhile in the public's view, the president is unlikely to gain much electoral traction from it because people will probably have gone on to other concerns by the time of the next election.

The ability of Congress to keep the president from deploying troops is similarly constrained. It does have the constitutional power to declare war, of course, but that custom is now honored entirely in the breech rather than in the observance: as far as I am aware, there have been no formal declarations of war anywhere in the world since the Second World War. Sometimes Congress can reduce funds as it did for the Vietnam War—although this happened only after American troops had been withdrawn from hostile areas. Or it can issue restraining resolutions, as in the Boland Amendment which hampered Ronald Reagan's efforts to aid the Contras in Nicaragua. But once American troops are deployed, politics dictates support.

Casualty phobia, defeat phobia, proximate casualties

Written in 2007 when, as it notes, the war in Iraq was not going well, the article is not very hopeful for eventual success there. But it argues that even if there were to be continuous good news about the war, including especially a decline in the American casualty rate, this would not likely trigger a large rise in support for the war but cause the erosion in support to slow or even cease—an observation also included in a shorter version of this article published in *Foreign Affairs* two years earlier. As also noted in the article, Christopher Gelpi, Peter Feaver, and Jason Reifler have in contrast insisted that Americans are "defeat phobic" rather than "casualty phobic" and therefore that, as they put it in a 2009 book, "persuading the public that a military operation will be successful" is "the linchpin of public support."

As it happened, developments in the war provided a test of these contrasting perspectives. After 2007 things actually *did* improve in Iraq for various reasons to the point where, by 2009 or 2010, some could claim that victory had been achieved. The public clearly got the message: by late 2008, the percentage of people who thought US efforts were making things better had risen from 30 to 46 while those believing they were having no impact had dropped from 51 to 32. And the percentage holding that the US was making significant progress rose from 36 to 46 while the percentage concluding that it was winning the war rose from 21 to 37. Despite this change, however, as the updated figure on p. 199 (Figure 9.3) suggests, support for the war did not increase—nor did it do so on measures tapping those who favored the war, those who felt it had been worth the effort or the right decision, or those who favored staying as long as it takes. Successful prosecution of a war, it appears, is unlikely to convert people who have already decided it was not worth the costs.

American casualty rates also declined after 2007 but this, too, had no effect on support for the war, rather confounding predictions by political scientist Scott Gartner that decreasing casualty rates would cause an increase of support.

A change in casualty tolerance?

As noted in the article, tolerance for American casualties in Iraq was far lower than for the wars in Korea and Vietnam, and I suggest this was because the value of the stakes was lower in Iraq (see also proposition 4 in the previous article in Chapter 8). It does not appear that there has been a general decrease in casualty tolerance over the years—the subject of something of a debate I participated in on the pages of *Foreign Affairs* in 2006. Quite a lot of poll data suggest that Americans, deeply threatened and in a rage after 9/11, were, as noted previously, willing to suffer enormous casualties in the drive against al Qaeda in Afghanistan.

Thus, Americans would likely react to another raid on Pearl Harbor in much the same way as they did in 1941. A degree of support for this proposition comes from data gathered in 1990 after Iraq took over Kuwait. Some American troops were sent to neighboring Saudi Arabia to deter an attack on that country, and the poll data arrayed on p. 175 (Table 8.3) of the previous article make it quite clear that if Iraq had attacked those troops, support for going after Iraq would have been overwhelming. Indeed, limited data reported in my *Policy and Opinion in the Gulf War* suggest that prospective support for going after Iraq in 1990 under those conditions was higher than it was before Pearl Harbor for going after Japan if that country were to attack Hawaii.

If the stakes are high enough, then, Americans will still accept considerable casualties. By contrast, in places like Somalia, Bosnia, Haiti, or Kosovo, the public clearly found the stakes too low to justify many casualties at all, while in Korea, Vietnam, and especially Iraq, the stakes proved insufficient as costs rose. And, as suggested in both of the articles in Part III of this book, if the public comes to consider a venture to be scarcely worth further American bloodshed (as in Vietnam in 1975, Lebanon in 1983, and Somalia in 1993), it has been quite willing to cut its losses and get out—that is, to rise above any postulated phobias and to accept defeat.

The anti-war movement during the Iraq War

In the article, I think I unjustifiably tended to underplay the importance of the anti-war movement during Iraq. Refusing to commit the mistakes of their counterparts during the Vietnam War, opponents of the Iraq War never became associated with anti-American values and, rather than expressing themselves in noisy and often unruly public demonstrations, they worked assiduously within the Democratic Party. As such, they were instrumental in engineering the party's 2004 nomination for the presidency of the most credible anti-war candidate, John Kerry. Then, in the 2006 and 2008 elections they fielded successful anti-war candidates for House and Senate, many of them Iraq War veterans, substantially increasing in each case the number of Democratic seats. And, in 2008, they were the cornerstone of the success of the only major presidential candidate in the field to have opposed the Iraq War, Barack Obama.

Reason and caprice (continued)

A particular problem for idea entrepreneurs is that the public not only substantially sets its own agenda—that is, decides what it wants to be interested in—but that it can be quite selective, and often rather unpredictably so, about which facts will arrest its attention and affect its opinion. This is particularly true in the case of war. Thus, as may be seen in the updated figure on p. 199 (Figure 9.3), support for the war in Iraq dropped at the time of Hurricane Katrina in 2005 as Americans were led to wonder about the nation's priorities, a decline that was more than reversed, it appears, by the successful Iraq elections of November 15. Within days of that event, however, war support dropped again to a level slightly lower than was registered before either event took place. Similarly, a decline in support in 2004 at the time of the Abu Ghraib prison disclosures was eventually mostly reversed. There was also a notable upward shift in support for the war when

Saddam Hussein was captured in mid-December 2003, as seen in the figure on p. 203 (Figure 9.7). However, the specific poll question tallied in the figure on p. 199 (Figure 9.3) failed to register that effect because it was not asked until a month after the capture, by which time the upward boost had evaporated.

The explanations I have supplied for the upward and downward bumps in war support are decidedly ad hoc. After the fact, an effort was made to consider what could plausibly have triggered each rise or fall—although some of these phenomena, of course, might simply be caused by sampling or other errors in polling procedures. However, taking the rises and falls at face value, it certainly seems that the events the public happened to consider significant were less than fully predictable.

Of particular note in this regard is that support for the war appears to have been affected on several occasions by events (or even non-events) that had nothing whatever to do with the war, though after the fact one can supply some linkages. Thus, as noted, support temporarily dipped in 2005 in apparent response to government action, or inaction, over Hurricane Katrina, a memorable event that took place thousands of miles away from Iraq. On the other hand, support temporarily rose after terrorist attacks in London in July 2005 and also at the time of the fifth anniversary of 9/11 in 2006, an event and non-event respectively that apparently reminded Americans of what the war was purportedly all about. However, other anniversaries or other notable terrorist events—such as those in Madrid or Bali—do not seem to have had an effect.

Other peculiarities show up in the later stages of the war. In September 2007, General David Petraeus issued a report which garnered great attention suggesting that the war had started to go well for the United States and that it was reasonable, though not guaranteed, that further progress would ensue. The report, as might have been expected, caused war support to rise, but this actually happened *before* Petraeus reported, presumably in anticipation of what he was going to say, about which there was considerable informed advance speculation. Immediately after the report was issued, support for the war actually dropped to about where it had registered previously.

Ultimately, democracy is based on the notion that "the people shall judge." Various "opinion leaders," including those in the media, bring out ideas and perspectives and try to sell them to the public. The public then "judges"—chooses which of the many issues before it are worthy of its attention and which of these it is willing to embrace. The process seems less one of "deliberation" than one in which reason is blended with a considerable amount of caprice, and it is distinctly inexact, in part because, far from being the attentive, if unpolished, policy wonks dreamed of in so many theories about democracy, real people in real democracies often display a lack of political interest and knowledge that approaches the monumental. However, as much of this discussion has suggested, people often seem quite capable of making up their minds without much reliance either on the media or on "opinion leaders." In his *Selling Intervention and War* John Western has looked at a variety of instances in which sellers failed as well as ones in which they were successful. He finds that the public has often "resisted persuasion," and that sales pitches work when the arguments made are ones "the public was willing to accept," when they "strike a chord" or "resonate" with the public.

Thus the murders at Fort Hood by a deranged Muslim psychiatrist in 2009 capture infinitely less attention than the O. J. Simpson murders. The public presumably ignored the Cambodian genocide of 1975–79 because it did not want to be reminded of the recently ended war in Vietnam. Despite considerable media coverage and impassioned advocacy by reporters and activists, little interest was roused in the public about the war in Bosnia in the early 1990s. The famine in Ethiopia in the mid-1980s inspired great attention, but not the far greater humanitarian disaster that transpired in the eastern Congo after 1997. The sex life of Madonna or Britney Spears or Tiger Woods is of more interest than those of figures of more historic importance, or even of other celebrities. And meanwhile, the often quite colorful terrorist plots rolled up in the United States over the years since 9/11 do not sustain much public interest.

Comparative syndromes

The article ends with some speculations about a possible "Iraq Syndrome." For present purposes, a "syndrome" can perhaps be efficiently defined as a general, even visceral, unwillingness, in the aftermath of a bad experience, to do anything that might lead to a repetition.

There was something of a Great War Syndrome in Europe in 1918. It failed to prevent the next massive war though, as argued on pp. 14–15, but for the existence of Adolf Hitler it might have. There was a comparable syndrome after the Second World War, and that one still shows signs of potency even two-thirds of a century later, even though there have been many dire predictions over the decades that the Syndrome would soon fail. Many of these are arrayed on p. 111 and in an appendix in my *Quiet Cataclysm*.

There was also a Korean War Syndrome. In the aftermath of that costly and distinctly unpleasant experience, theorists viewed it as a harbinger and geared up extensively for another "limited war"—a war like the Second World War but geographically constrained. Such a conflict never took place and the Syndrome was probably a key reason why.

Above all, there was the Vietnam Syndrome. I've argued in an article, "The Search for the Breaking Point in Vietnam," that the chief cause of the outcome was the fact that the United States was up against an enemy almost unique in the history of modern international and colonial war in its willingness and ability to suffer casualties. The lesson learned from that experience, however, was not to pick your adversaries more carefully, but to avoid anything that looks like that kind of war, and counterinsurgency was substantially expunged from military training and theorizing. There never was another Vietnam for the United States during the Cold War, though the Soviet Union stumbled into one of its own in Afghanistan in 1979.

For the United States there was something of a respite in the Gulf War of 1991. Before it began, many were worried about "another Vietnam," but few of these were in the military. The war went exceedingly well for the Americans, and in its aftermath the military was inclined to credit its success to weapons, modern technology, excellent training, high troop quality, "fantastic host nation support," "superior intelligence and airpower," "new allied tactics and weapons," "the revolutionary potential of emerging technologies," and the "power of coherence and simultaneity." In an article, "The Perfect Enemy," I have suggested that the war chiefly showed how easy it is to run over an enemy that has little in the way of effective defenses, strategy, tactics, planning, morale, or leadership. Whatever the reason for its outcome, the war's chief instigator, President George H. W. Bush triumphally exclaimed at its end, "By God, we've licked the Vietnam Syndrome once and for all."

Within three years, however, the country had picked up another syndrome. A couple of dozen American military personnel were killed in scraps of armed conflict while trying to police an anarchic situation in Africa. In consequence, Americans succumbed to the Somalia Syndrome, and thereafter troops were sent into such situations only when the environment was "permissive" or when they seemed likely to be able to rely on high-altitude bombing alone.

The experience of 9/11 changed this in the sense that it brought out an enemy that the American public was willing to take on regardless of the costs as noted earlier. However, given how the war in Afghanistan turned out initially, the public's tolerance for US casualties was never tested.

With that encouraging experience under their belt and well remembering the splendid little war of 1991, American forces, with a few allies in tow, plunged into the war in Iraq in 2003. It began like the Gulf War, but then disintegrated into something like, but much worse than, Somalia. To top this, by the end of the decade the occupation of Afghanistan began to look like another Iraq as dedicated insurgent forces became ever more threatening and capable.

Unlike the situation after Vietnam, military planners seem to be anticipating that the next war will be like Iraq and Afghanistan, and counterinsurgency has again become all the rage. Whether there will be the political will to venture into experiences like Iraq and Afghanistan again is yet to be seen. Certainly there is none for launching Iraq-style invasions of the current devils du jour, Iran and North Korea.

Andrew Bacevich espies in the experience since the Second World War the rise of what he calls a "new American militarism." However, it seems to me that his analysis puts too much weight on the temporary successes of the stridently hawkish neoconservative movement in the early part of the George W. Bush administration, an issue covered in the "Faulty correlation, foolish consistency, and fatal consequence" article (Chapter 7). As demonstrated in the article under current discussion, Bush was unable to boost support for going to war despite a lack of much opposition from the Democratic leadership. Moreover, as seen in several of the articles reprinted here, there has never been much support for sending American troops into hostile situations in the last decades—or maybe even century—unless there was a decided provocation like Pearl Harbor or 9/11. By now even support for the once-popular, 9/11-induced war in Afghanistan may be waning (p. 200).

Relevant to this consideration may be a new data point. Trends in a set of public opinion questions about internationalism posed between 1945 and the end of the twentieth century are shown in the figure on p. 176 (Figure 8.3). The question most asked throughout that long period is "Do you think it would be best for the future of this country if we take an active part in world affairs, or if we stayed out of world affairs?" At the end of the century, as seen in the figure, the "stay out" option was chosen by 28 percent, something of a historical average.

In the wake of 9/11, this number dropped to 14 percent, the lowest it has ever attained. It rose some thereafter, but then declined again to 14 percent with the Iraq War in 2003. Since that time, however, the "staying out" option has become considerably more popular so that by 2006, the latest time the question was asked, fully 38 percent embraced the sentiment, the highest ever registered by the question.

This is not necessarily an indication that old-fashioned isolationism will emerge—the US is unlikely to withdraw from participation in the global economy or political organizations. But it could well be fertile ground for an Iraq Syndrome, or an Iraq-Afghanistan Syndrome, to flourish.

Reflections references

Andrew J. Bacevich, *The New American Militarism: How Americans Are Seduced By War*. New York: Oxford University Press, 2005.

Scott Sigmund Gartner, The Multiple Effects of Casualties on Public Support for War: An Experimental Approach. *American Political Science Review*, February 2008.

Christopher Gelpi, Peter D. Feaver, and Jason Reifler, *Paying the Human Costs of War: American Public Opinion and Casualties in Military Conflicts*. Princeton, NJ: Princeton University Press, 2009.

Jon Western, *Selling Intervention and War: The Presidency, the Media, and the American Public*. Baltimore, MD: Johns Hopkins University Press, 2005.

Publications by John Mueller referred to in the introductions and reflections

1973. *War, Presidents and Public Opinion*. New York: Wiley.*

1980. The Search for the 'Breaking Point' in Vietnam: The Statistics of a Deadly Quarrel. *International Studies Quarterly*, December.

1985. The Bomb's Pretense as Peacemaker. *Wall Street Journal*, June 4.

1985. *Astaire Dancing: The Musical Films*. New York: Knopf.*

1986. Containment and the Decline of the Soviet Empire: Some Tentative Reflections on the End of the World as We Know It. Paper Presented at the Annual Convention of the International Studies Association. Anaheim, CA, March 25–29. Available at http://polisci.osu.edu/faculty/jmueller/links.htm.

1988. The Essential Irrelevance of Nuclear Weapons: Stability in the Postwar World, *International Security*, Fall.

1989. *Retreat from Doomsday: The Obsolescence of Major War*. New York: Basic Books.*

1994. *Policy and Opinion in the Gulf War*. Chicago, IL: University of Chicago Press.

1995. *Quiet Cataclysm: Reflections on the Recent Transformation of World Politics*. New York: HarperCollins.*

1999. *Capitalism, Democracy, and Ralph's Pretty Good Grocery*. Princeton, NJ: Princeton University Press.

2004. *The Remnants of War*. Ithaca, NY: Cornell University Press.

2005. The Perfect Enemy: Assessing the Gulf War. *Security Studies*, Autumn.

2005. The Iraq Syndrome. *Foreign Affairs*, November/December.

2006. The Cost of War. *Foreign Affairs*, January–February.

2006. *Overblown: How Politicians and the Terrorism Industry Inflate National Security Threats, and Why We Believe Them*. New York: Free Press.

2008. Dead and Deader. *Los Angeles Times*, January 20.

2010. *Atomic Obsession: Nuclear Alarmism from Hiroshima to Al Qaeda*. New York: Oxford University Press.

2010. Capitalism, Peace, and the Historical Movement of Ideas. *International Interactions*, April–June.

2011. (with Mark G. Stewart) *Terror, Security, and Money: Balancing the Risks, Benefits and Costs of Homeland Security*. New York: Oxford University Press.

* For reprinted, and in some cases updated, versions of these books, see edupublisher.com.

Index